# Don't Spit
# *the Good Stuff*

*Cheers !!*

# Peter Ward

Published by

**GENERAL STORE
PUBLISHING HOUSE**

Box 28, 1694B Burnstown, Ontario, Canada  K0J 1G0
Telephone (613) 432-7697 or 1-800-465-6072

ISBN 1-894263-86-3
Printed and bound in Canada

Cover design, formatting and printing by
Custom Printers of Renfrew Ltd.

©General Store Publishing House
Burnstown, Ontario, Canada

**National Library of Canada Cataloguing in Publication**

**Ward, Peter, 1930-**
     **Don't spit the good stuff / Peter Ward.**

**ISBN 1-894263-86-3**

     **1. Ward, Peter, 1930- —Travel.  2. Wine and wine making—Anecdotes.  3.
Wine tasting—Anecdotes.  I. Title.**

**TP547.W37A3 2003          641.2'2'092          C2003-905704-6**

# Don't Spit
# *the Good Stuff*

## CONTENTS

# FOREWORD

After close to thirty years of making, tasting and sometimes spitting wine, Peter Ward has sensibly decided to commit the gastronomic grind and the hedonistic demands of a wine writer to a book.

It's a journey that began with my invitation to write a weekly column in *The Ottawa Citizen* about "learning in public" the mysteries of laundry-tub winemaking. In the early '70s wine drinking was not yet a national pastime. We have grown up oenologically since then with the help of columnists like Ward.

From the basement of his Ottawa home, wine has taken Ward literally around the world, wherever wine is made, culminating in the personal pinnacle of confronting sixty-six glasses of Port in Oporto to be tasted in one day.

As a working international journalist before wine took over his life, travel had alerted his taste buds to its rewards. He has included some of these experiences as a context for the mid-life career move that changed his life, and that of many of his readers. Anyone who has ever experienced the frustration at their local LCBO store the day after Ward recommended a particular wine in his Friday column will know the influence, and the trust, that he inspired.

*Don't Spit the Good Stuff* heeds its own advice . . . It's all here, like a good Shiraz—robust, rich in flavour with a lingering aftertaste.


Noel Taylor

# ACKNOWLEDGEMENTS

Without prodding from my daughter Wendy, this book would not have gone past the thinking stage. Once I got going, she eased off a bit, then gave the manuscript a first critical read. My wife Jane put up with writer's procrastination, skilfully sending me back to the computer by discovering unattractive household tasks for me to perform.

Tim Gordon of General Store Publishing House thankfully decided to take a flier on this book, and Jane Karchmar was a fast, thorough, sympathetic editor.

Of course, thanks are due the *Ottawa Citizen*, responsible for getting me hooked on wine, and to the readers who watched me learn about wine in public.

# INTRODUCTION

Wine has been an enjoyable accidental journey for me, beginning more than sixty years ago. This book is a collection of wine experiences, notes on grape types, and drinking stories from around the world. Some of the stories don't have much to do with wine, so please accept the fact that they are included on the grounds that a good story itself is very like a good glass of wine: sometimes complicated, sometimes light, sometimes heavier, and always good for an experimental sip. This collection of stories is called *Don't Spit the Good Stuff* because even on the most demanding wine tours, I always had trouble spitting out wine that I really liked.

Here's how I got started as a wino.

In a basement crock, my grandmother made wine that was red and very sweet. In another crock, Grandfather made white wine that was cloudy and sour. They both used Ontario grapes. I was allowed sips on special occasions before I was a teenager, so my thoughts on wine rated Grandmother's sweet red as the best of a bad lot.

Then, in the early 1960s, *The Toronto Telegram* sent me overseas to Europe on assignment, where I met the joys of German white wines from the Mosel; or Beaujolais with a sandwich at a Paris sidewalk café. What wonderful experiences. As I explored the mysteries of mixing wine with food, there was always room on the expense account for a bottle of wine with dinner, provided my taste didn't run to the better Burgundy or Bordeaux wines.

Once back home, my taste for wine was firmly entrenched, but there was no expense account, so the only answer was to make my own wine. Truly, I made every mistake in the book, including the creation of an infestation of fruit flies that almost ended an otherwise happy marriage.

Once I bought a load of California white grapes and decided that the three kids should have the experience of tromping grapes. I lugged the grapes and a big tub into the bathroom; then, one by one, I loaded barefoot and washed kids into the grapes. They didn't like it one bit. The grapes were cold, the grape stalks hurt their feet, and there was this yucky squishy sensation between their toes. They still remember that experience—along with the one when a five-gallon carboy of embryo white wine slipped out of Dad's grasp to shatter on the basement floor, which left him dancing about ankle deep in broken glass while the children learned all sorts of interesting new words.

When *The Toronto Telegram* moved us to Ottawa so I could work in the Parliamentary Press Gallery, I took with me several cases of homemade wine, plus half a dozen cases of empties that I planned to fill with this new hobby. Looking for a house in Ottawa, Jane was impressed because I showed so much interest in the quality of laundry tubs in the houses we saw. Didn't she realize the importance of good laundry tubs for a home winemaker?

Like many home winemakers, I thought my basement stuff was pretty good, and getting better as I learned from many mistakes. I tried concentrates of grape juice, real grapes, and juice bought in season from one of those stores that caters to winemakers. As the wines got better, we inflicted homemade wine on patient friends at dinner parties; and in time the complaints diminished.

When *The Telegram* ceased publication in October 1971, I decided to stay in the Press Gallery and run my own business, servicing American newspapers with Canadian news, and broadcasting for the CBC. Thank fortune there was a stock of homemade wine, because there wasn't much time for a newly minted free enterprise guy to make wine in the basement. Nor was there the budget to buy it from the LCBO.

Then a friend, Noel Taylor, who was at that time the *Ottawa Citizen*'s entertainment editor, asked if I would be interested in writing a weekly wine column for the paper.

"Gosh, Noel, I really don't know much about wine," I confessed.

"You make your own, and it's not bad," he said. "Besides, what we want is somebody who isn't afraid to learn in public, and can write."

That began twenty-nine years of writing a weekly column, without missing a week. This book talks about some of the things I experienced while I was learning about wine in public, and throws in some of the experiences of a travelling freelance journalist. The flavour is certainly complex, and I hope you'll find the bouquet's not bad.

# MAKING WINE

It's difficult enough to even carry a five-gallon pail of grape juice. Try loading it into the trunk of your car and driving home. This very first adventure of what became The Ward Basement Winery was very nearly the last. Sticky floors, pungent odours, broken glass, and a permanent fog of appreciative fruit flies almost brought things down to a choice between the survival of a marriage and my career as an amateur winemaker. There were three small Ward children at the time, and I felt that Jane really needed a hobby she could share with me to make constructive use of her spare time.

As an observant news reporter, I had noticed that at certain times of the year in certain sections of Toronto, whole neighbourhoods had a peculiar and delightful smell. During the course of several assignments in west-central Toronto, the opportunity arose to sample a variety of basement production wine. Some of it was excellent stuff, and I was impressed. Wine I knew something about, because on overseas assignments I'd established a real fondness for wine with meals, courtesy of an expense account.

My new Toronto acquaintances with the Italian genius for winemaking explained to me how I, too, could become an artist of the grape. Every winemaker had his own formula for success. There was such a diversity of advice that I fell back on the simplest of recipes.

When the season came for California grapes to go on sale at the St. Lawrence Market, I lined up with other prospective winemakers and bought my first five-gallon can of juice.

It had slopped over slightly out of its plastic bag and pail into the trunk of the car on the trip home. Some spilled down my pant legs as I hoisted it inside and downstairs. I'd been warned about having an airlock and a big glass carboy to hold the wine while it fermented, so those were waiting in the basement. There was enough grape juice left in the pail to almost fill the glass carboy, which I had carefully washed, so it didn't take long to fit the airlock; and there we were. All I had to do was wait patiently, and within a few weeks we'd be drinking this wonderful wine. That's what I'd been told.

That's not the way it happened.

By the next morning, there were several tiny, pesky flies flitting about in the basement. There was slight activity in the grape juice, because the occasional bubble of air glugged itself through the airlock on top of the carboy.

On the second morning, there was a semi-alcoholic aroma in the bedroom when we awoke. It became stronger as we approached the basement door, and you almost needed a mask to go downstairs. The carboy was awash in purple-pink foam, not unlike the scum that mother used to skim off the top of her jelly saucepan when making raspberry jam. Periodically, more of this semi-solid glop would spurt in gobbets from the airlock, flow over the cork, and slide down the sides of the carboy to the growing lake on the basement floor. It was difficult to focus on any one aspect of the scene, because the whole was fogged by a roiling cloud of fruit flies, driven to a state of frenzy by this feast of the grape. We must have collected every fruit fly for ten blocks in all directions.

I went back upstairs to think.

When Jane brightly enquired about the progress of our home-brew wine in a supportive way, I answered in a distracted manner; but there was no sidetracking her obvious interest in the art of making wine in a basement on laundry day. The ensuing brief discussion over shared labour in this, our new hobby, was not totally rational. It was perhaps for the better that I had to leave for work just as Jane's fascination with the eating/mating habits of the fruit fly reached its peak.

Subsequent home winemaking efforts in the Ward basement were a few notches lower on the Richter scale, because never again were so many lessons learned so quickly in what not to do in making wine. And it was damn decent of Jane to help with the cleanup. I'm glad we went through the pain of learning to make adequate wine at home. It was an excellent way to find out things about wine in general, from the importance of the grape, to crushing, pressing, fermenting, and bottling.

The basic principle behind winemaking is the fact that yeast cells will "feed" on the sugar in grapes to convert the carbohydrates to alcohol, provided you keep oxygen away from the chemical reaction. That fine dusting of powder you see on grape skins is yeast, occurring naturally in the vineyards. Break the skin of a grape, and those yeast cells will go to work on the sugary juice inside. If air is allowed to get at the "must" while it is working, oxygen will join the fermentation party, producing acid instead of alcohol, so the must has to be shielded one way or another from exposure to air.

For every one percent of sugar in the must before fermentation begins, roughly half a percent of alcohol will result when the yeast has converted all the sugar. Once the alcoholic content of the fermenting must gets to fifteen percent, it will be of sufficient strength to kill off the yeast cells, or at least send them into a happy, dormant state. The point of alcoholic content at which fermentation stops depends on the type of yeast. Some yeasts can hold their liquor better than others.

If you measure the sugar content of grape juice before it begins to ferment, you can calculate the alcoholic strength that will result if yeast is allowed to consume all that sugar. Harvested ripe grapes are considered to have good wine potential when they contain twenty percent sugar or more. In general terms, a wine must be at least ten percent alcohol to keep well, and selected wines may run to thirteen percent. In some cases, grapes are dried to concentrate their sugar, and special yeast nutrients are used to push wines as high as seventeen percent. Wines like Port and Sherry, which run up to twenty percent alcohol, are so strong because they have been fortified with brandy.

There are areas in the world where the same grapes have grown in the same vineyards for years, and few, if any, strains of unpredictable wild yeast are present. In some of these cases, winemakers harvest their grapes, crush them, and let the natural yeast present on the grape skins work its fermentation magic with the grape sugar. That system leaves a few things to chance, however, so most wine producers these days sterilize the must to kill all natural yeast present, and then inject a true strain of yeast to do the fermentation work.

Yeast takes a day or so to work up to its maximum authority, so it may be thirty-six hours or more before those little cells, munching on sugar and happily subdividing as they go, take hold firmly of the process. The ideal temperature for fermentation is 18 to 22 degrees Celsius. When it's colder, the action of the yeast cells slows up; when it's warmer, they work faster.

Interestingly, yeast cells that are madly reproducing and converting sugar give off considerable heat; so left to itself in large quantities, a fermenting must will tend to gallop away out of control. The first phase of fermentation is violent and produces all manner of seething foam. If the must gets too hot, the wine can pick up a burned, bitter taste, which most of us have discovered in a bottle or two. These days, a great many wines are "cold fermented," which merely means the winemaker arranges to have water trickling down the outsides of the huge fermenting tanks. Evaporating water cools the tank and neatly balances the heat produced by the active little yeast cells. By regulating the flow of water, a winemaker can control the temperature of his must to avoid the unpleasant effects of a hot fermentation.

It's quite possible to make delightful wine out of a wide variety of fruits and vegetables. Wine hobby books offer a legion of recipes for rhubarb wine, dandelion wine, wheat wine, potato wine, apple, plum, and elderberry wine, and even sake, made with a combination of rice, raisins, oranges, sugar, and one of your wife's good pillowcases—a formula that has been known to cause trouble.

With these few basics of winemaking in mind, consider the situation in the Ward basement that opened this chapter. Mistake number one, there had been no sterilization of the grape juice lugged home in the five-gallon pail, nor was there injection with a pure strain of yeast, as there should have been.

Mistake number two was the failure to clean up the odd splotch of grape juice spilled on the basement floor, hence the attraction of our own private fruit fly farm. Mistake number three merely compounded the other errors. I filled the glass carboy absolutely full, failing to leave any room for the inevitable foam of the first violent fermentation. That guaranteed the churning must would bubble out through the airlock and in fact turn that narrow aperture into something akin to a vertically held hose, spraying sticky, fermenting foam like an out-of-control fountain.

Ah, but the fruit flies loved it, as they trailed their germs through everything, just in case that wine had any faint remaining chance of staying clean.

If the easiest way to make your own wine is with a bucket of juice, bought from one of the establishments that cater to wine hobbyists, easiest is certainly not best. You never know whether your pail of juice has come from the bottom of a vat or the top; hence it might be thin and low in sugar, or it might be gumbo-thick with potential sediment. Usually pails of juice purchased like that have already begun fermenting by the time you get them home, so you are also likely to have some frisky wild yeast problems.

If you buy pails of grape juice for your homemade wine, sterilize the juice before you add cultured yeast. Use exactly measured quantities of sulphate chemicals, or Campden tablets, to sterilize the must before fermentation begins. If you use too much sulphur, your wine will smell like a packet of burned matches, so obtain directions from a wine hobby store for the particular type of wine you intend to make, and follow them carefully.

The next easiest winemaking technique involves using tinned concentrated juices, which must be mixed with the right amount of water, sugar, yeast nutrient, citric acid, and other chemicals suggested in various recipes. In my time, I've added yeast nutrient, sterilizing agents, acid balance powders, and cultured yeast mixed with orange juice. I learned early in the game that packagers of grape concentrate invariably tell you to add far too much water, in order to convince potential buyers that they are getting more for their money than they actually are. When using concentrate to make a basement wine, always cut the amount of water to be added by ten to twenty percent, depending on how heavily bodied you like your wine.

Commercial wine producers know all about adding water and/or sugar to stretch their grape juice, particularly in Ontario, where that heinous practice used to be quite legal and almost universally practised by the larger wineries.

Making a passing-grade wine from grape concentrate is relatively easy, once you've cottoned on to the fact that your equipment must be clean. You sterilize everything with just the right strength of sulphate solutions sufficient to kill the bugs. You ensure that your juice has plenty of room for a violent primary fermentation, without an overflowing excess, and you guard the temperatures carefully. With the proper bottling care, and reasonable storage conditions, a drinkable result will reward these labours. You have no right to expect more.

Grapes that are capable of creating first-rate wines are used to make first-rate wine; they are not concentrated in jars or tins to sell to wine hobbyists.

The Ward Basement once obtained a white grape concentrate from California that promised to produce an angel of a white wine. I remember carefully suspending a muslin sack of elderflowers in the tub for thirty-six hours as this paragon went through its violent primary fermentation. Elderflowers as an additive can impart a really decent bouquet to a homemade white wine, but be careful to ensure that the muslin bag is tightly tied, or you could be in for a messy session of straining out sodden flowers from fermenting grape juice.

I took the five gallons of semi-fermented white wine from the large tub in which it had gone through elderflowering and primary fermentation, and transferred the golden liquid into a nice, clean five-gallon glass carboy. The three kids sat on stools nearby, I recall, watching with idle amusement.

The glass carboy was heavy, wet, and awkward to grip. I had to lift it from the floor onto a stand I used to keep fermenting wines close to eye level. As I straightened up in the approved non-rupture stance, clutching the carboy to my waist, it started to slip. There was nothing I could do about it, save swear with increasing vehemence as the heavy carboy slid out of control towards the concrete floor. The kids' interest picked up considerably as Daddy began to yell strange words and dance ankle-deep in a mixture of broken glass and half-made wine. Each youngster remembers that scene from a slightly different perspective, and each of them retains a different set of words from the selected language Daddy used to describe the stupidity of an amateur winemaker in too much of a hurry with a full carboy.

It would have been a prize-winning wine if the damn carboy hadn't slipped.

Hobby winemakers will go to remarkable lengths to create quality in a bottle. Some have been known to add oak chips to their fermenting wine, on the theory that an oak flavour will be imparted, leaving the finished product laced with tannin, the way a barrel-aged wine would be. Others, with real zeal for perfection, belong to clubs that have arranged at considerable cost to import barrels of French oak from French coopers. First-class grapes, carefully fermented in professional style and barrel-aged in the best French oak, can produce wines that rival the best of California, France, or northern Italy. I've tasted wines made by Ottawa amateur winemakers that would easily sell for $30 a bottle or more. I've also tasted some awful stuff. And I've also learned that it's dangerous to be a judge at the annual Little Italy winemakers' contest. Everybody who is not a winner wants to rip out the judge's taste buds.

I never reached a superior degree of skill in the Ward Basement Winery. My brawn wasn't well coordinated enough; my patience and skills never attained the necessary heights.

Commercial wine producers don't have the same problems as the amateurs when it comes to making wine the way it should be made—with grapes. In a winery, huge screws and mangles crush the grapes; enormous plastic pipes throb like giant arteries as they carry the must to the correct vat; filters cleanse murky juice; vast bladder presses squeeze the last possible drop from crushed grapes; and thermostats keep temperatures at ideal levels.

You make red wine by allowing the juice and skins to ferment together for periods that can be slightly longer than a week. The skins roil about in the fermenting must, usually collecting on the top of the fermentation vessel, which is one of the reasons that the skins are called "the cap." Skins and juice are mechanically mixed, and the temperature is controlled, so that colour and flavour can be extracted from the cap.

When sufficient colour, flavour and tannin have been extracted, in the judgment of the winemaker, the juice is drawn off and the soggy pulp is pressed to extract any remaining juice, before the liquid is allowed to continue its fermentation. In some cases, contact between juice and skins lasts for merely a day or so, resulting in light ruby- or garnet-coloured wines. When only a few hours of skin-to-juice contact is allowed, the result can be a delightful rosé wine, like some of the Zinfandel rosés being made in California.

When making white wine, the usual practice is to crush and press the grapes in the same operation, so that there is little or no contact of the skins and the juice during fermentation. Some winemakers have discovered they can produce white wines with a deeper, fruit-rich bouquet and taste by allowing as much as thirty-six hours of fermentation with the skins, so with some grape varieties that practice is being adopted.

Making wine with real grapes presents problems for home winemakers, who don't produce wine in quantities large enough to make the expensive crushing and pressing equipment economically viable. That's one of the reasons hobbyists form wine clubs. Members can share expensive equipment, and they sometimes get better prices for winemaking materials through group buying.

I once became involved in a group-buying scheme that brought several large crates of excellent California white grapes to the Ward basement. I didn't have a grape crusher, or the inclination to borrow one. I was sure I could wash them carefully, de-stem them, and crush them by hand. After all, there were only a few boxes of grapes.

I set up several buckets of water in the basement, and co-opted Jane's laundry tubs for the operation. At first the grapes would squish out of my hands any old which-way, threatening to reduce the potential volume of the wine, so I came up with the idea of putting a few pounds of grapes in a large plastic bag. I'd put my hands inside and squish away until all the skins were ruptured, then empty the mess into my primary fermenting tub, and repeat the hand crushing process with more grapes in the plastic bag.

It took most of a full day to de-stem, clean, and crush those grapes. By the time I was finished, my fingers were cramped into stiff claws like the witch's hands in *Snow White*, and from the wrists down I was stained as if dipped in walnut juice. It was virtually impossible to type next day, because my fingers had developed grape crusher's rickets. However, although there were splotches of grape in the laundry section of the basement floor, by and large it had been quite a tidy operation.

One could not say the same for the several hours that followed. It got downright messy as the pulp of these crushed grapes yielded its juice through a small portable press. In theory, you twist a worm gear on a grape press, and juice is forced out of the pulp to dribble sedately down the sides of the press and collect in a moat sort of thing around the base of the press. There's a spout at one end of the moat, allowing the juice to run tidily into a container. But my juice had a tendency to spurt from the sides of the press straight to the floor or walls. In a matter of half an hour it was impossible to walk within ten feet of the press without the soles of your shoes adhering to the cement. Had a case or two of vinyl tiles been handy, we could have set them straight down and they would have stuck for life without any glue save the escaped grape juice . . .

It took a day or so to restore some order to the basement, which was once again proving to be a magical attraction for the neighbourhood fruit flies. What was left of the California white grape juice happily bubbled its way through primary and secondary fermentation, tasting better by the day. When the last bubble eased its way through the airlock, and the wine was clear in the carboy, it had a gorgeous golden colour and was tinged with sweetness on the palate. I carefully bottled it, using old-fashioned screw-top bottles, salvaged from some domestic plonk we had favoured during an earlier period.

Oh, it would be such a pleasure to drink that wine when it had settled a little.

Several months later, on a periodic inspection tour of the wine cellar, I noticed a suggestion of moisture around the cap of one of those three-dozen bottles of white California wine, resting there in the cool gloom. I picked up the bottle and there was a slight hissing sound from the cap. The wine was clear, save for four or five brown nubbles of something lying on the bottom. I twisted the cap, and it came off in my hand. White foam sprayed the wine cellar and the winemaker with some violence. Defensively, I opened my mouth to direct as much of the foam as practical out of harm's way. It was delicious—just like Champagne, or, at the very least, Spumante Wardello.

There was enough wine left in the bottle for Jane and me to share a proper glass. She agreed that we had a success on our hands—but a dangerous success.

Undoubtedly there had been a secondary fermentation in the bottles. These were your everyday domestic type of bottle, with no added strength. If all the bottles were in a secondary bottle fermentation, we had a collection of three dozen bombs in the wine cellar, each capable of bursting to spray broken glass about with lethal force. We'd better check the others.

Sure enough, there were brown pellets in each bottle, deposits of yeast from a secondary fermentation inside those bottles, none of which were designed to contain the force of carbon dioxide in solution that had built up in the wine over three months. Only one safe solution was possible. It was Friday evening. Could we drink the dangerous three dozen by Sunday?

We did—with the help of courageous neighbours. Ours was a short and friendly street, filled with curious people. The next two days saw a steady stream of neighbours arriving to see if the rumours of Ward wine distress were true. They stayed by the twos and fours to help us defuse the liquid bombs in the wine cellar. We had a dandy block party.

That's how we found out about making our own sparkling wine. In fact, if you don't stabilize homemade wine when fermentation is done, there is always the danger of a second bottle fermentation, which could have explosive results.

Champagne makers create their bubbly in more or less the same way, only they do it on purpose, injecting some sweetened wine into a bottle and encouraging bottle fermentation.

Many wines go through a slight in-bottle fermentation, often in spring or fall, because the wine in the bottle is a living thing, and it "works" a little in sympathy with the elements of nature. There's little danger of an exploding bottle when it's stoppered with a cork. Building pressure inside a corked bottle would merely force out the cork and spill the wine, but beware of screw caps, and of corks securely wired down to the necks of bottles.

We don't make wine in the basement anymore. My palate has been spoiled by sipping some pretty fair stuff for professional adjudication. I think Jane approves of the decision not to practise the basement fermentation arts, but sometimes I'm wistful for the smell of fermenting juice drifting upward through the hot air registers.

The lessons learned by making your own wine—the triumphs and the disasters—give you an inside track as a wine critic. Fooling with grapes in the basement makes you better able to understand what's right and what's wrong with commercial wines. Once you've created a wine of your own, you've got tannin under your nails, so to speak, and you're doomed to a perpetual love affair with the grape.

# CABERNET SAUVIGNON

The world's most popular red wine grape is Cabernet Sauvignon—which can be either an aristocrat or a commoner when it comes to making wine, depending on where it's planted, how it's grown, and how heavily the vines are allowed to produce. You can pay $100 or $5 for a bottle of Cabernet Sauvignon, and the wine can give you everything from a trip to heaven to near-terminal heartburn.

It's popular with consumers because it partners well with a wide variety of foods from ham, chicken and veal, to lamb, and most cuts of beef. Grape growers like it because the vine is hardy; so is the small, blue-red grape, which has big pits and a thick skin that is very resistant to rot. The vine flowers late and the berries ripen late, so—although Cabernet Sauvignon produces great fruit in moderate climates—there can be a problem when spring is late and autumn is early.

Cabernet Sauvignon is planted in most of the world's wine-producing countries, particularly France, where it is the backbone of most famous Bordeaux wines. The grape variety did not come into its own until corks made bottle ageing possible; to be at their best, Cabernet Sauvignon wines need to bottle age to mellow their tannic flavours. Rule of thumb: the better the vintage year and the better the producer, the longer the wine will have to age to reach its peak.

Cabernet Sauvignon has done so well in California that wines produced there have even topped the best French Bordeaux wines in blind tastings by French wine experts.

It has done well, too, in Ontario's Niagara district, although its sister grape, Cabernet Franc, does better. Most, but not all, Cabernet Sauvignon wines go through some barrel ageing to enhance complexities with the vanilla, woody flavours of oak. French oak is the preferred variety for barrels, but some wines are aged in American oak.

If you meet a wine with a deep red colour, a bouquet like blackberries, raspberries, or even bell peppers, chances are you're facing a Cabernet Sauvignon. When the crop is kept low, the soil is suited, and the year's climate is just right, the fruit and structure of a well-aged Cabernet Sauvignon wine can be ambrosia. When the vine has been too heavily cropped or the vine's foliage allowed to become too vigorous, the wine can taste like week-old broccoli with a thin overlay of underripe raspberries. Usually you get what you pay for, although there are some real bargains around in low-priced Cabernet Sauvignon wines from Eastern Europe.

# GEORGIA

On a mountainside overlooking Tbilisi, capital of the Soviet Socialist Republic of Georgia, stands a huge, white stone statue of Mother Georgia. One hand holds a sword, threatening enemies; the other offers a wine cup, no doubt ready to challenge any friends to drinking combat. The ability to ingest large quantities of alcohol and stay on your feet is regarded as proof of manliness in much of the Soviet Union, and as a guest, it becomes virtually impossible to avoid competing. In Georgia, that region of the old USSR lying between the Caspian and Black seas, drinking prowess can assume extreme macho competitive proportions, to the point of being juvenile—and extremely dangerous to your health.

Georgia claims to be the birthplace of wine. Certainly an unhealthy degree of bacchantic behaviour is quite common, as we five Canadian journalists visiting the Soviet Union in the late fall of 1974 were to discover. Stewart MacLeod, Press Gallery president, was our leader. The troops were Archie MacKenzie, Jean Marc Poliquin, Peter Thompson, and myself, Peter Ward. Our Georgian hosts introduced us to some wonderful wines, and sent us away after three days with our saturated livers literally throbbing for a rest.

Before leaving Canada, we had all heard horror stories about bowel ailments rampant in the Soviet Union, particularly in Moscow; so immediately on arrival there, we commenced a prophylactic regime of 1,000 milligrams of vitamin C dissolved in vodka each morning, and four ounces of straight Cognac just as we retired each night. The idea was to kill off any stray bugs picked up during the day, simultaneously enhancing bodily resistance to disease with vitamin C.

Our hosts in Moscow and Leningrad were eager to prove they could drink stronger, longer, and more, whilst staying relatively more sober and on their feet. Suckered into competition by our own attitudes, we managed to out-perform the Soviet side in Moscow, before being passed on to Leningrad for round two, which we also survived. Georgia and Tbilisi was round three of the drink-a-thon, sort of the Stanley Cup finals, you might say.

We flew via domestic Soviet aircraft from Leningrad to Tbilisi. Inside the aircraft, there was a raised platform with a couple of steps in the centre of the passenger cabin, because the passageway had to go over the main wing spar. There were rope luggage racks over the seats, very like Canadian railroad passenger car luggage racks of the 1930s. Soviet airline passengers threw their packages and suitcases into these rope racks, and there was nothing to prevent packages from flying about in air turbulence. Fortunately ours was a relatively smooth ride. Besides, we had had a drink or two to say farewell to the Leningrad drinking team before boarding the aircraft. Loose luggage? So what?

The in-flight meal was a lump of cooked beef, served with a chunk of dark bread, on a hand-carved wooden tray. There was some paper on which to wipe your hands, but no knives, forks, or spoons. The bread was excellent; the beef was cold, and was one of the tastiest and most tender beef chunks I've ever attacked. We were served a choice of ginger ale or cola as a beverage.

The stewardess nonchalantly piled used food trays and cases of soft drinks at the rear of the cabin as we prepared to land. The wheels touched down, the pilot threw his engines into reverse thrust to slow the aircraft, and an avalanche of wooden trays, broken bottles, and soda pop cascaded down the aisle. We left the plane ankle deep in dripping debris, without evoking the slightest sign of astonishment from anyone. The situation must have been quite normal.

Three limousines waited for us on the tarmac, under the charge of a friendly middle-aged bear of a man named Koko, who was president of the Union of Journalists of the Republic of Georgia. Flashing identification that had the ground crew practically bowing, Koko's three drivers intercepted our baggage as it came from the belly of the aircraft, and stashed it in the limos. We whooshed away from the airport while the rest of the passengers were still walking to the terminal.

Crisp autumn air made the city lights sparkle as we approached the Kura River from the east bank. Tbilisi is built to straddle the river, with bridges laddering across every quarter mile or so. Our hotel, apparently, was west of the Kura, and the first bridge we approached was blocked by some fierce-looking troops cradling submachine guns in a very businesslike way. On the other side, we could see heavy tanks and troops grinding about in the streets. Koko cursed and directed our three-car parade to the next bridge.

The problem, he explained, was that tomorrow the parade to celebrate the anniversary of the Revolution would take place, and troops were using most of the west side of the city to practise. Somehow, he said, we'd get across the Kura to our hotel.

More troops with submachine guns greeted us at the next bridge. They had already stopped an ambulance, with a patient on board, refusing to let it cross to a hospital on the west bank until the parade rehearsal was over.

Koko cussed again, and left the car. He flashed his impressive identity papers at the guards, who leapt back at the salute, then pointed to an officer at the other end of the bridge. Koko marched angrily towards the officer, who stood waiting with his arms cocked on hips, in the arrogant manner of armed authority common the world over.

Koko's ID papers worked a miracle of changed attitude. Immediately we were waved across the bridge, past saluting guards. The ambulance remained blocked and waiting on the east side of the river. For some reason, we suspected that Koko had been flashing more than a simple press pass at the troops. Turned out he was the brother-in-law of the republic's justice minister, and didn't hesitate to use that family connection.

Enjoying a beer break in Tbilisi, Georgia, are (L to R) Jean Marc Poliquin, Koko, president of Georgia's union of journalists, Archie MacKenzie, Peter Thompson, and Stewart MacLeod, then president of the Ottawa Press Gallery

Koko made sure there was a bottle of vodka in each of our hotel rooms, and left us sipping vodka on our balconies as we watched the rehearsal parade for Revolution Day thunder past outside. It was after two a.m. The tanks, rocket carriers, missile launchers, guns, and trucks were full of troops, practising to ensure that every ceremonial detail would be perfect next day. Koko said he'd meet us at eight a.m. to guide us through our first day in Georgia.

Having fortified ourselves against disease with vitamin C and vodka, we faced the Georgian custom of cold cuts and beer for breakfast with good cheer. Koko was there on schedule, to take us on a walking tour of Tbilisi churches, while providing disapproving editorial comment. It seemed on every street Koko met dear friends or close relatives, greeting them in the Georgian way with a bear hug and a kiss full on the lips, whether they be male or female.

At ten-thirty a.m., Koko announced that it was beer break time. We joined a throng of others at a coffee-house-cum-beer joint, where knots of men stood in circles at small chest-high tables, munching pretzels with their beer, feet cocked comfortably on circular brass rails. There were businessmen, construction workers, artists, truck drivers, soldiers, and older men. Beer break was obviously a regular Georgian morning ritual.

With foam still on our lips, we went to a civic reception where the mayor had half a dozen bottles of sparkling Georgian wines, red and white, ready for us on ice. He poured and drank during conversational breaks while our translator from Moscow did his stuff. So did we. Conversation became quite jolly. The mayor demonstrated considerable respect for Koko, who was delighted that we liked Georgian sparkling wines. Truthfully, it was very difficult to assess actual quality, because we were expected to drink a glass straight down once we had picked it up, and the moment you set a glass down empty, some minion would fill 'er up again.

We were relieved that Koko only insisted on two vodkas before lunch, and a mere trio of wine types with lunch. We should save ourselves, he explained, because that afternoon we would be touring a "Kognac" factory in Tbilisi.

Russians freely appropriate famous beverage names, like Cognac or Champagne, and happily stick them on their own products. We discovered that Georgian Kognac is made mainly from Spanish white grape juice, shipped to Black Sea ports by tanker. The Spanish have plenty of white juice left over, because in making their sparkling wines, they use only the best fifty or sixty percent of what is pressed from the grapes. Leftovers come by tanker to Georgia for Kognac making.

The Georgians ferment that Spanish juice, mixed with some of their own excess, and then distill it into eighty percent alcohol. After five years or more in oak, this firewater loses some of its razor edge, and becomes quite drinkable. Proprietors of the Kognac establishment marched us through the production process of their product, and then sat us down to sample everything from five to twenty-five years old.

"Just a little sip of each," they coaxed.

Koko didn't join us for the Kognac tasting, and that wasn't fair. I swear he was out getting his stomach pumped in preparation for evening drinking combat. He'd left instructions with our drivers to take us directly from our firewater sampling to a luxury restaurant high on a mountaintop just west of the city, where we could relax and have a drink before dinner. There was a balcony facing the city, with access through French doors along the length of a huge banquet hall. Lights were reflected in the river as dusk arrived; inside, an orchestra began to play.

In this enormous room, the size of half a football field, there was an orchestra playing, and one table, set for twelve people—our party.

Koko arrived with a few friends, and we sat for the preliminaries of dinner. Apart from us five Canadian journalists, there were Vladimir, our translator from Moscow; Koko; and five other Georgian journalists, one of whom was a young woman who announced she would not be drinking that evening. Obviously she had been involved in dinners like this before. Koko said we'd be saving the empty bottles, trying for a new record.

Georgian dinners are much like a Greek *meza*. Dish after dish of food arrives, and each guest is expected to take a little from each plate, thus munching and sipping for perhaps three or four hours of conversation. Ours was an auspicious occasion, because it was the first visit ever of an official delegation of Canadian journalists to Georgia. Early on in this dinner party, we discovered that all the Georgians spoke pretty good French, and could understand even the fractured French of the English Canadians. One of our number, Jean Marc Poliquin, was a Quebec journalist, flawlessly bilingual. With communication in French, the only person at the table who understood nothing was our guide from Moscow, provided as our minder because he spoke both Russian and English. These talents were obviously coupled with a marvellous memory to facilitate report-making for the KGB. The Georgians thought it was hilarious that our Russian bird dog couldn't follow what was happening. An official visit would be reason enough for plenty of friendship toasts; the added benefit of no report being made to Moscow increased everybody's enthusiasm for toasting.

In turn we were each required to stand and deliver a brief toasting speech. We drank to Canada, to Georgia, to Canada-Georgia friendship, to beautiful women, to Tbilisi, to Ottawa, to everything we could think of toasting. Each time a toast was made, everybody had to empty the eight-ounce crystal goblet of wine that stood at each place.

We were required to invert our glasses after each toast, and each time to bang the rim on a thumbnail to demonstrate that the glass was empty. The wine was a delicate Georgian white, with a happy floral bouquet and fresh fillip of acid in the taste. It might as well have been beer. There was no way our hosts would allow sipping. Wine, they said, is to be gulped back. That's also what they wanted us to do with the vodka and Kognac that appeared at intervals for the more serious toasts.

As the evening progressed, the line of empty bottles beside the table grew longer and the party picked up speed. I know that the non-drinking lady journalist left early. I dimly recall arm wrestling with Koko at the head of the table, while crystal glasses smashed on the floor, and there's evidence to suggest that we all had a turn trying Georgian squat-kick dancing. I know my rump was bruised next day, I assume because of lost balance.

Our count for dinner was thirty-two bottles of white wine, two bottles of Vodka, and two bottles of "Kognac." Two Georgians were under the table by the end, and one Canadian, so I guess we won. I have faint memories of travelling down the mountain in a cable car at two a.m., swaying and singing, and even fainter recollections of arriving at the hotel for a few hours of sleep. Koko said he'd be there again at nine a.m., but nobody really believed him.

We were a sorry lot when morning wake-up calls came, although most of us made it to our feet. Missing was Vladimir, the man Moscow sent to keep an eye on us. Three of us went to investigate his room, and managed to wake him up. We spent the next half hour laying cold cloths alternately on his forehead and neck nape, while from his knees in the bathroom he up-chucked everything that had crossed his lips during the past three days.

"Please don't tell Moscow about this," he pleaded between the surges of spontaneous action from his digestive system. "They would not be pleased."

We were a few minutes late in the hotel lobby, but it didn't matter, because Koko was a few minutes later. When he arrived at about nine-thirty a.m., one of our Canadian troop was leaning with eyes closed against a large marble pillar, forehead pressed tightly against the soothing, cool stone. The others were spread about in various stages of catatonia, sitting, standing, leaning—mostly with eyes closed. Koko would have been more comfortable with his eyes closed, too, by the appearance of them. Collectively, we were all suffering from severe alcohol poisoning—gigantic hangovers.

Koko let us know that if we could make it through the first few hours of the day, we'd recover. He led us off, symbolically, to inspect a Georgian cemetery, which was resplendent with flowers. At each gravesite there was either a statue, or a bust of the departed, or an engraved picture. Raised marble stones formed the border around small coffin-sized patches of grass, and in many cases there were flower blossoms on the enclosed grass. Koko explained that the custom was for families to come for a visit to the departed, picnic at the graveside, and often share sandwiches or a drink with the deceased by scattering food morsels or pouring refreshment on the ground.

We went for a beer break after the cemetery visit, and everybody began to recover. Koko guided us through various tourist sites in Tbilisi, and we noticed, as we walked down the streets, that many men claimed his relationship, unabashedly kissing him full on the lips after loud and friendly greetings.

Koko showed us churches, drove us to the best of views, and at one point stopped beside an old spring. There was a stone-rimmed pool beside an ancient wall, with water flowing freely through a pipe jutting from the stone wall.

"Take the cup and have a drink," said Koko.

We each did as he said, and wondered what his point was.

"This is where Tamerlane and his Mongol warriors watered their horses in the fourteenth century when they conquered Tbilisi," said Koko. We were impressed.

Koko arranged a marvellous lunch, naturally with the appropriate drinks, and we discussed plans to visit Stalin's birthplace, in Gori, that afternoon.

The tiny cottage where Stalin was raised by his drunken shoemaker father has been preserved as a museum, because Stalin is still a hero in Georgia, his birthplace. There's a stone pavilion with marble pillars entirely surrounding the cottage where Iosif Vissarionovitch Dzhugashvili—Stalin—was born, and next to that, there's a mammoth stone structure jammed with Stalin relics, portraits, and statues, many of them in white marble.

Koko hustled us away from Gori, because he had a special place on the route back to Tbilisi reserved for dinner. Our three cars stopped at a restaurant in the foothills of the Caucasus Mountains, where there was a series of wooden pavilions spread around a large central building. We would be dining outside, in one of the gazebo-like structures set in the woods a few hundred feet from the central building.

When our cars arrived, Koko began busily supervising the erection of the reel-to-reel tape equipment he had brought. On a sound system that might have come from the early 1950s, he planned to play his collection of American Western music for us during dinner, because he knew that was the sort of entertainment we would like.

He pointed to the white wooden rail surrounding our dining shelter, and announced that tonight we would be filling the rail with empty wine bottles (the thought was enough to set my stomach a-churning). Dinner was Georgian style again, and so was the drinking. The wine was red and excellent. Tossing back tumblers of smooth, dry, red Georgian wine for every toast rapidly lost its charm and became a competitive matter. We Canadians had to speak rather sharply to our stomachs to quell rebellion, and I'm sure the Georgians had to do the same.

The food came in a never-ending procession of dishes, and a waiter kept pouring the wine. Koko and his two allies refused to let anyone put down a glass with any wine left in it, and the moment a glass touched the table, the eager waiter filled it to the brim. The line of bottles along the rail of our gazebo grew, and Eddy Arnold's quavering voice mirrored the way we were beginning to feel.

Koko had some vodka brought out, just in case we were thirsty, and had a shot or two poured for special toasts. His hospitality was on the verge of drowning us. He was treading water in an extremely unsteady way himself. At about eleven p.m. he announced that dinner was over. The bottle count around the rail was twenty-seven empties of red wine and two empties of vodka. Next, our host said, we were going back to Tbilisi to visit a nightclub.

Enthusiasm for this project was only moderate with the Canadian contingent; however, you can't disappoint your host. There was some concern lest we collectively pitch our cookies during the floor show, but two of our number quickly brightened up when a couple of gorgeous gals arrived at the next table.

We might have partied at the nightclub till dawn, but for the fact that the two lovelies had Russian escorts of apparently high rank who decidedly didn't care for the progress the amorous Canadians were making with their dates. Koko encouraged us to finish off the bottle of Kognac he had ordered, so he could take us home to the hotel. We all made it to bed. I'm not certain what time it was.

Mornings were not the best time for us in Georgia, at least until we each had downed one of those fizzy vitamin C tablets, dissolved in vodka. The process, recommended to kill stray bugs in the intestinal tract, thus preventing the trots, also gave us a jumpstart on the day.

Koko had another full day of sightseeing organized, and he promised that the evening would be one of moderation because we had an early morning flight scheduled to take us to Moscow for a reception at the Canadian embassy. The morning passed in a blur of statues, churches, and riverside vistas. We had the usual beer break about mid-morning, and I know we had lunch somewhere, with the inevitable wine. Koko was suffering red-eye himself, and he suggested we might grab a nap in our hotels before dinner. Where would we dine? Koko surprised us by announcing he was taking us all to his home for dinner and the evening. A Soviet citizen almost never takes foreigners to his home, so this was something special.

Our cars picked us up just as the sun was dipping behind the mountains, and threaded through the business district into a network of dusty side streets. Paint was peeling from the door of the dirty, mud-brick building where the cars stopped, making us wonder if the driver had made a mistake, or if we were being taken for interrogation, or if Koko was really a pretty poor man.

Past the grubby door there was an entrance hall, containing a few tables and chairs, where things didn't look quite so shabby. Next there was another door, which opened into a new world of thick carpets, polished furniture, and the smell of sandalwood. There was Koko, arms wide in the gesture of the perfect Georgian host, lips and scratchy beard ready for the embrace and kiss that a Georgian offers to good friends. He'd been munching a little garlic snack to lay a base for the party. Hell of a way to start the evening.

There was no sign of Koko's wife, but an extremely attractive, dark-haired girl of about twenty-five was introduced as a relative and the wife of the Soviet ambassador to Cuba. There was also a newspaper editor, a friend of Koko's, and a man who had been a regular with us at Georgian meals, no doubt because he seemed impervious to alcohol.

The dining room seemed small, chiefly because of a solid, circular walnut table, about ten feet in diameter, apparently lifted from King Arthur's castle. There was a matching sideboard, trimmed with gold curlicues, and perhaps a dozen chairs, each of ornately carved walnut, and each with a solid gold angel, perched with wings outspread, on either side of each chair back.

On the lace tablecloth were solid silver flatware and silver-trimmed plates, matched by a set of unique drinking glasses. Each tumbler was a perfect cut-glass crystal cone, standing in a filigreed silver holder, and there were several sizes of matching glasses like that at each place.

There could have been a quarter of a million dollars worth of furniture, crystal, dishes, and flatware in the room. Koko was pleased that we were impressed.

"Where did all these lovely things come from, in a communist country, where such treasures are only fit for museums?" we wanted to know.

"These things have been in the family for over three hundred years," said Koko. "The same people are running Georgia now as have always been running Georgia. Communists are here because we want them.

"You know, for more than 2,000 years, wars have been fought over and through our country. It's been the invasion route for those from the east heading west, and for those from the west heading east. For the first time in our history, that's not going to happen anymore. Moscow looks after our foreign policy and our defence, and that's the way we like it. We look after our own internal affairs, and we like that, too."

Georgian politics and lifestyles made excellent conversation over dinner, particularly as the rules about draining your glass for each toast had been relaxed. I think Koko wanted to avoid another post-dinner arm-wrestling session, which had proved so hard on crystal and chinaware two nights earlier.

The food was super, and we commented on the fact at some length. Koko was appreciative, and after dinner he called out to the kitchen. Two women wearing aprons answered his summons, blushing and bobbing shyly as Koko translated our appreciation of the food into Georgian for them. He introduced the two as his wife, and his sister-in-law, the wife of the Minister of Justice for the Georgian republic. The women were allowed to stay and have a drink with us before returning to the kitchen.

When they were finished washing up, they were allowed into the living room while the men talked over cigars, and the beautiful twenty-five-year-old played Georgian dances on a highly polished grand piano; another piece of furniture with a lengthy family background. Koko's wife and sister-in-law seemed very appreciative of being allowed into the social part of the evening, but neither of them said a word, except perhaps a few whispers to each other, probably about women's liberation, Georgian style.

We took our after-dinner drinks up a winding metal staircase and onto the roof of Koko's home, to watch the lights of Tbilisi sparkle in competition with the extremely bright stars in the velvet sky. We stayed up there, talking and testing Georgian Kognac, until well past midnight, reluctant to leave despite the fact that Koko was to pick us up at six-thirty a.m. for the airport and our flight to Moscow. The flight wasn't until nine a.m., but Koko had one final treat for us. He promised a real Georgian experience—breakfast at a special hangover restaurant.

We packed and fell into bed back at the hotel, leaving wake-up calls for 5:45 a.m. so there would be time for showers before departure. Promptly at six-thirty a.m. we appeared in the hotel lobby, with baggage, and there was Koko, looking, like us, as though he needed the services of the hangover restaurant.

Tbilisi was coming to life as our motorcade threaded through traffic towards the early morning eatery. Big French doors were swinging with customers as we approached, and Koko had some difficulty finding a suitable table for us. A peculiar smell floated through the restaurant. There was a cup on the table, filled with something that looked like horseradish. It was minced garlic—the source of the smell.

At that point a waitress plunked down steaming bowls before us, distributed eight-ounce tumblers, and proceeded to fill them from an iced bottle of vodka. The bowls were filled with stewed tripe and onions, cooked in butter and milk. Koko showed us how to lace the stewed tripe with several spoonfuls of minced garlic; and in truth, unless you were a devoted fan of stewed tripe, that was about the only way you could choke it down.

There were no menus. All this place served was tripe stew, garlic and iced vodka, although I did notice some steaming cups of strong Georgian coffee floating about the room. And the place was packed with men obviously in need of the restorative powers of a hangover tripe stew breakfast, with vodka. Hold that stuff on your stomach and you could face anything.

Certainly Koko appeared to perk up considerably as breakfast progressed. He downed his tripe stew, well laced with garlic, and happily went through two tumblers of vodka, successfully removing the red from his eyes almost as effectively as a bucketful of eye drops. The treatment worked for us, too, I guess, because we were certainly pretty jolly by the time we left for the airport and our flight to Moscow.

There was passion in our farewell embraces at the Tbilisi airport, and we vowed to do it again soon in Canada, because Koko was scheduled to be part of a return visit delegation of Soviet journalists to Canada. Let us rest up for a year and we would we show him a thing or two about Canadian drinking on our turf.

The return match never took place. Next year, on his way to Canada, at Moscow airport, Koko suffered a heart attack. He died back home in Tbilisi.

# CHARDONNAY

Wine made with Chardonnay grapes has become so popular worldwide in the past forty years that the name of the grape variety has almost become synonymous with white wine. Consumers can't get enough Chardonnay; consequently you'll find the name of the grape on labels of bottles from superb through mediocre to lousy. *Caveat emptor*—let the buyer beware!

Most wine experts agree that making a good Chardonnay wine requires not only good soil and a moderately temperate climate for the vines, but strict control so that no more than 4.5 tons of grapes are produced from each acre of vines. Half that volume of crop is usual in French Burgundy, where they claim the world's best Chardonnay wines are produced. There's some truth in the saying that Chardonnay wines are made in the cellar by the techniques of the winemaker.

Chardonnay is available in a wide variety of styles, from relatively inexpensive wines with little or no ageing in oak barrels, through to wines with moderate barrel ageing; wines that have been fermented in oak barrels; or some of the Australian and Californian Chardonnays that are so heavily flavoured with oak that sipping them seems to leave wood splinters in your tongue.

When there's little or no oak barrel ageing, Chardonnay wines often taste like Granny Smith apples, grapefruit, lemon, or tropical fruits like mango, pineapple or papaya. If the vines have been too heavily cropped, expect a watery aspect to the taste, as opposed to the concentrated fruit flavours that should be present.

If Chardonnay grapes are left on the vine past their prime stage of ripeness, they lose acidity, and the resulting wine will taste flabby, although it may be higher in alcohol. It's crucial for a winemaker to keep temperatures cool during the fermentation process in order to preserve fruit flavours.

Ferment Chardonnay grapes in oak barrels and the result is a creamy texture/taste. If they have been aged for lengthy periods in oak barrels, they will offer vanilla, caramel, and buttery flavours that will increase in intensity depending on the length of oak barrel ageing, and on how heavily the barrel has been toasted—charred inside to add a measure of caramel to the wine's flavour. Wine aged in American oak barrels, which cost half the price of barrels made with French oak, smells and tastes something like Bourbon, because American oak barrels are used to age American corn whiskies. Moderate to heavily oaked Chardonnay wines will partner well with everything from medium to heavy-bodied fish—salmon, halibut, and swordfish—to pork, veal, chicken, and even lamb when there's lots of oak flavour. Moderately oaked and non-oaked Chardonnay wines can pair well with light- to medium-bodied fish and shellfish, and with pork, veal, and chicken when they are served plain or with light sauces.

# WINE CELLARS
# AND SELLERS

Years ago, six wine tasters helped me to prove that wine is distinctly better after two months of storage in a decent home wine cellar than it is if you drink it while the ink on the wine store receipt is still wet. We blind-tasted identical wines, one decently cellared for two months and one opened the moment it came home from the wine shop. The stored wine won hands down.

That's dramatic evidence that a wine cellar in your home can pay big dividends in return for a modest outlay. You might drink more wine, because it's handy, down there in your cellar, but you'll drink better wine for the same price per bottle. Proper storage facilities give you better value from what you buy, and will also allow you to buy bargains by the case.

A home wine cellar can be anything from a protected box to hold a dozen bottles, to one of those fancy, climate-controlled cabinets advertised in gourmet magazines for prices ranging up to $5,000 and more. Wine cellars, like the wines you drink, can be tailored to your budget, and you can have at least a modest wine cellar whether you're an apartment dweller, a townhouse person, or a homeowner. The price will range anywhere from $100 to several thousand, depending on what you want.

Ideally, wine should be stored at a constant temperature of about ten degrees Celsius, in a place that guards against rapid temperature fluctuations. Wine must be stored lying down, so that the cork will stay moist and flexible, protecting the wine. There should be some gentle air circulation, and the space should be dark. Strong light can quickly ruin the best of bottles. The space under your basement stairs is a less than ideal site for a wine cellar, because vibration is the enemy of resting wine. Rapid increases and decreases of temperature will also spoil a wine, but your best bottles will tolerate a steady eighteen to twenty-two degrees quite comfortably. Changing temperatures can cause leaky bottles, as the slight amount of air in the bottle expands and contracts, exerting pressure on the cork.

My own wine cellar gets down close to freezing in the dead of a winter cold snap, and rises to the twenty-five-degree range in a July heat wave, without damaging the wine. In summer, I often move the best bottles to a lower, cooler level of the cellar shelves, and in winter, better wines live on the upper shelves, where temperatures are a few degrees higher. The colder the storage temperature the more slowly a wine matures; wine in warmer conditions ages more quickly. Heat of thirty degrees and more will spoil wine, and so can temperatures cold enough to freeze it.

With those factors in mind, design yourself a wine cellar. If you have a basement, insulate a section of an outside wall, as far away from the furnace, hot water tank, and stairs as possible. An outside basement wall will stay at a relatively constant temperature, because the earth outside your home foundation varies very little in temperature as the seasons change. Build a frame around the insulated wall section, and put in shelves.

I used twelve-by-one boards (in the days before metric measure) and made a series of fourteen-inch boxes, each of which will hold about eighteen bottles of wine, lying on their sides. In retrospect, I wish I had made the boxes into diamond shapes by angling my twelve-inch boards at forty-five degrees from the floor, so they would cross in a checkerboard fashion. That way the wine bottles would stay solidly in place, instead of developing a tendency to roll about when only a few bottles are left in a box.

Some wine devotees construct a wine cellar by stacking concrete cylindrical tiles in piles, with a bottle to each tile. The concrete of each tile changes temperature very slowly, and insulates each bottle from temperature trouble very effectively. That's a great way to store wine, but it takes up a huge amount of space. It also means there's a temptation to pull out each bottle periodically to see what it is, thus disturbing the wine. That, of course, is counterproductive, because shaking a bottle of wine around breaks one of the cardinal rules of ageing wine correctly. When I move wines from top to bottom shelves in my cellar to adjust for seasonal temperatures, I do it very carefully. If you've got the space, and you label each concrete tile carefully, individual tiles for each bottle can be a good system.

In most basements, space is at something of a premium. You can use very little of it by building an insulated box that will hold a dozen or two bottles, or you can construct a small room, designed to hold 1,000 bottles or more. You can spend a heap of money installing temperature control, or you can simply leave a small gap at the base of the door, and a small space near the ceiling of the wine cellar. That will provide ample air circulation.

Space is even tighter for apartment dwellers. If your budget does not run to a fancy wine chest with climate control, consider building a small box, with Styrofoam insulation, either in a closet, or against an interior wall. You can easily build something to hold a few dozen bottles. Choose an interior wall for wine storage if your wine cellar is to be above ground level, because above ground level, exterior walls are subject to extremes of cold or heat, while interior walls change temperature less readily. When you must store your wine in a space above ground level, avoid stashing it high up in a closet or cupboard, where it will risk the heat that spoils wine.

Now to fill your cellar. Wine is a very subjective matter. It takes time and the basics of tasting know-how to purchase the right wine stock in your personal taste, so it's important to make your selections with care. Remember that except for fine white Burgundy wines, fine Sauternes, and Chardonnay wines of good character, red wines generally need more ageing than white wines. Wines from a good vintage year need the most ageing. Usually, the higher the calibre of the winemaker, the more his wine will improve with age.

Think of a wine's maturing process in terms of the line on a graph that begins at a low level of "drinkability." The roughness of youth in a new wine needs some quiet time to smooth off the edges to a fit state for contemplative company. A wine's drinkability curve gradually climbs upward as it rests in your cellar—as ageing brings it towards its best—and then the graph line flattens out, indicating a period that can last for a couple of years, when a wine plateaus at its peak of consumer quality. Once a mature wine begins to slide off that plateau of quality, it goes downhill rapidly, sending the line on our graph plunging towards the point where it has become senile with too much age.

Heavier red wines need more ageing to reach that peak plateau than white wines, and the more ageing at the winery a wine has had in oak casks, the more bottle ageing in your cellar it will require to mature to its best. Some folk like their wines with plenty of the bite of tannin left in them; some like a red wine to taste slightly of caramel, an effect that comes at the edge of the ageing plateau. Learn your preferences and drink your cellar accordingly.

Never buy ordinary Beaujolais for lying down in a cellar. It should be consumed when it's young and fresh. It's also a waste to buy light, fresh white wines for ageing, because that very freshness prized in young white wines disappears over the course of a year.

The key to stocking a wine cellar successfully is to learn about the good vintages, so buy a wine book that lists the calibre of recent vintage years and buy for your cellar accordingly. Bordeaux reds from good cellars and in good vintage years need ten years or more of ageing to approach their peak. Good Burgundies need less time, although some can last for several decades. Some red Italian wines—Barolo, Barbaresco, Gattinara, and Spanna—also need at least five to ten years of ageing. Brunello di Montalcino often takes twice as long to reach its potential. I've tasted Brunello wines that were twenty years old and still puckery with tannin. A wine wag once remarked that Brunello is really a battery wine—never ready. That's going too far. A Brunello di Montalcino from a good vintage year will become a true king of wines after the proper resting time in your cellar.

Vintage Port is another wine that requires a decade or more of cellar ageing to deliver its true worth; and again, Ports from excellent years require the most ageing. A Port bottling house only declares a "Vintage Year" when it judges the quality of wine from a specific year to be extremely good.

The old British tradition was for a father to buy a "pipe" of Port for his sons each time a Vintage Year was declared. Meanwhile, Dad would be able to drink the Port laid down for him by his father. That sort of thing is all very well for baronial mansions. I find that every time I put a few bottles of Port of recent good vintage in the cellar, my sons lick their lips.

If I were setting up a modest cellar, I would buy at least three bottles of each type of wine. I'd also get fairly heavily into Ontario red wines, particularly the Reserve Baco Noir made by Henry of Pelham and the Reserve Cabernet Franc from Pillitteri. Choose good vintage years, which will probably cost a bit more. Depending on your budget, pick three good Bordeaux wines from decent chateaux from recent vintage years. When you've got three bottles of each on hand, you can wait the time you think would be proper, then open a bottle to test. That would still leave two for a dinner party.

I'd buy some vintage Port, hoping to live long enough to drink it, and, failing that, expecting posthumous gratitude from my heirs. Don't figure on drinking a vintage Port until it's at least twenty years old. I'd buy a few bottles of white Burgundy of recent good vintage—expensive, but worth it for special occasions three to five years hence. I'd also check the various neighbourhood wine stores to see what good California Chardonnays I could afford, and cellar them for a couple of years. I have enjoyed twelve-year-old Chardonnay wines from Ontario that were still sound with enhanced complexity, and Ontario Cabernet Sauvignons of the same age that were magnificent. Red Burgundies are regarded as a must for any decent wine cellar, and they are lovely at their peak.

Frankly, there are wines more to my taste that are better buys. When you travel, take time to sniff the labels at wine stores wherever you go. Sometimes the bargains can be astounding. I remember once buying a Margaux for a song at a small store in upstate Maine. It had been stored upright, and in the light, but at the price it was worth taking a chance. We drank it at a Prince Edward Island barbecue and it was delightful.

If there is any room left in the cellar, and funds in the budget, buy some Spanish Rioja wines costing $20 or less a bottle, and some good Italian Chianti Riservas. For current drinking, buy some of your favourite red wines, and some of your favourite whites, with the idea of letting them sit a minimum of a couple of months, and then drink from your cellar according to the occasion.

Keep track of the wines you have in your cellar in a cellar book, or set up a computer program that will show you when and where you bought each wine, and what you paid for it. When you try a bottle from each batch, note down the date and your impressions. That's the way you learn about which wines are your personal preferences, and how long they should age. An ordinary business ledger makes an excellent cellar book, or you can buy one in most major bookstores.

Some of the best places to shop for cellar stock are the wine shows that now take place in increasing numbers in most major cities. They offer the opportunity to sample many wines in a short length of time, and to make comparisons, tasting similar brands against each other. Keep in mind the rule of wine merchants: To get the most objective result in tasting, use only dry bread or plain water to clear your palate between samples. You sell wine by having people nibble cheese or pâté as they taste. Wine really does taste better with food, so the idea is to avoid influencing your judgment. When tasting a number of wines at a single session, it's a good idea to stay with a particular type of wine—perhaps even a selection of wines made from the same grape—rather than have your taste buds hop from red to white, from sweet to dry, and back again. When you taste a number of wines of the same type, your nose and palate have a good basis for comparison.

Powerful bouquets and flavours can blunt your senses, so taste white wines before red; dry wines before sweet; and young wines before old. You might decide to sample a number of light dry white wines first, and then move to whites with more definite flavour, like those made with Sauvignon Blanc grapes. Save heavier-bodied Chardonnays for last in the white wine department.

Test the younger, lighter red wines—like Beaujolais, Valpolicella, or Barbera—before you get into Cabernet Sauvignons, Burgundies, or Barolo wines. Save tippling on Port, brandies, or liqueurs until your taste buds have given their best on table wines.

Examine the shade of colour carefully as you sample. Brownish tinges in either a red or white wine can betray either venerable old age, or something drastically wrong with the wine. Swirl wine in your glass to release the maximum bouquet possible, and sniff with care to sort out the various facets of the scent. You can best examine the taste of a wine by rolling a small amount around in your mouth to warm it, then breathing a small amount of air through the wine to magnify the flavours. Write down what you find: what you like, and what you dislike.

Be reluctant to buy a case of a light, fruity white wine for your cellar, because the very freshness that you like won't last. Avoid buying white wines for your cellar when they contain less than ten percent alcohol. They usually won't keep for many months. Red wines that will profit most from cellar ageing often taste terrible when they are young. That bitter, cold tea taste flaunted by some young red wines is tannin, which comes from the grape skins and from the barrels in which the wine was aged by the producer.

Tannin softens as wine ages, and adds to the complexity of flavours that is so prized in the great wines, so a cold tea bitterness in a recently bottled red wine with lots of underlying fruit flavours is usually an indication of future high quality. Those are the wines that will pay the best dividends from ageing in your cellar, provided you have the patience to let them rest until they are ready for the table.

Plan on replacing what you drink from the cellar. That way you'll have a continuing source of well-treated wine for the table that will give you top value for dollars spent. And you'll have grateful heirs. We've told our kids that the one who cleans out the basement gets first crack at the wine cellar.

One of the joys of a wine cellar is the fun you can have deciding what to serve at a dinner party. Matching wine with food is like making music: the right combinations can be exquisite, and unsuitable mixtures can jar your palate with a taste discord. That being said, different palates spark to different tunes. That's what makes the appreciation of wine—like music—highly subjective.

Wines should blend smoothly with the food they accompany, because a balance between wine and food, with neither being dominant, is the recipe for a successful dinner evening. Sometimes contrast can also create the necessary balance. I remember one elegant dinner that began with the host serving a bowl of hot shelled hazelnuts, matched with a delicate, icy Soave. Perfect.

Serve wines in the right glasses and at the right temperatures. It makes a considerable difference in how they are received. Sherries and Ports go in smaller glasses of about four-ounce size, and you should fill the glass half full. Sparkling wines go in flutes, white wines go in glasses of four, five, or six ounces, about three-quarters filled. Lighter red wines require glasses of the same size or slightly larger, which should be half filled, and big red wines go in large goblets—I have some that are twenty-ounce size—and the wine should fill a third of the glass or less.

There are no hard and fast rules for achieving a successful balance between wine and food at an elegant dinner, but there certainly are useful guidelines to be followed unless you want to deviate from them for a specific reason. Serve white wines before red, lighter-bodied wines before heavier-bodied, and dry wines before sweet. There's always that rule about serving white wine with fish and poultry and red wine with meat, which some people defy for the sake of being different. The rule holds true in most cases. Some fish—hake, sole, turbot—have a chemical component that reacts badly with red wine to spoil both the food and the drink. Some fish, particularly when cooked in tomato-based sauces, can go very well with lighter-bodied red wines.

Serve white wines chilled but not iced; serve light-bodied red wines slightly chilled. You can drink white wine with anything you like—from oysters to baron of beef. I know one chap who boasts that he drinks nothing but Champagne with everything, although that might be more an expression of personality than good taste. Champagne, or an elegant sparkling wine of other origin, might well be the perfect way to begin dinner, served with caviar if you're flush, or with pâté and crackers if you're not. Serve the Champagne and caviar iced; the crackers and pâté merely chilled.

The purpose of a drink before dinner is to set up the taste buds so they are ready to appreciate good things ahead. That means Sherry, white wine, or perhaps one of those bitter aperitifs like St. Raphael, would be the ticket. Stay away from martinis, Scotch-on-the-rocks, and the like, unless you have a guest who simply must have one to unwind. Hard liquor is like hitting your palate with a sledgehammer; it deadens your taste buds.

Suppose you begin dinner with some smoked salmon, capers, and sour cream, served around the fireplace. A dry white wine would go well, provided there was sufficient bite to it, because smoked salmon is strong. A patsy wine wouldn't do, and a dry Sherry might be slightly discordant.

Sherry would be perfect with a selection of pâté, though, and again, great with the right selection of canapés. Serve dry Sherry ice cold, by the way. In Spain they bring a bottle to your restaurant table in an ice bucket, and it's gorgeous. We keep a bottle on the inside of the refrigerator door. Sherry goes well with many hot soups, too.

If there's a fish course, select a white wine with body and flavour to match— light for something delicate, heavier for a spicier creation. We had baclau in a tomato sauce at a recent meal, which was excellent with a light red wine.

I'm opposed to serving wine with most salads, because vinegar in a dressing spoils wine. Powerful white wines, like a Fumé Blanc or Chardonnay from California, can follow if your main dish is fish, provided you remember the dictum that wine and food should complement each other, not get into a flavour war. Chicken, veal, or pork give you a choice of white wine or a lighter-bodied red wine as partner.

In general, when the spicing of such food is modest, white wine goes best. When you lay on the extra spicy flavours, you should think about red wines.

There's a temptation to pull out the big red wine guns for a main course, and that can be a mistake. In my opinion, top-rated Bordeaux, Burgundy, northern Italian, and the best California reds should be served with cheese at the end of a meal, so they can be savoured and appreciated, rather than buried in an avalanche of flavours.

When it comes to your prized bottles of well-aged vintage red wines from excellent years and first-rate producers, it's sometimes wise to keep such wines for special tastings dedicated to examining the facets of fine wines alone. Think about choosing second-tier wines for most dinner entertaining.

With ham, a good Bordeaux wine is the best match, and perhaps that's a personal prejudice because of one delightful experience with this combination. The type of spicing used is again the key to selecting the right wine for heavier main courses made with game, ducks, geese, lamb, or beef. Burgundies are soft and rich; Bordeaux wines are more austere. Côtes-du-Rhône wines can be quite peppery, and California Cabernet Sauvignons can be as big as all outdoors.

Spanish Rioja wines, particularly the Reservas and Gran Reservas, are usually big in flavour and value, providing an excellent balance with most beef dishes. Italian Barolos, Barbarescos, and Chianti Reservas can be rich in tannin with plenty of heft. They go best with the richer red meats, like lamb, or with goose, venison, or wild duck. And remember, good red wines are best served at a temperature of between twenty and twenty-two degrees Celsius.

Appropriate partnership of wine and food is particularly important with dessert, because that's the last impression your dinner leaves. Contrast can be a useful tactic here, perhaps setting ice-cold Sauterne beside an orange mousse, or a fine Mosel Auslese with fresh fruit. There are some delightful late harvest wines, Riesling and Vidal, from many Ontario wine producers. Frankly, the perfect end to dinner for me is wine and cheese. The cheese can be a selection and the wine can be heavy-bodied red; or the cheese can key to something like Italian Gorgonzola or British Stilton, in which case a good bottle of Port is required drinking.

Prejudices like that can lead a fellow happily into the danger of gout, I suppose, but until the big toes start to ache, it all seems worthwhile.

# CABERNET FRANC

If ever there were a grape variety that could take on different characteristics depending on how and where it is grown, Cabernet Franc is that grape. It's one of the major building blocks for some of France's great Bordeaux wines, and it's the chief grape in great wines like Chateau Cheval Blanc, but usually in France Cabernet Franc makes a thinner wine than its cousin Cabernet Sauvignon. It carries a harsher flavour, with—according to the experts—the smell of pencil shavings.

I'm very much a fan of Cabernet Franc as produced in Ontario, where the finest examples come from production held back to as little as two tons an acre of production. Pilliterri's reserve Cabernet Franc, as made by Sue Ann Staff, is one of the best I've tasted. Chateau des Charmes makes a top-flight Cabernet Franc, as do Inniskillin and Henry of Pelham. In the best of these there are complex, deep fruit flavours of plum, raspberry, and even fig, often producing bell pepper smells and yes, the smell of a pencil, freshly sharpened in one of those rotary devices.

Cabernet Franc does well in cooler climates, ripening even in a cool autumn. That characteristic makes it a super insurance grape for Bordeaux, where a bad autumn can ruin the Cabernet Sauvignon crop, and an ideal vine for Niagara and B.C., where growers sometimes need an extra week or two of ripening time. It's rated by many Niagara growers as one of the best plants for the region, one that certainly rates major study at Brock University's cool climate oenology centre.

Drink it with red meats, strong cheeses, or spicy Tex-Mex dishes.

# IRAN

One of the perks of belonging to the Parliamentary Press Gallery used to be foreign travel with a cabinet minister, courtesy of the Canadian government. The Press Gallery would be informed of a ministerial excursion and there would always be a limited number of seats available for the media. These days, media organizations like the CBC, the Globe and Mail, CTV, or The Toronto Star insist on paying the commercial rate for a seat to travel with a minister. As a low-budget freelance reporter, I was always grateful for the chance of a free lift. Most of my media customers were newspapers in the US or South Africa, so foreign affairs were interesting to them, which made it practical for me to travel, whenever I got the chance, with Mitchell Sharp, then Minister of External Affairs. Besides, as a Canadian I could go to some places that were off limits for Americans.

One of the most memorable of such trips took place in the early 1970s, starting in Rome and including Istanbul, Tehran, Jerusalem, Nicosia, and Cairo. Standing out in memory are stops in Tehran, in the days when the Shah still ruled Iran, and Cairo, where the remains of the 1967 war with Israel were apparent even in the Cairo museum.

When you're slightly jet lagged, Tehran really jangles the senses. From the airport, we rode in a minibus at the back end of the official ministerial cavalcade, led through the traffic by a wedge of police motorcycles. While Sharp met with the Shah's ministers, the Canadian media contingent was entertained by Iran's Ministry of Information.

First we went to the famous Persian Market Place, a bazaar of nearly ten miles of winding aisles, roofed over with a dirty glass and metal covering, much like that of London's Victoria Station. In the 1970s, visiting Tehran's market was an exciting experience. You could buy almost everything, all of it with an exotic slant. There were piles of nine-by-twelve-foot Persian carpets, woven with wonderful designs in work so fine that even by folding the edges back as hard as possible, you could barely distinguish the knots of the individual threads. This fine work went into carpets worth more than $1,000 each, and in many booths there were stacks of them five feet high. There were even some carpets made with silk, which were incredibly expensive. The smells and the noise of bargaining battled each other for command of your senses. We did some shopping for jewellery to bring back home, quickly learning the market's favourite phrase—"*Bari Shaman*"—which means, "but for you . . ." That was the line we heard from every merchant hoping for a sale, the preliminary words to a fierce session of bargaining. I couldn't afford much, but Jane did get a few pieces of jewellery when I got home.

I'll never forget one sight at a jewellery store next to our hotel. Just inside the door, open to the street, sat a jeweller with a large silver box on a table. Beside him was a tray containing pearls, sapphires, rubies, and emeralds in separate sections. He was mounting these gems on the sides and lid of the box with a pair of tweezers and a tiny hammer. The box, we were told, would be a present for the queen of Morocco. The jeweller was quite happily working with several millions of dollars in cut jewels, open to the street from which any passerby could have performed a grab-and-run act.

Most Tehran streets were flanked by ditches that acted as sewers as well as catchments for any rain runoff. The smell mingled with diesel fumes and the odours from sidewalk food vendors to give the centre of Tehran a very distinctive aroma. You could amuse yourself endlessly just watching the traffic, which was a cross between the chaos of Paris and Beirut, with some teenaged drag strip racers thrown into the mix to make it interesting. Iranian drivers in those days drove at seventy to eighty kilometres per hour on downtown streets. Drivers didn't use their brakes until the last possible moment, preferring a combination of speed and invective yelled from the window to intimidate other drivers. They paid little attention to stoplights, and had yet to discover the purpose of the white centre lines on the road. Pedestrians rich or poor either in silk suits or tatters crossed through this mayhem wherever they chose, behaving like matadors without capes in a traffic bullfight.

Our first brush with Iranian cuisine came at a luncheon thrown for us by the Ministry of Information. There were huge bowls of fresh black caviar, nestled in chipped ice, for the first course. I'd had caviar before, the salty tinned stuff, and considered it overrated. Iranians serve their caviar with finely chopped onions, finely chopped boiled egg, and fresh, flat pita bread. Cautiously, we Canadian newsmen spooned a bit onto our pita bread and tasted. Wow. This was fresh caviar, smooth as silk, and almost beyond description in flavour. With a squish of lemon and a sip from a glass of ice-cold Iranian vodka it was culinary heaven. With some regret we moved on to the small pieces of fried sturgeon, served with a super Iranian white wine, then to tempting chunks of filet with a reasonable red wine.

Then that evening came the Iranian foreign minister's state dinner. Rain was falling softly as we arrived at the foreign minister's palace. Outside was an impressive staircase, tapered from more than fifteen metres wide at the base to five metres at the top, and covered with a magnificent Persian carpet, with nobody showing the slightest concern that this treasure was open to the elements. A swarm of limousines milled about waiting turns to deposit loads of dinner-jacketed guests. The entrance was at the base of a three-storey turret. Inside, stairs followed the curves of the walls upward and the whole was alive with light because the walls and the domed ceiling were lined with chips of mirror that bounced the light from a huge central chandelier back and forth so brightly that it looked like a laser light show.

We climbed the curved stairway and were greeted at the upper entrance by a major-domo who swept out his arm, inviting us down a long, wide hall. Spaced ten metres apart were a series of fireplaces with chesterfields, chairs, and tables grouped around each one to make a string of living rooms without walls, each open to the other, to provide for small pre-dinner conversation groups, or for guests to wander from one group to another. Silver cigarette cases filled with black and gold cigarettes, and larger cases with cigars wrapped in gold foil, were everywhere. Each wrapped cigar bore the crest of the Shah.

While we settled in, waiters came by with every imaginable drink, from icy cold vodka through several types of Scotch, to wine—red, white, or bubbly. A second layer of waiters offered canapés. It was the sort of setting that made jaws drop in wonder, even for well-travelled reporters.

When dinner was announced, the dining room was even more impressive. A huge table at least six feet wide was spread with white linen, crystal, gold (plated, I think) flatware, candelabras, gold-trimmed plates, and an array of glasses that promised a good part of dinner would be liquid. There were about 100 of us for dinner, with a waiter for each guest, standing behind the chairs to help seat us. Mr. Sharp, at the centre of one side of the table, faced his Iranian counterpart on the other side. Minions of each minister were seated in descending order on either side of their bosses, although I'm sure there were some additional Iranians to flesh out the Canadian side. I could see very well because I was seated at the end curve of the table, as far below the salt as it is possible to be.

Big surprise! We began with fresh caviar and ice-cold Iranian vodka, surely a match made for the gods. When debris was cleared from the first course, each waiter produced a plate of steaming spiced rice with a raw egg in its half shell perched on top of the rice. My waiter mixed the raw egg and a dab of butter into the rice, which was so hot that it cooked the egg, producing a delightful, flavoured rice, partly bound together by egg.

I was so impressed with this procedure that I vowed to try and duplicate the dish for Jane and the kids. At home in Ottawa, I was not a success. Having described in detail for them the dinner in Iran, I then prepared for each of them, Jane and the three kids, my own plates of rice, spices, and a bit of butter with a half shell of raw egg on top. When I mixed the raw egg into the rice the result was a gluey mess of raw egg and rice. No question, my eggs were bigger and colder; their rice in Iran must have been hotter and their eggs warm and smaller. They might even have been quail eggs.

I was so taken with the egg-and-rice routine at that grand Iranian dinner that I don't remember dessert. I do recall that the wines were exclusively white and varied from slightly sweet to bone dry. No question about it, these wines would rate rave reviews wherever they were served. Each matched the food perfectly, at least from the perspective of my vodka-numbed palate.

There were brief speeches of mutual friendship from Mitchell Sharp and his Iranian counterpart, with waiters ensuring that we all had something in our glasses for the toasts. As people rose from their places to head for the exits, it seemed remarkably early to call it quits. But nobody had any intention of going home. The crowd moved past the long hall of fireplaces where this adventure had started, and on to a large room with more than a hundred overstuffed armchairs surrounding a stage. There was plenty of room between the chairs for waiters to come through with coffee and a selection of Cognacs, liqueurs, and more of those gold-foil-wrapped cigars. A small Iranian orchestra played while we settled in with our after-dinner business.

As the last waiter delivered his goodies, half a dozen very attractive girls appeared on stage, all dressed à la harem in transparent pantaloons, bare midriffs, and winning smiles. They danced wonderfully for a good hour while we puffed on those great cigars, sipped our coffee and Cognac, and wondered at the good life of the Iranian elite. What a first taste of the Shah's Iran!

Next day we had been promised a look at some of the trinkets given to the Shah and previous rulers over the past 100 years or so, a visit to the underground vaults that held the crown jewels of Iran, and a look at the Iranian Parliament.

The deputies were not in session when we viewed the chamber, about the size of a small provincial- or state-elected body. Desks and chairs were set in several ascending rows in a semi-circle facing the speaker's chair and rostrum. These deputies debated just as ours did, we were told, the difference being that their advice did not have to be taken by government unless the Shah said so. The impression left was that the deputies provided a good forum for taking the political temperature of the country. Its effectiveness in that function certainly fell down in the months before the Shah was forced to flee. Either that or he wasn't listening. Not even his notorious secret police could stem the tide of protest.

No wonder the Shah was unaware of public opinion until too late, living as he did in the insulated world of a potentate's luxury. That had been the Iranian way for centuries, a fact we found underlined by the opulence of the Iranian crown jewels, and the gifts received by Iranian rulers over several hundred years.

The entire first floor of a large office building had been turned into something like a museum to display the Shah's gifts, from royalty to royalty. We were faced with a blaze of gold, silver, diamonds, emeralds, pearls, rubies, and the like. There were country scenes done with combinations of precious metals and gems, golden horses with ruby eyes, and gilded statues galore. One piece will live forever in my memory. It was a gold and silver model about two feet high and two feet around, intricately worked to represent an English country scene with a brook running through it, and over a waterfall. When the clockwork mechanism was wound, the waterfall appeared to be actually flowing, because behind a fine silver grid there was a revolving drum set with diamonds that flashed at you through the grid like falling water. This was a gift from Queen Victoria to the Shah's grandfather.

These wonders were a prelude to viewing Iran's crown jewels. We were told that the crown jewels formed the basis of value for Iran's currency. They technically belonged to the Shah, but were housed in the sub-basement of the main Bank of Iran building. We had to go two floors below the surface, past several guard desks for identity checks, before arriving at the entrance of the largest vault I've ever seen. Visitors had to pass two separate steel bar gates that were suspended overhead. We were warned that if anyone touched any of the cases inside the vault, it would trigger an alarm, and bring the portcullis-like gates crashing down to seal the room. Past the two gates, a right-hand turn, and there was a room almost the size of half a football field, brightly lit, and shimmering with the jewels on display. Around the outer edges of the room were glass cases lined with jewelled swords, sabres, scimitars, and scabbards, each encrusted with every gem imaginable. There were several display cases of jewel-encrusted pottery. I'll never forget the sight of one vase, about three feet high, set with lapis stones in spirals so that the smaller stones were at the base and neck, with the size of the stones expanding and contracting as the spirals reached the wider parts of the vase.

On one side of the room there were four glass cases, roped off so you could not get too close. Each case had three shelves, and on each shelf there were golden dishes filled with cut but unset gems. In one glass case the stones were all rubies. In another case the plates held emeralds, in another, sapphires, and in the fourth, diamonds. These were not your everyday gems. Not one was smaller than a couple of carats. Each plate was filled to overflowing, so that gems dripped over the edges like fire.

At the far end of the room stood the Peacock Throne of the Shahs of Iran. A good eight feet tall, it is covered with hammered gold from the square base to its cathedral peak, and set with precious gems all over. The blazing colour of the gems is why it's called the Peacock Throne. You simply stand there in awe, however uncomfortable it must be for the seated ruler to use this treasure. Close by the throne was a pedestal-mounted globe of the world, about four feet high, and also heavily golden—covered with hammered sheets of gold, we surmised. On the globe, the oceans of the world are all set with emeralds, and the land masses with rubies—except for Iran, which is done in diamonds.

In a glass case close by the throne and globe are the jewelled objects used by the Shah and his wife for state occasions, including a selection of wonderful tiaras, a pendant with a tear-shaped diamond of at least forty carats, and the belt worn by the Shah for formal occasions. It's made of chain link gold, the work so fine that it is difficult to see the individual links. The buckle is one enormous emerald the size of the palm of a large man's hand.

There has been no attempt to estimate the value of this collection; at least there had not been until that time. A former *Toronto Telegram* photography technician, Lee Warren, had left that newspaper some years previously to work for the Royal Ontario Museum, and from there he had been commissioned to photograph some of these jewels. The ROM had also put an estimated value on a few of the pieces. One in particular was a snuff box, two inches deep, five inches long, and three inches broad. Every edge was set with pearls, while the silver of the lid was sprinkled with set precious stones. The box was displayed on a mirror so you could see that the base was one whole emerald. The ROM team estimated the 1970 value of this trinket at $3 million.

As we wandered through this astonishing display of wealth, we asked our guide where all these precious things had come from. Many had been brought back to Iran from long-ago raiding wars into India. I kept strolling back to look at the jewelled globe of the world, to examine the Peacock Throne, and to marvel at the beauty of the huge tear-shaped diamond pendant. Some of these gems had undoubtedly been around at the time of Alexander the Great, and from there into the treasury of some Indian rajah. Each would have a story to tell probably as dramatic as its monetary value.

After more than thirty years, my rich memory of those jewelled symbols of power is almost as vivid as it was next day. Each time I think of them I wonder what happened when the Shah was ousted and the Ayatollahs took power. The collection was obviously the property of the people of Iran, a valuable economic resource as well as the cause for emotional pride. One would assume that the crown jewel collection still sits in that huge vault two storeys beneath the streets of Tehran, backing the nation's currency, but certainly not destined for public display again in the foreseeable future. Such beauty should be displayed, no matter what the politics of the regime.

That evening, with our heads still full of jewelled memories, we went to see a demonstration of whirling dervishes in an arena resembling a small bullring. The music was fittingly Eastern—flutes and strings with a few drummers—and the dervishes were white-robed, turbaned, and very tall. They wove through intricate dance patterns, spinning as they went. The music picked up pace; so did the spinning, until each dancer was almost a blur of motion. How they keep upright and overcome vertigo is, I suppose, one of the points of being a dervish. We were a small part of the crowd that had gathered to watch, so you could equate the dervish display to something akin to a North American sporting event or theatrical occasion—half ballet and half arena football without the physical contact. There was something of controlled violence about the dance, and from the audience, a sensed reflection of fierce involvement. In retrospect, this might well have manifested some of the discontent that we now know was beginning to appear on the streets of Iran. At the time I certainly wasn't shrewd enough to spot it. As was the intention of our political hosts, we were dazzled by the displays of wealth, and the friendliness of our official guides, who kept us far too busy to be asking any difficult questions in the street. It was even arranged that some of us could buy the best fresh caviar, supposedly on the black market, for $15 a kilo.

We flew out of Iran, heading for Egypt, with our most pressing worry being how to keep that luscious batch of sturgeon's eggs cold enough to last until we got home.

Cairo was a quite different experience. Our group had a police escort through the crowded streets, clearing the way through mad traffic and streetcars festooned with people, packed inside and hanging from anything available on the outside. We went to the famous Shepphard's Hotel, enjoined to be ready for a pickup in about an hour for a reception at the Canadian Embassy.

It quickly became apparent that the journalists would not be part of the official party, because we were taken to a sub-reception and buffet at the home of the military attaché, an officer who looked after us as though we were family. It was a small but wonderful party that went on until the small hours of the morning. About midnight our host asked if anyone would like to see the pyramids. We all expressed enthusiasm. It was a cool but wonderfully clear night, with the moon just past full. We drove south from Cairo to Giza, and the car stopped a few hundred yards from the Great Pyramid. All three huge monuments were bathed in moonlight to make a sight so beautiful that it struck us all dumb. Then the desert around the pyramids came alive, and in an instant, the car was surrounded by Arabs, many of them brandishing rifles. That sure got our attention.

Our host spoke to one of the Arabs through the open car window, then turned to us with a smile.

"They want to know if we need a guide to see the pyramids," he said. "These guys sleep out here all night, and they don't miss a trick. There's nobody else here at this time of night, and they are competing for our business. I told them we'd be back tomorrow."

And indeed we were. Right after breakfast there was a tour arranged for us. We climbed partway up the Great Pyramid, paid our fee and crawled up the sloping entrance to the centre, hunched over in the four-foot-high tunnel, so we could gaze at the totally bare central chamber, where Pharaoh was said to have been entombed. There are now ruts in the passageway, worn smooth by millions of tourist feet.

We had lunch in the café that sits beside the Sphinx, eating on the patio so we had a clear view of the three pyramids beyond the crouching man-lion. Two of us decided to pay the high cost so we could ride around the pyramids on a camel, and we have the pictures to prove it.

Peter on a camel at the pyramids in Giza

Our guide from the Ministry of Information then piled us all in the minivan and headed down the dusty road, even farther south of Cairo. Villages are spaced at regular intervals along the green belt of fertility that the Nile creates. Farmers work their fields, and donkeys are urged through the streets with staggering loads on their backs, just the way things have been done for centuries.

In less than half an hour we turned right, away from the Nile and into the desert towards a looming shape—the Step Pyramid. It sits at the end of a partly excavated square, rising in steps to the sky. From a distance it appears you might be able to climb, as though the "steps" really were meant for mounting. Good luck. These are ten-, fifteen-foot steps, crumbling on the edges from age, because the Step Pyramid predates the famous ones at Giza.

Behind the pyramid, almost obscured in the desert, is the entrance to an enormous underground chamber, several hundred feet long and at least 100 feet wide. There's an elevated walkway down the middle, with large stone compartments on either side. In each compartment there was a huge sarcophagus, far too big to hold anything human. Our guide explained that this was the burial place of the sacred bulls and that each stone chamber had contained the remains of embalmed mummy bulls—rather a contradiction in terms, we thought.

Outside in the sand I picked up a small piece of polished alabaster stone and fantasized that it might be the broken ear from a statue of some ancient Egyptian cat.

Next day we had time for a quick look at Cairo's famous museum, where artefacts from the ancient world are so crowded together they tumble over each other. There must have been more than 100 royal mummies on display, in glass cases, with the paraphernalia of ancient royalty around them. There was half an entire floor devoted to King Tut, the boy king whose golden visage has become synonymous with Egypt. Golden chariots, boats, thrones, weapons, and the like competed for your attention.

We were visiting five years after the 1967 war that the Arab nations fought with Israel. To preserve the ancient treasures from anticipated Israeli bombs during the war, sandbags had been piled around many of the glass cases. The fabric of most of these was rotting, so that sand spilled out in irregular torrents, for all the world as though the desert were reclaiming the buried treasures and bodies that the archaeologists had exhumed.

In those days an aircraft could not fly directly to Israel from Egypt, so we made a diplomatic refuelling stop in Cyprus, then flew on to Tel Aviv, the last stop on Mr. Sharp's tour. We stayed at the King David Hotel in Jerusalem, where we met Israeli Foreign Minister Aba Eban, a man who impressed us all as being that rare creature—an ardent Israeli nationalist with moderate views towards the Palestinians.

I had been to Israel before, in 1964, with Canada's then Defence Minister, Paul Hellyer. On that trip with Canadian troops in the United Nations, I'd had a chance to explore the Gaza Strip, Palestinian Jerusalem—then under Jordanian control—and even the Christian holy sites at the Mount of Olives, Church of the Holy Sepulchre and Bethlehem. In 1964 in Bethlehem I had met two Lebanese brothers from Dallas, Texas, who were operating a holy relics store right next the Church of the Nativity. I wanted to see how these amiable characters had made out since the 1967 war.

They were still operating the same store, offering much the same wares to pilgrims, although on the southern outskirts of Bethlehem, a large barn-like building that once advertised itself as a "Holy Relics Factory" had lost its sign. The two brothers from Dallas actually remembered me, but were very loath to talk in the shop. They urged me into their office, where they said a freer conversation would be possible.

"Things are not the same since 1967," said one of the brothers. "Yes, we can still operate, but under strict Israeli control."

I privately reserved judgment on a move that may well have made things much better for the customers, and asked what were the major changes.

"Our personal lives are okay," said the other brother, "but we have lost many of our friends. Since 1967 the Israelis have had 25,000 Arabs moved out of the Bethlehem district and over the Allenby Bridge to Jordan. Once someone goes over the bridge, there's no way he can get back to his home. There's a strong policy of reducing the number of Arab Palestinians in the country."

We chatted for perhaps half an hour over those tiny cups of strong Middle Eastern coffee, and then I said my goodbyes. I've often wondered what happened to those two brothers from Dallas with their prosperous, and perhaps slightly shady, business. I'll bet somebody is still selling fragments of the true cross, plaster statues, and olive wood crosses to the tourists.

Back in Jerusalem, I was offered the opportunity to join a party of half a dozen US state governors and their wives visiting Israel. We travelled in a small bus with a charming Israeli army major as our guide. As we headed east out of Jerusalem, he pointed out some battle sites of the 1967 war, when the Palestinians were swept out of the west bank, Gaza, and the Sinai, too.

We were heading towards the Dead Sea, Jericho, and the river Jordan.

"There's a limited amount of time," announced our guide. "Which would you like to see: Jericho, the Dead Sea and the archaeological diggings at Qumran, near where the Dead Sea Scrolls were found, or the Allenby Bridge?"

Consensus was clearly in favour of visiting the Allenby Bridge, which crosses over the Jordan River from Israel to Jordan.

"Okay," said our guide as the bus started downhill towards the Dead Sea. "We'll start with Jericho, then the Dead Sea, and then Qumran. It's much more interesting than the Allenby Bridge. We're now going below sea level, so everybody please roll up your windows."

Most of the bus passengers started to do just that; then, distracted by our guide's charm and good humour, we avoided insisting on the political potential of visiting the Allenby Bridge and began our tour of Jericho.

Yes, the Israelis managed the news, and they were very good at it. They still are.

# SHIRAZ

Lovers of big, gutsy red wines are turning in legions to the pleasures of Shiraz red wines, made with a grape variety that the Persians originated and the Australians made into an international fashion. Those great ripe plum, blackberry, and spice flavours of Shiraz must have been a hit in biblical times, because tradition has it that the seafaring Phoenicians brought Shiraz grapevines to France's Rhône valley in those days, where it still flourishes today as Syrah. Think of the great Rhône wines like Hermitage and Cornas, then thank the gods for Shiraz/Syrah.

Australia unquestionably made Shiraz fashionable today, thanks to a chain reaction that began in 1832 when James Busby took some Syrah cuttings down under, where they restored the old Persian name to the grape. Syrah reaches its peak of perfection in France's Hermitage wine. In Australia, Shiraz hits just as high a mark in Grange Hermitage. There are several Shiraz/Cabernet Sauvignon blended wines available in the $10 to $15 range that are excellent value. Today Shiraz is the most grown red grape in Australia. It's also grown in California, South Africa, parts of South America, and even Ontario. The joy of Shiraz is that you can buy a good bottle for a reasonable price and drink it with dinner that evening, or you can blow the budget on a pedigreed Shiraz/Syrah, lay it down in the cellar, and wait as it improves with age.

Shiraz makes a super partner with roasted red meats, particularly lamb or pepper steak.

It fits well with strong cheese, too. Be careful with some Australian Shiraz wines because they can be very high in alcohol content. Aussies like big, strong wines, so some vineyard managers leave the grapes longer on the vine to increase sugar content, producing a higher alcohol content when the grape juice ferments. Shiraz is a grape that can lose acidity quickly when left too long on the vine, so some Australian Shiraz wines will taste "jammy" to North American palates. If you find a Shiraz that you feel is low in acidity, try adding a drop of lemon juice to your glass to correct the balance.

# PLEASE PASS THE PORT

Thank fortune for the serendipity of history, which is responsible for so many good things in life. Port in particular. The word "Port" has a plummy sound to it. The very name of this famous wine conjures up visions of gouty British gentlemen sipping away at glasses full of glowing, tawny liquid, spinning tales of dubious accuracy about empires of the past.

In a tenuous way, Port wine has been connected with Britain from the very beginning, because the Phoenicians were responsible for creating the vineyards of the Douro River Valley. They started the Oporto wine business on their way to Britain. These intrepid mariner-traders made the first substantial Mediterranean contact with Britain—Cornwall, to be precise—and their discoveries helped them to corner the ancient world's bronze market, something that was far more economically rewarding in those days than a monopoly on Port wine.

Tin was vital to the Phoenicians' metallurgical craft—you mix tin and copper to get bronze—and when a mariner-trader is out exploring for raw materials, thirst can be a distracting thing. The sensible Phoenicians made a point of organizing wine stops along the Atlantic coast as they planned their trade routes from the Mediterranean to the Cornwall tin mines. One such stop was the mouth of the Douro River, at what is now Oporto, the city that gave Portugal's greatest wine its name.

The steep vineyards of the Douro River Valley produce a huge variety of Port wines, ranging from youthful ruby, guzzled by the gallon around the world; complex tawnies of varying ages; aristocratic vintage Ports; and a whole lexicon of late-bottled vintage Ports, *colheita*s, tawnies with special qualities, and white Ports ranging all the way from quite sweet to bone dry.

My first trip to Oporto in 1986 was the beginning of a love affair with Port that will last a lifetime. I liked Port before that first trip. Two weeks on site turned me into a total enthusiast, thirsty to learn all I could. On the first day of that first trip we tasted sixty-six Ports at five Port-producing houses. I'll never forget the tasting at Ferreira, where we sampled a variety of Ports, finishing with a 1917 vintage that was simply superb.

There were five wine writers on that 1986 trip. We visited a dozen Port producers in Vila Nova de Gaia, across the river from the city of Oporto, and everywhere there were legions of glasses of Port to taste. It was all good, but you had to taste and spit, or there was no way of lasting even an hour. Port is heady stuff.

Port may well be identified with the British, but the United Kingdom is in fact only third on the list of Port-consuming nations, behind France and Belgium.

North Americans lag far behind, as any Port lover knows who has pleaded in vain for a glass of Port with waiters in otherwise decent restaurants in cities all over the continent. Not many offer Port for sale, and those that do usually have a stingy selection. Such misadventures bring to mind the happy contrast of the Oporto club bar of the Instituto do Vinho do Porto, in Oporto. Every Port producer is allowed to have two types of his wine on sale. It's the best Port bar in the world.

Stand on the north bank of the Douro River in Oporto in the evening, and you'll see a marvellous sight. Reflected in the oily waters, neon lights announce the locations of most of the world's famous producers of Port wine: Cockburn, Warre, Graham, Sandeman, Kopke, Calem, Croft, Offley, and others, all named in flickering neon, adding colour to the soft evening darkness.

The city of Oporto, at the mouth of the Douro River, gave its name to Port wine, and perhaps that was unjust, because Port's true home is on the south side, in Vila Nova de Gaia. I doubt that the wine would have sold nearly so well had it been called "Gaia." The great Port blending and shipping houses are crowded together in the designated district on the river's south bank, the only area where the blending, storage, and bottling of Port was allowed by law, until a regulation was changed in September 1986.

The Port business was first established in Vila Nova de Gaia because there were plenty of empty storage sheds from a cod fishing industry that was in a slump, and because of tax advantages. The Bishop of Oporto wanted more customs duties than government authorities on the Vila Nova de Gaia side of the river, so it was cheaper to operate on the south bank.

The compound for the Port blending and shipping houses is unique, in that it's a collection of walled estates. Stone walls cut off any view as you drive through Vila Nova de Gaia, and the entrance to every Port shipper's property is designed so it can easily be guarded. Security was the aim. At one stage armed guards patrolled the controlled area, to ensure that no lesser liquids were smuggled in to adulterate the Port.

The wines from the Douro were originally heavy-bodied, and they didn't always travel well. Through the centuries the art of growing grapes and making wines waxed and waned along the Douro River, until sometime in the seventeenth century when the international wine trade first became extremely competitive, and Port production became lucrative.

The first record of Port as a fortified wine was in the western Douro in 1678, when the Abbot of Lamego served a Port-like wine to two young Englishmen. The wine came from grapes grown near Pinhão, today the largest town in the Port district. Not until the 1830s did Port shippers regularly dose their wines with brandy to stabilize it before the casks were loaded on exporting vessels.

Brandy made Port wines much stronger, and left them sweeter. The resulting wine was a huge marketing success.

Modern Port exists because drinkers of the industrial revolution rapidly acquired a taste for this strong, sweet wine that could offer such amazing depths of taste and character. Port, as yet unfortified, became so popular in the mid-eighteenth century that profitable wine frauds nearly spoiled the business. At one stage, although the letters might have said "Oporto" on the barrel, the customer might very well have been getting vinegary stuff from the flatlands, thickened up with a bit of yeast sludge and tar.

That great Portuguese hero, the Marquis de Pombal, saved the Port business from ruin in 1756 by ending the frauds. Appreciating Port as a beverage, and realizing the long-term foreign exchange benefits it could bring to his country, the Marquis of Pombal set out stone markers to denote the legal grape growing areas for Port, and he policed his edicts so carefully that sometimes the death penalty was imposed on cheaters. Armed guards were empowered to shoot when they suspected monkey business with the wine. Good thing, too. Capital punishment for fooling around with the Port is an idea that would appeal to many devotees of that special wine, even today.

The Marquis de Pombal's rules for Port were the first tough wine laws that the world had ever seen, governing where grapes could legally be grown to make a specific wine. You can still find some of the stone markers he erected marking the zones where grapes can be grown for the making of Port. The stone walls surrounding Port houses in Vila Nova de Gaia were built to prevent juice swapping. Security almost as tight as that still surrounds the districts where grapes for the making of Port can be legally grown, but without the death penalty. It is possible, however, for the Instituto do Vinho do Porto to ruin a Port House if it breaches the laws. The Instituto is the regulating body for all Port wines, and financed through the Institute, by the producers of Port.

After the Marquis de Pombal died, periods of strict control over Port alternated with wine anarchy down through the years, depending on the state of international markets and the interests of government. When the profits became big enough, there was always some extra silver around to pay off a few officials. Then, once adulteration became too blatant, there would be a shying away of buyers, until the rules were once again enforced to control quality; then sales would pick up, and the cycle would recur.

The Napoleonic wars gave Port its first really big push in the UK, what with difficulties in getting French wines, and the Duke of Wellington in the Peninsula. Admiral Horatio Nelson is even supposed to have drawn out his plan of attack on the French and Spanish fleets at Trafalgar before the battle, on a table with a finger that he had dipped in Port wine.

In 1907, new rules on Port were imposed after a period of free trade and laxity that had lasted for forty-two years. Those 1907 regulations form the basis of the regulations now in effect. In 1932–33 the rules were tightened, and enforced more closely. Those regulation changes were designed to control the quantity of Port produced each year, and to ensure that the many small growers had economic protection against the powerful blending and shipping companies that dominated the trade. Today Port is subject to probably the most complete wine laws in the world, so much so that it helps to have a lawyer's ability to grasp intricate rules when you make a living through the growing and blending of Port.

Grapes for the production of Port can be grown only in a limited area on the banks of the Douro River and a few of its tributaries, approximately 100 kilometres upriver, east of Oporto. The Instituto do Vinho do Porto keeps a file on each of the 34,000 authorized growers of the grapes for production of Port wine, including extensive notes on the soil, type of grapes grown, type of viticulture, fermenting methods, etc. There are regular vineyard inspections.

Peter being inducted into the Confrerra do Vinho do Porto as the first Canadian member

Port is made of both red and white grapes, usually blended to the formula of each individual shipper. There are almost 100 grape varieties grown in the Douro region and allowed in the production of Port. Some grape types are "recommended," some are "authorized," and some are "tolerated." Experts maintain that such a wide variety of grape types is necessary because climate and soil along the Douro vary so widely, according to altitude, the direction in which the slopes face, and prevailing winds.

Until a few years ago, most vineyards were planted with a mixed variety of grapes, which were harvested and made into wine together. By the 1970s a new system was taking over. Now each grape variety is planted separately and vinified separately. That works better because different grape varieties ripen at different times. Blending in most houses now takes place after the separate varieties have been made into wine. One of the best Port tastings I ever attended was at Symington's, where they create Graham's, Dow, Warre, and a number of other brands.

We tasted wines made with Tinta Roriz, Touriga Nacional, and Touriga Francisca, the chief grape types used by Symington. We then tasted the major brands, and were able to see how each achieved its style through the proportion of each grape used in the blend.

Port's vines are planted in strip terraces, contouring the steep banks of the river. Flinty rocks—known locally as schist—and lumps of granite have been powdered into soil by pickaxes over centuries of work to give the roots of the vines holding ground. When a new vineyard is planted, they often make individual holes in the rock for new vines with dynamite. The worse the soil, the better it is for growing grapes to make Port. For nourishment, vines must thrust roots deeply into crumbled rock. The deeper they go, the more mineral complexities can be passed upward to the grapes and, eventually, to the wine.

Production from each vineyard is rated in a complex system that takes into account every conceivable factor governing how the grapes are produced. The soil, altitude and location of the vineyard, slope of the land, exposure to sunlight, spacing of the vines, production volume per hectare, grape type, the way the vines are trained, age of the vines, and even the degree of shelter the vines get from prevailing winds—each factor is assessed. Sometimes the growers must curse the bureaucrats, who have so much power, yet take so little of the farmer's risk. Officials record everything but the names of the donkeys that patiently pull small ploughs to till the terraced Douro vineyards. The hills are so steep that in places there's room for no more than one row of vines on each terrace. The physical conditions of the land almost prohibit any use of tractors for cultivation. Yet in some areas grapes for less expensive Port are planted in vertical rows, and cultivated by machines from bottom to top, so that soil washed down by the rains can be restored to the upper levels.

Each of the twelve factors involved in rating Port grapes is weighted with a percentage figure, and a complex calculation is made so the Instituto can decide on the grade of Port that will be produced from each vineyard. The Instituto awards each farmer an annual production quota, based on the predicted overall sales for the year, to ensure there won't be excess production; then it sets the price for each farmer's production, depending on how his vineyards scored on the scale of the twelve production factors.

Most harvesting is done by hand. Panniers of harvested grapes, each weighing sixty kilograms, are carried as far as the nearest road on the sturdy backs of peasants. Tractors and trucks balance precariously on these dirt tracks to pull the crop to the fermenting tanks.

Juice for making the best Port is still trampled out of the grapes by the same peasants who do the picking and carrying. The crop is dumped into huge stone cistern-like affairs, called *lagares*. Two lines of barefoot peasants start squashing, each group working towards the other from opposite ends of the *lagar*. This treading of the grapes is performed like a military exercise, each man with his arms around his neighbour's shoulders as they high-step it back and forth through the thigh-deep layer of grapes. It's hard work, and by the time the four hours needed to crush each batch of grapes are over, the crushing team is exhausted. Next day some of the treaders return to mix up the must again, until fermentation has reduced sugar in the juice to the right stage for adding brandy.

Fermenting of the juice is brief and violent in the making of Port. It is vital that the maximum amount of colour be extracted from the skins of the fruit quickly, without the grape pits or stems being crushed to bring bitterness to the wine. Human feet are still judged the best tools for meeting this requirement. For making less expensive Ports, fermenting juice is pumped up to be sprayed over the top of the fermenting must, continually exposing the skins to new molecules of yeast.

The grapes are fermented in wine cellars close to the vineyards, and several different fermentation methods are used. The aim is to accomplish a fairly rapid fermentation of the grape must, down to the required level of sugar, while mixing the juice and the pulp thoroughly, so that maximum colour is extracted from the skins. Most wineries now operate with temperature control to avoid any "cooked" flavour to the wine. Still, in most cases fermentation to the required sweetness level takes only a day or two.

Wine masters watch the fermenting must carefully. The moment it reaches the desired level of sweetness—depending on the style of the individual producer—the new wine is mixed with seventy-seven percent alcohol brandy. That's as much of a shock to the wine as it would be to you and me, were we to knock back a glass of such potent stuff. It stops any fermentation instantly by killing off the yeast.

The standard amount of brandy added is 100 litres per 450 litres of wine. That results in new Port which is somewhere between seventeen and twenty-two percent alcohol. If the must is still very sweet when brandy is added, then the end result will tend to be on the sweet side. If the must has been allowed to ferment further, there will be less sweetness, and the finished Port will be of a drier style.

All brandy used in the process of fortifying new Port wine must be obtained through the Instituto do Vinho do Porto, which ensures purity.

The new wine requires time to recover from the addition of brandy, time to meld into a whole personality. It is mellowed until spring in barrels called "pipes" and then shipped downriver to Vila Nova de Gaia for blending and eventual bottling. Pipes of Port used to travel downstream in picturesque *rabelo* boats, shooting the rapids, propelled by a huge single square sail, and steered by a long stern oar. Construction of hydro dams on the Douro ended the traditional springtime voyage of the flotilla of Port boats. These days wine travels to Vila Nova de Gaia by truck or rail.

*Rabelos* still race once a year in a picturesque contest to celebrate June 25—the day of St. John, patron saint of Vila Nova de Gaia and Oporto. Each sail carries the name of a Port company as the flotilla surges from the sea up the Douro to the pool of Vila Nova de Gaia, sailors and spectators all well-greased with hookers of Port.

*Rabelo* boats hit the watching crowd at the annual race on the Douro River

One year I was accepted as a crewmember on the Graham *rabelo*. We were towed to the starting point at the river's mouth with at least fifty other *rabelos*. Each craft anchored against the incoming tide, and we waited, with the northwest wind quartering across the stern. On signal, each *rabelo* slipped its anchor rope, leaving each craft's motorboat tender to salvage anchor and rope. Away we went, charging up the river in chaos, helmsmen and crew yelling at competitors as each *rabelo*, pushed sideways by the wind, threatened to foul its neighbour. *Rabelos* are flat-bottomed, so they go to leeward like a dead leaf in a crosswind.

There's a narrow gap in the Douro where the new bridge crosses the river, making the docks along the southern shore an ideal place from which to watch the race. As we reached that gap, several cursing helmsmen found their vessels pushed into the rows of pleasure boats moored alongside. Owners of those endangered craft joined in the yelling. We managed to squeeze by with two feet to spare, clear of the gap.

There aren't many rules for this *rabelo* race, but one regulation states that any craft touching shore, or a vessel moored to shore, must wait until all other racing *rabelos* have passed, and then it can be towed out to midstream by its motor tender to resume the race. Our vessel, Graham's *rabelo*, was one of the largest in the fleet, consequently known as "the aircraft carrier," and size helped us stay away from the shore. We barely made it through the gap without touching anything, and then surged away as the wind increased. We passed our last threatening competitor a good quarter of a mile from the finish line, and as we got the winning horn, gleefully downed a few hookers of Port to celebrate.

As we crossed the pool to land at Vila Nova de Gaia, one of the other boats, right out of control, hit us broadside, her bow running up over our side. No serious damage, but I learned some interesting new Portuguese words. Then we all repaired to the riverside facilities of Sandeman for the traditional post-race lunch, which is a never-ending buffet served with Douro table wines and a veritable ocean of Port.

It takes the fruit of approximately 1,000 vines from a top-rated vineyard to produce enough wine to fill one pipe barrel with Port. There are several differing versions of the size of a pipe. Up the Douro, where the grapes are grown and fermented, a pipe is 550 litres, whereas down at Vila Nova de Gaia, where the wine is blended, bottled and shipped, a pipe is only 534 litres. The huge Port blending and shipping houses buy pipes of wine at the Douro measure of 550 litres, and sell pipes by their own scale—534 litres per pipe. The difference is said to be from evaporation.

Until 1986, all Port produced and vinified near the vineyards along the Douro had to be shipped to Vila Nova de Gaia for ageing, blending, and bottling. In September 1986, the Instituto do Vinho do Porto changed that regulation to allow ageing, blending, and eventual bottling to be done up the river, close to the vineyards and fermenting facilities. The move has allowed the formation of many new small Port houses upriver. That's quite a switch, considering that only a few years ago Port shippers were required to locate within a specific area of Vila Nova de Gaia, and armed guards patrolled the district to guard against hanky-panky. Blending and bottling facilities upriver will be more difficult for the Instituto to control, but the relaxed regulations will certainly reduce some of the congestion now strangling Vila Nova de Gaia, and bring some new taste sensations to Port lovers.

I can remember sampling some Port made up the river by a company that decided to try ageing Port in French oak barrels. Sure made the Port taste different.

Port shippers are under all manner of restraints. During any given year, each Port shipping company is allowed to sell by volume only one-third of the amount of wine that it had in stock on Dec. 31 of the previous year, according to the Instituto's books. A company that oversells can be fined, or even prohibited from shipping. The regulation induces Port shippers to buy heavily from the growers in autumn—sometimes almost to the extent of panic buying in December. That assures a decent cash flow for the grape growers of the Douro. It also means the Port shipping companies, not the farmers, are required to hold wine while it ages, shouldering the necessary capital investment burden.

The first two years of the life of a Port wine are critical. Each shipping company has the option of "declaring a vintage" when conditions of a particular year have been such that an excellent wine has been produced. In a given year, some vineyards may produce superb wine, while others might miss the mark. If a shipper wishes to "declare" a vintage, samples of the wine must be submitted for testing to the Instituto do Vinho do Porto between 1 January and 30 September of the second year after the vintage. That means a 1985 Port, for example, had to be submitted as a potential vintage between 1 January and 30 September 1987. Having passed inspection by the Instituto, vintage Port must then be bottled by the shipper between 1 July of the second year and 30 June of the third year.

Port shippers are notoriously close-mouthed about their intentions of declaring a vintage year. When asked in 1986 for an opinion on the excellent 1985 vintage, which has been rated as one of the best of the century, one company's expert cautiously replied:

"It is not inconceivable that this wine might develop into a wine which may approximate the character of a vintage Port."

And his colleagues thought he was going out on a limb.

The act of declaring a vintage year by a Port shipper involves aspects of the trade not connected with the quality of the vintage in question. Vintage Port can be sold out of a shipper's hands after slightly less than three years in his cellars, improving cash flow. And the law insists that each shipper sell no more than one-third of the company's wine stock in any given year.

That means a shipper with a low total wine stock is less likely to declare a vintage and more likely to save stock for making tawny with indication of age, or *colheita* Ports. It also means that shipping companies are likely to buy considerable quantities of wine from the growers in the year following an excellent year, so they can enjoy the flexibility of being able to sell heavily a wine from a vintage year. The rules are designed to encourage shippers to keep a large stock of wine in their cellars.

So there are many hurdles for the Port blending and shipping houses before they can sell their wares. Every batch of Port must pass the inspection of a professional Instituto do Vinho do Porto blind-tasting panel before winning a permit to be exported as Port. About one-third of the wines submitted pass the panel's blind-tasting test. The rest must be downgraded and sold as Ruby, or later as Tawny.

Looking at the flames of the fireplace through that glass of Port, you'd never guess this marvellous royal liquid had to suffer so much, just to brighten a winter's afternoon. No wonder the best Port is pricey.

And you can do more than drink it. My wife Jane has a recipe for Port jelly that is absolute heaven with roast chicken, turkey, veal, or even pork. It's not bad spread on your morning toast, either, but a word of warning. Don't try driving to work if you've had more than two slices of toast and Port jelly!

## Jane's Port Jelly

2 cups Ruby Port

3 cups white sugar

Half bottle Certo™

Cloves

Lemon rind

Gently heat the Port in the top of a double boiler, add sugar, and stir to dissolve thoroughly.

**Do not** allow the Port to boil, or you will drive off the alcohol. Remove from the heat and immediately stir in the half-jar of Certo™.

Place a couple of cloves and some lemon rind, to taste, into sterilized jelly jars.

Fill the jars with the jelly mixture, and allow to cool. When set, cover with tight jar tops or paraffin wax.

You can also make this with tawny Port, which gives a better flavour, but not as attractive a colour. Limit your intake of Port Jelly on weekdays, or your work will suffer!

# Types of Port

*Ruby Port*

This is the mainstay of the Port business, and the most commonly sold type. Named for its colour, ruby Port spends a brief, limited time in oak casks, and is blended by the cellar masters of each shipping house so that the exact colour, bouquet, taste, and finish is maintained from year to year. It's a relatively cheap wine, because it doesn't spend much time in the hands of the shipper. Port lovers drink it plain, or with a wedge of lemon, or mixed with lemonade; after dinner, or as an afternoon drink, or as an additive to mulled wine after a bracing day on the ski slopes.

*Vintage Reserve*

Many shippers have begun bottling a ruby Port that has been blended with some well-aged wine so that the colour is still ruby, but the bouquet and taste have some oak to them. Such wines have something of the nuttiness found in tawny Ports and are priced higher than plain ruby Ports. They will be called things like Vintage Reserve, Director's Choice, or President's Favourite. Generally, they are worth the extra money.

*Tawny Port*

As the name implies, tawny Port has a brick-red brownish or orange cast to it, depending on age. Tawny spends years in Yugoslavian oak casks, and as it ages, the ruby colour fades to tawny. Tawny Ports are blends, and a single bottle might contain a mixture of wines anywhere from five to fifty or more years old. Blending tawny Ports is like blending Cognacs—an art passed down from generation to generation in the same family. The object is to produce a wine of the same appearance, bouquet, taste, and finish as the one that wore the same label twenty-five years ago.

Tawny Ports offer complex bouquet and taste, characteristics gathered from the Douro vineyard soils and from the oak barrels in which they have matured.

The recent demand for cheaper tawny Port has been answered by shippers with a blend of ruby Port and white Port. You can spot these wines because they'll be cheaper—about the price of a ruby Port—and because they'll be pink in colour, rather than truly tawny. It's a nice wine, but remember, with Port as with anything else, you get what you pay for.

*Tawny Port with Indication of Age*

There are many Ports on the market with labels claiming that the contents have "the character" of ten-, twenty-, thirty-, forty-, or even fifty-year-old Port. These are the products of blending, achieved almost in the same way as the *solera* system for making Sherry. The task of the cellar master is to create a wine through blending Ports of disparate ages, which will taste like a tawny that has been held in barrel and matured for the stated number of years.

Tasters from the Instituto do Vinho do Porto use their expert palates to carefully check that such wines do indeed reflect the character advertised on the label.

*Dated Port—Colheita*

This is not vintage Port, but a wood-aged tawny, which must be at least seven years old, with the vintage year displayed on the label along with the bottling date.

Ruby Ports, tawny Ports, and tawny Ports with indication of age have all been aged in oak and are ready to drink when they are bottled. They'll keep well in the bottle, provided they are properly stored, but they will not improve. Nor will they throw a deposit.

Once opened, they'll keep in a well-stoppered bottle or decanter for a number of weeks, depending on how much air space is left in the container with the wine to oxidize it.

*Vintage Port*

Vintage Port is the elixir bought by aristocrats to stock their cellars for the next generation. That's almost the way to handle it. Good vintage Port takes twenty years of careful ageing to reach its best. I've had vintage Port 100 years old that still had plenty of life. It's up to individual shippers to decide whether to declare a vintage year for their product. When they do, the wine is bottled two-and-a-half to three years after the harvest, and sold in bottles. It must mature gracefully for ten years or more before being consumed. The length of ageing required depends on the excellence of the vintage. Good years require longer to mature, and can last for a century. As it matures, vintage Port throws a deposit in the bottle, so it is imperative that the wine stay undisturbed in the cellar while it ages. It must be brought up from the cellar with great care and decanted to separate the deposit from the wine.

Vintage Port will keep for a limited length of time once opened—perhaps a week or so in a well-stoppered decanter. Great vintage Port can be the high point of the art of winemaking.

*Late Bottled Vintage (LBV) Port*

This is a less expensive offshoot of vintage Port. The wine has been held in cask by the shipper for a minimum of almost four years, and has thrown its deposit in the cask. It does not need decanting. Shippers do not usually offer an LBV Port dated with the same year as a declared vintage. LBVs are therefore usually of lower quality, but thank fortune for them. They are favoured by restaurants because it's easy to handle them. That fact improves available selections of Port.

## Crusted Port

Shippers blend a variety of Ports to produce crusted Port, which can be ready to drink in three or four years. It shows some of the characteristics of vintage Port, but is considerably less expensive. Not a bad choice if you want decent Port, ready to drink in a year or so. The label will show the date of bottling. Like vintage Port, crusted Port can be stored in the cellar for a number of years, and should be carefully decanted before serving.

## White Port

White Ports come in a range of styles from sweet to bone dry and they are extremely popular in Europe as an aperitif. White Port is priced about the same as a good ruby, and can be enjoyed in the same way. Or you can add a cube or two of ice, a slice of lemon, and discover that it sure beats most of those patent aperitif wines as a tipple before dinner.

# VINTAGES OF THE CENTURY

Spit happens. Yes, there are times when you have to spit the good stuff. Such an occasion was a Port lover's dream come true—more Port than the thirstiest enthusiast could handle—on June 12, 1999, at the 150-year-old Bolsa Palace in Portugal's northern city of Oporto. It was the largest tasting ever of those marvellous wines, a tasting billed as the Vintages of the Century, an affair impossible to duplicate. Imagine the best Port vintages of the twentieth century, 271 Port wines, from forty-seven renowned producers, ranging from the vintage year 1900 to the most recent at that time, the 1996 vintage. Spread these wines, bottles, and several thousand glasses over almost 100 metres of tables in the four-storey main Hall of the Nations in the Bolsa Palace, and then turn loose sixty-two international wine journalists for a marathon daylong tasting.

Imagine. Sitting in front of you are eight glasses of Port, four from the 1934 vintage and four from 1935, both years of outstanding quality. Any Port lover would be ecstatic to share one bottle of either vintage with a dozen friends. One such bottle would cost today more than $1,000, if you could find it. I'd never before even *sniffed* a glass from either year—and I've tasted a lot of Ports.

Tasting and comparing these eight glasses of Port, four '34s and four '35s, you examined the colour of each, sniffed the bouquet, made some notes. Next you sipped each wine in turn, rolling it around your mouth, and then—sigh—you spat out the wine, with regret, so your judgment for subsequent wines would not be warped by the twenty percent alcohol content of each glass.

When you'd finished with that flight of Ports, a waiter came, took away the precious remains, and set another eight glasses in front of you. Those glasses of '34 and '35 you had sampled, still holding a substantial quantity of wine, were poured away as waste. Sob! If only a taster had thought to smuggle in a few empty water bottles, to act as liquid doggie bags . . .

Preparation for the Vintages of the Century tasting had begun several years earlier, as an idea spawned in the chambers of the Instituto do Vinho do Porto.

The concept was to celebrate the arrival of the millennium, from a Port perspective, and also to strike a mammoth public relations blow for Port, attracting most of the world's big names in wine writing (plus a few smaller fish like me) to a Port tasting so grand, with wines so rare, that any writer who cared about Port could not resist coming.

Some of the world's best-known wine writers, like London's Jancis Robinson, a particular idol of mine, were there, impressed and sipping along with the rest of us.

When it was decided to hold the tasting, Port producers began checking their cellars to see what vintages of their Ports they could make available. Some

Peter as a happy taster at the Vintages of the Century tasting, about two-thirds of the way through sixty-three types of Port tasted that day

houses, like Sandeman, Ferreira, Calem, and Ramos Pintos went all out. Sandeman found Ports from forty-five vintages, starting at 1900, but got badly stung by a supplier who passed off something considerably younger for a 1900. Ferreira presented thirteen wines from a legitimate 1900 through 1904, '12, '20, '34, '45, and '47 to 1995. Calem's offering of sixteen Ports began at 1908, went through '20, '31, '34, '47, '63, and on to 1996. Ramos Pintos showed nineteen vintages, beginning at 1917 through '21 to '24 inclusive, then '34 and '35, with '52, '60, the '70s and '80s, to 1995. Other remarkables included the 1927 Niepoort (which I thought was best of the lot), to a whole flight of Ports from the great 1963 vintage.

Vintage Port is born from the grapes of the best Douro vineyards, trodden into juice by human feet, usually, in a stone vat called a *lagar*. It gets fermented to just the right degree of sweetness, then dosed with brandy to bring it to twenty percent alcohol, and to stop fermentation. It then gets stored in casks to rest and to be evaluated to see if it is good enough to become "vintage."

A Port company can "declare" a vintage two to three years after the harvest, but before this Port is bottled, it must be passed as being fit quality for sale as a "vintage" by a blind-tasting panel of the Instituto do Vinho do Porto. Once passed by the panel, the vintage Port must rest for many years in bottle before it is ready to drink. It begins life as a thick, red-purple, fiery liquid, a wine heavily dosed with brandy. As the years pass, solids deposit in the bottle and the wine gradually changes colour, first to a ruby red, then a brick red, then a reddish umber, and finally something slightly brown, rather like an old Madeira.

This tasting taught me that old Vintage Port is not necessarily worth the high price demanded for it. Once Vintage Port gets to be thirty or forty years old, you're much better off to buy a good tawny Port with indication of age, or to buy a *colheita*—a Port of a particular year that has been kept in barrel until just before you buy it. There certainly are exceptions. Excellent vintage years bottled by excellent Port producers can be magnificent for seventy years, as demonstrated by the Niepoort 1927.

Timing for the Vintages of the Century tasting was crucial, so the Port Institute decided to have the tasting just a few days before Vinexpo, nearby Bordeaux's famous wine show, which attracts many of the world's wine writers. If wine writers would be there for Vinexpo, they would almost certainly come early for a Port tasting like this.

The Vintages of the Century tasting brought journalists from most European countries, from Brazil, Hong Kong, Japan, Russia, the US, and Canada. The largest delegations came from countries where quality Port is most popular, namely Brazil and Holland. Those who were interested were invited to spend two days up the river Douro, at some of the Quintas where Port grapes are grown.

I went to Burmester's Quinta Nova and Ramos Pintos' Quinta do Bom-Retiro, both about a two-hour drive east of Oporto, and both producers were well represented with wines at the Vintages of the Century tasting.

It's always a thrilling experience to visit the Douro vineyards, with their terraced plantings on stony slopes of up to sixty degrees. You travel in four-wheel drive vehicles, straining on narrow twisting tracks that often overhang the vines below, so you look out the passenger seat to see no road, only the magnificent view.

It's prudent to get out and watch when the driver has to turn around. The biggest change since the last time I visited was that an increasing number of growers were now planting vineyards vertically, the rows going straight downhill, instead of on terraces that follow the contours of the hills.

Erosion? That's the obvious question. The answer at Ramos Pintos, which first planted vertical vineyards twenty-five years ago, was that the stony schist soil doesn't shift much, and that mechanical cultivators can bring what soil is eroded back up the hill. The advantage is that the three main varieties of red grapes to make Port can be planted in the same vineyard, with the slower ripening varieties at the warmer base of the slopes, and the faster ripening grapes at the upper levels. Some Port producers claim that fermenting the three varieties together gives better end results.

Interesting though the vineyards were, it was wonderful to enjoy that Ramos Pintos swimming pool after a hot day on the slopes. We made an important discovery there. A half-empty Champagne flute will float beside you in the pool, provided you make no waves. There were ice buckets containing bottles of Champagne, cold bottles of beer, and iced white Port scattered around the edge of the pool, with dishes of toasted almonds, all within reach of the pool so you didn't have to climb out to have a drink. The French Champagne giant Roederer now owns Ramos Pintos, so it seemed fitting to sample the proprietor's wares, if only to prepare for the onslaught of Port that was coming the next day.

We arrived at the Bolsa Palace shortly after nine a.m. to watch the experts of the Port companies decant their precious vintages. Vintage Port throws a bitter-tasting deposit and must be carefully poured into a decanter or another clean bottle, leaving the deposit behind. For older, more precious vintages, a pair of Port tongs is sometimes used. The iron sides of the tongs are heated red hot, then clamped over the neck of the bottle to heat the glass. When the tongs are removed, a cloth dampened with cold water is applied, and the neck of the bottle will snap cleanly off below the cork. The Port is then carefully decanted into another container. For the Vintages of the Century tasting, in many cases the original bottles were thoroughly cleaned after decanting, and then refilled with the Port they had held, less the deposit. Journalists and photographers swarmed to the tables to watch.

By ten-thirty a.m. all Ports had been transferred to the great Nations Hall of Bolsa Palace, and set on tables around the perimeter. Thousands of tasting glasses were ranked behind the bottles, and each glass fitted with a paper collar, identifying the type of Port and the vintage. Fifty or so staff stood behind the Port tables or circulated through the twelve tables of wine writers. Each of us had a stack of tasting request sheets. We'd fill in a sheet naming eight Ports, their producers, and the vintage. A waiter would bring our requested wines almost immediately.

We each were given a hardcover tasting book, plus a vintages book that included tasting notes from the company that produced each Port. We were also each given a litre of water to clean palates between sips, and a spit bucket. Swallow too much Port at twenty percent alcohol, and your judgment quickly disappears.

You must decide in advance on some logical approach to a tasting like this, an approach made with the full knowledge that no person could possibly taste through 271 Ports in a single day. I decided to start with Burmester and Calem Ports, because I have friends with both companies, and I like their Port style. Burmester 1970 was super, with a good balance between fruit and wood, with good depth of flavour. The 1935 Calem was even better, with a surprising red brick colour still strong, a bouquet of blossoms, apricots, and dried fruit, and loads of figs and apricots in the taste, mixed with nutty flavours.

Bottles of Port and tasters at the Vintages of the Century tasting

Next came the Ports of Ferreira. The 1920 won three stars in my tasting notes for a deep umber colour and a great concentration of fruit in balance with the tannin and acid. The 1908 was at least as good, with flavours of raisins, figs, honey, and tobacco. The 1900 Ferreira was the anticipated star of this tasting, and with its intense dried fruit flavours, and deep umber and caramel colours, it lived up to expectations. Tasting that wine blind, I would have sworn it was an old Madeira.

It seemed about time to taste some recent vintages, so I tried the 1996 Ports on offer, and was surprised to find that I liked the Quinta doVista Alegre best, because the producer was unknown to me. It will be ready for drinking in ten years, and last three or four decades in your cellar.

Best of four 1977 Ports was the Smith-Woodhouse, closely followed by the Sandeman. Pocas was the best Port of the seven available from that great year, 1963, and Sandeman tied with Croft as the quality of the 1945 vintage. By this time I had sixty-two Ports listed in my tasting notes. Like the rest of the tasters, my mouth was raw from tannin and alcohol, my judgment slipping. But before quitting, I simply had to try the 1900 Sandeman.

What a surprise! You could tell by the ruby, slightly brickish colour, that this was no 1900 Port—far too much colour, and quite lively. It tasted like a good twenty-year-old tawny. I talked to a couple of fellow tasters, who all agreed that this was more like something from the 1960s, or a tawny.

I headed for the Sandeman area and quickly found a senior spokesman. He blushed, but quite readily explained. When Sandeman heard about the Vintages of the Century tasting, there was no 1900 vintage in their cellars, so they put out the word to other companies that they would like to buy some of their 1900 vintage. A dealer in London claimed to have found two cases. The labels and corks looked authentic, so Sandeman bought. By the time the company discovered this was not a 1900 Port, but something from a much later vintage, all the material for the tasting had been printed, so Sandeman allowed the professed 1900 vintage to stand at the tasting.

After the tasting, we had to shower and change for a gala dinner. More wine, rich food, and gorgeous Portuguese Sera cheese with tawny Port at the end. As dinner concluded, word came that some of the leftover vintage Ports were available, if anyone was interested. You'd think we would have had enough, but there was almost a stampede for the Port tables. It's hard to get too much of a good thing.

# RIESLING

If you smell apricots, peaches, pears, or fruit blossoms in your wineglass, chances are pretty good you've got Riesling wine about to cross your palate. Germany and France's Alsace region made this great grape variety famous; it's been adopted in wine growing countries around the world, particularly in the cooler northern/southern hemisphere areas where moderate temperatures fit best with the grape variety's hardy vines and late ripening habits. Riesling can be very sweet or very dry. It can even be semi-sweet and taste dry because of its superb natural acidity. It makes wonderful ice wine that can improve with age.

It's said in the wine business that Chardonnay is made in the winery and Riesling is made in the vineyard. That's so right. Some say that on the shale-based, thirty-degree southern slopes of the banks of Germany's Mosel, Saar, and Ruwer rivers, Riesling grapes reach their winemaking perfection, producing an elixir loaded with fruit flavours, tingling tart on the palate, yet capable of improving in the bottle for several decades. Others argue that Riesling is best grown on the south-facing slopes of Alsace's hills, where they make a wine so steely dry it almost tastes of stainless steel, yet it flaunts its fruit in both bouquet and flavour, again ageing well for decades. Make it steely dry or semi-sweet, even as sweet as late harvest wine or ice wine. It can be a delight in all those forms.

Riesling grapes made the first decent Ontario wines, back in the late 1970s, and winemakers have improved since then as growers take advantage of that stony, mineral-rich soil on the bench between the Niagara escarpment and Lake Ontario. In recent years some large new Riesling vineyards have been planted by Vineland Estates on a field of shale not unlike some of the soil in the Mosel-Saar-Ruwer. Early results from those plantings show new promise for Ontario Riesling wines.

A Riesling wine should be clean in your mouth with just enough acid to perk up your palate. It should smell of apricots, peaches, pears, or even citrus, sometimes with blossom fragrances. Drink it in delight with things like shellfish, light-bodied fish, lighter chicken dishes flavoured with fruit, or oriental food—Thai, Chinese, or Indian.

# VIETNAM,
# NORTH AND SOUTH

A trip to Vietnam with Canada's then Minister of External Affairs, Mitchell Sharp, was extremely important to me in early 1973, because the US was pulling out, after more than a decade of bloodshed, and I was writing for half a dozen large American newspapers. Normally, newspapers like my customers—the *Boston Globe*, the *Miami Herald*, the *Baltimore Sun*, the *Detroit News*, the *Washington Star*, and the *Buffalo Evening News*—were interested only in Canadian news from me, and would naturally depend on American reporting for everything else. But Mitchell Sharp and the Canadian delegation were not only going to Saigon, but also to Hanoi. American journalists didn't get into Hanoi in those days, because parts of the city were still repairing bomb damage from US raids in late 1972.

Mr. Sharp was going to Vietnam to discuss terms of the temporary multinational force that would be in place to save US face as their forces were withdrawn, leaving the government of the South to fight alone, armed with US equipment. Canadians were part of that multinational force, and were already in South Vietnam, so it was important for top-level Canadian input through talks in Saigon with the failing government there, and in Hanoi, where the North could hardly wait for the US to withdraw so it could demolish the faltering South Vietnamese army.

Landing at Saigon's Tan Son Nhut Airport was something of a homecoming for me, because I'd spent two months in Vietnam in 1965, covering the war for the *Toronto Telegram* and *Weekend Magazine*. The smog and noise of thousands of Honda motorbikes was just the same as it had been eight years ago—perhaps a bit worse. In those earlier days, I'd been through the routine of paying off officials to get permission to file news copy, buying Vietnamese money on the black market, attending a few of the news conferences run by US information impresario Barry Zorthian—events known in the press corps as Zorthian's Five O'clock Follies—and finding a cheap place to stay. No problem in finding quarters when you're travelling with Canada's Minister of External Affairs; we were billeted at Saigon's Continental Place Hotel, a landmark since French colonial days, and once the haunt of Graham Greene.

There's a charming verandah that goes around two sides of the Continental, where patrons sit over breakfast, lunch, coffee, or cocktails. This balcony extends deeply into the body of the hotel, crowded with tables and patrons. Invariably the tables closest to the street displayed a healthy sprinkling of high-priced hookers, so that since the early 1960s the hotel's verandah has been known as the Continental Shelf.

Peter with Saigon's Continental Palace Hotel in the background

Unfortunately we were billeted in the annex, a rabbit warren across the street. My room was large, with a cracked washbasin, and the shower was rudimentary. One morning I caught an extremely large insect retreating down the drain. All veteran travellers in our group followed the accepted practice of brushing our teeth with beer, because not even the bottled water was totally safe, thanks to Saigon entrepreneurs who have been known to collect empty water bottles, fill them from the taps, and then sell them as the real thing. We were allowed, however, to eat our meals in the hotel's delightful courtyard dining area, an oasis of quiet, palm trees, fountains, and soft music in the heart of the Continental's main floor. No wonder the French loved the place.

One of our small band of reporters did get into a touch of trouble. Late one afternoon he came pounding on my door asking for some money. It seems he had invited one of the girls from the Continental Shelf to his room, where she immediately demanded payment for services about to be rendered. He paid, and as the banknotes went into her bra, a heavy object hammered on his door wielded by the policeman who apparently worked with the girl. He whisked girl and cash from the room, then demanded payment from our colleague of more than he had, else he would be taken to the cells—not a pleasant prospect anywhere, and particularly undesirable in Saigon when you're travelling with the Canadian Minister of External Affairs. We helped him out with a loan, he paid off the police con man, and that was that.

Mr. Sharp's talks in Saigon went well. We spent some time with Canadian troops who would be keeping the peace for a few months while the American troops withdrew, and then prepared for the flight to Hanoi in our Canadian government aircraft.

As we circled to approach the landing, everybody pressed foreheads against the windows, looking for evidence of past US air attacks. Yes, there were filled bomb craters straddling the runways, and several burnt-out vehicles. There was some obvious damage to the main airport buildings, hastily repaired. Considering it had been a month or so since the last American attack, the cleanup was efficiently aimed at getting things working again, rather than at cosmetics.

A camouflage-painted bus waited for us. As we boarded the bus, we met the smiling guide who would be with us for the duration of our short Hanoi stay. He was about thirty, loaded with enthusiastic energy, eyes sparkling through medium-strength glasses, and about five foot five inches tall. He offered a running commentary in pretty good English as the bus rumbled towards Hanoi over rough, patched pavement.

Without warning, we drove into the middle of severe bomb damage. To our right, we could see through the windows that rubble was heaped in a hodgepodge mess. You could see the odd railway wheel box upside down, shattered rail cars, and the mangled remains of several locomotives. Not very long ago this had been a major railway marshalling yard. Now it was filled with scrap metal and pulverized masonry. On the left side of the road, and at both ends of the ruins, stood houses with their windows blown out. The blast of bomb explosions had been their only damage. The bombing had been not merely accurate, but surgical.

We turned left, over the main Red River bridge into Hanoi, where bomb damage was obvious at both bridge approaches, and several sections of the bridge were new, showing evidence of recent repair. Our guide, who had been describing the bomb damage as we went, became almost lyrical with understandable pride as he explained how the people had restored this major link between Hanoi and Haiphong within hours of each American bombing raid.

The bus took us through one of Hanoi's better residential districts, where gracious old plane trees joined branches in a leafy arch across lovely wide avenues, lined with colonial-age homes. We newsmen came to the common conclusion that this must have been where senior French civil servants enjoyed their lives in the old colonial days before World War II, when Ho Chin Minh was a youngster, pleading for French, then British, then American support for his nationalist movement in French Indochina. As a very young man, Ho Chi Minh made his first international plea for independence at the Paris peace talks of 1919, where his representations were ignored in spite of US president Woodrow Wilson's fourteen points, one of which said there should be ethnic self-determination for nations affected by the war. When France was allowed by the allies to resume colonial rule at the end of World War II, Vietnamese nationalists, who had freed their country from the Japanese with virtually no outside help, resisted French reoccupation with guerrilla warfare. The communists, with the most effective organization, rapidly became the nationalist leaders.

We were taken to one of a series of massive buildings, each five storeys high, and divided into suites consisting of two rooms each with beds for six people, both rooms sharing a bathroom with washbasins and several toilets. Without question these had been barracks for French troops, built sometime between the two world wars, probably in the early 1930s. A rough calculation suggested that these buildings had been living quarters for about five thousand troops.

I said something to our guide about how well the Vietnamese were maintaining these old French barracks, using them for their own purposes. He drew himself up to full height, eyes blazing, and told me that these barracks had all been built by the Vietnamese after the French had been defeated in Vietnam.

What he said was so obviously untrue, that I was momentarily flabbergasted. We were standing in the doorway of one of the suites, right beside the old toggle light switch, connected to wiring tacked to the door moulding. There was printing on the housing of the switch.

"If you built these quarters," I said, "why does it say on this old light switch, in French, 'made by the Shanghai Electric Company'?"

He stared at the switch, gave me a venomous look, stamped his foot, wheeled, and marched away, head held high. In Hanoi, those days, you didn't question the Big Lie.

Our guide returned in half an hour, acting as though nothing had happened. We were to go to a luncheon held by the government's Minister of Information, and our bus was ready. The route wound through another residential district of the city, just as elegant, with no bomb damage visible. We stopped at a spacious complex centred on one large single-storey building whose walls were lined with windows. Inside there was a horseshoe-shaped table, seating perhaps seventy people, with a head table, slightly elevated, closing the top of the horseshoe. That's where the Minister of Information sat, with his senior aides. Our guide sat next to me to translate. We'd been warned, but the shock of straight alcohol distilled from rice wine still hit our systems hard in the first toast as the minister made his short welcoming speech.

The food was Vietnamese, and excellent—bits of chicken, crispy noodles, stir-fried vegetables. The plates were trimmed with what looked like small poinsettia flowers. Our Vietnamese neighbours were munching on these, so I gave one a try. Never before or since have I had anything so spicy hot in my mouth. The "poinsettias" were actually small Vietnamese red peppers, their outer shells sliced with sharp knives so they curled open like petals, leaving the yellow seed-bearing centre to mimic the yellow at the heart of a poinsettia bloom. The Vietnamese were highly amused by Canadian journalists' way of meeting the local taste for spicy stuff with their food.

Despite red peppers, luncheon was a welcome experience. We listened with attention as the minister gave us the North Vietnamese version of the events of the war that was winding down because of the agreement signed in early 1973. One of the things he told us—several times—was that there were no North Vietnamese troops fighting in the South, and never had been, but that the people who had fought the Southern government, and the Americans, to a standstill were all people from the South, whose opposition to government and will to join the North had finally been successful. We took copious notes of this briefing, because it would be important to show exactly how far official Hanoi stretched the truth.

After lunch, back on the bus for a scheduled trip to some of Hanoi's sights. We made a stop in one of the less prosperous neighbourhoods, where a funeral was taking place—a victim of American bombing who had died of injuries, our guide said. The body was lying open to view in a glass-cased hearse, elevated so the crowd could all see. The expected mourning was taking place, while flowers were strewn about, almost as you would expect at a wedding, We were shown a house hit by a bomb, curiously the only evidence of any destruction in the entire district. It looked as though at least one bomb had gone astray from the precision destruction the Americans claimed.

Our next stop was a beautiful park, with paths winding alongside small lakes, canals, and small green hills. Children watched by their mothers played the games kids play around the world. What jolted our senses was the number of men in uniform, sitting on benches or wandering the park, each with a leg or an arm missing.

These, said our guide, were soldiers who had been wounded in the hard fighting in the South.

"How can that be?" I asked. "Your minister just told us there were absolutely no North Vietnamese soldiers fighting in the South."

He glared at me again, and then went into the now-familiar denial routine of a stamped foot, about turn and an indignant walk away from this troublemaker.

Our next stop was a visit to that hospital where Jane Fonda had posed for pictures in late 1972 amidst the bomb damage. As we approached, there was an area the size of a good city block that had been bombed to rubble. Nothing was standing much more than six feet high. You could see the remains of machinery, heavy lathes, punch presses, and huge gear wheels scattered through the wreckage. At the far side of this ruin, across the road, stood the hospital, again the size of a large city block, and about five storeys high. We were taken to the main entrance, inside, where Jane Fonda had stood to model for that famous picture. One bomb had come through the ceiling at the entrance to the hospital, no more than fifty yards from the bombed factory. As far as we could determine, that was the only bomb to hit this hospital, obviously a stray from the bombing of that heavy equipment manufacturing plant next door. Could Ms. Fonda have missed seeing the damage next door when she went to pose for pictures? I suppose so, if you stretch credulity.

We left Hanoi shortly after that, crowding around Mr. Sharp as he gave us a post-trip briefing. We all wrote on the way to Tokyo, where we would be able to file our stories on Hanoi. My American customer newspapers were extremely interested in what we'd seen. It was a successful trip, both in terms of what we'd learned, and in earnings that would eventually roll in from the stories filed. One of my stories in the *Baltimore Sun* about the accuracy of American bombing was even quoted by former US secretary of state Henry Kissinger in his book about the final stages of the Vietnam War.

# PINOT NOIR

It's called the heartbreak grape because it presents so many pitfalls for growers and winemakers. When climate, soil, and winery skills combine successfully, Pinot Noir can be transformed into some of the world's finest wines. It can be made into Champagne, rosé, early consumption quaffing wine, or aristocratic treasures that improve for several decades in a wine cellar and require a bank loan to purchase.

Pinot Noir vines bud early, so they can't tolerate spring frosts. The vines are prone to most vineyard blights. They produce their best fruit in cool climates; they thrive best in limestone soils.

High quality Pinot Noir can wrap your senses in a kaleidoscope of sensations from rich spicy strawberries, cherries and violets; then after lengthy ageing, the wine can produce barnyard smells and gamy meat flavours. Less expensive Pinot Noir wines usually offer strawberries and cherries with intensity varying according to the amount of fruit the vines have been allowed to produce. Depth of colour in the wine depends on how long the juice has been allowed to ferment with the skins. Too brief a period and the wine will be pale in colour; too long and it may have picked up some disagreeable tannins. In Champagne, they press Pinot Noir berries as soon as they are harvested. Still, sometimes there's a slight pinkish tinge to a Champagne that's 100 percent Pinot Noir.

The Pinot Noir grape has probably been around for two millennia. Areas of east central France, Burgundy and Champagne are the variety's ancestral homes. Burgundy produces the world's most expensive Pinot Noir wines, but California (Josh Jensen's Calera Winery), Oregon, and Ontario (the best from Inniskillin, Herb Konzelmann, and Jim Warren) are producing excellent wines at much more reasonable prices.

A wide range of Pinot Noir wines in the $10 to $20 price bracket is available in most Canadian centres. There are even some priced lower from Eastern Europe that will serve for a barbecue.

Duck, goose, wild game, turkey, chicken, and beef are my favourite foods with Pinot Noir, which seems correctly to indicate I'll drink it with almost anything.

# FRENCH CATALANS, WINE, AND BULLFIGHTS

As we flew above southern France, into the Languedoc-Roussillon region, the air was so thick with smog that you could barely see the ground from 10,000 feet despite a clear sky and sunshine. This was the beginning of a ten-day tour of the vineyards of southwestern France, arranged for a half-dozen wine writers by Sopexa, the organization charged with promoting French wines in Canada.

We were all pretty tired, having flown overnight from Toronto to Paris, and then changed planes for Perpignan in Roussillon. Our understanding guide, tall, willowy blonde Christine Bach, had scheduled a little sightseeing that day, with no work—work for us being the marathon wine tastings that take place on such a tour. Most wine writers follow the rule that they'll accept a promotional wine tour trip paid for by a country, a district, or a consortium of many wineries, but not from an individual winery, because that might compromise objectivity. Wine writers find that there are usually three, four, or even more such invitations each year. I found I could make time to accept perhaps two such trips a year.

Our first task on this trip to Languedoc-Roussillon was to check into a hotel. We had arrived on a Sunday, so Christine had scheduled an afternoon drive in our minibus along the Mediterranean coast to the Spanish border, then back to a restaurant perched on the beach near the coastal road. About four in the afternoon we drove into a small seaside town where the road stayed close to the coast, beaches to the south, parks and open space to the north. We slowed at a spot where a small orchestra was playing.

There was a square paved with stone tiles, five musicians in a small bandstand, tables around the edges with scattered glasses, wine, and beer bottles, and several hundred people dancing in the square. Some of the dancers looked to be in their seventies; some were schoolchildren. Every age was represented. We all wanted to stop for a beer, so our driver obliged. The dancers were in circles, arms around each other's shoulders, dancing first in one direction, then the other, some circles of as many as forty people and some with only half a dozen. In no time at all we were served with beer, and invited to join the dancing. Strange language. It wasn't French, but Catalan, the language that is either first or second tongue for most of the people in that band of Mediterranean coastline from well west of Barcelona, Spain, almost to Marseilles. In places Catalan country reaches several hundred miles inland.

We left the dancing Catalans, drove on to the Spanish border, and then turned back. We returned to that dancing village no more than an hour after we had left it. There wasn't a person remaining in the square and bandstand was empty.

When we stopped briefly to ask a few questions, we were told that every Sunday afternoon the entire village comes to that square to dance and socialize before going home for Sunday dinner. What an introduction to Roussillon! No wonder great artists like Picasso, Matisse, and Georges Braque loved the area.

Every meal we enjoyed on that trip had something of a Catalan tone—hearty bean and meat dishes, frequently some goat, garlic, lots of rice and spice. In one restaurant we were challenged to use that great Catalan drinking tool, the jug with a spout. You fill it with wine, start pouring into your mouth while the jug is held close, then extend your arm while the wine still flows, running smoothly into your mouth in an unending stream. At least that's the theory. First time you try it, you should use white wine or wear an old shirt—or perhaps you should do both. The difficulty is that when a newcomer is challenged to perform this feat, it's usually after more than a few glasses of wine, which limits the discretion, and the wine is invariably red.

We visited several wineries with a Catalan slant, too. At that stage the emergence of quality wine in the Languedoc-Roussillon area was just beginning, with many producers fighting an uphill battle over labels with their betters in Bordeaux and Burgundy. Both these august wine districts objected strongly to any French producer using the name of the grape type—Cabernet

Peter using a Catalan drinking jug at dinner while
Christine Bach laughs

Sauvignon, Cabernet Franc, Merlot, Chardonnay, Pinot Noir—on any label, because those, of course, are the grape varieties of Bordeaux and Burgundy, where wine is named for the property at which the grapes are grown, not for the grape variety. That rule has long since been overturned, but at the time of this visit, almost every producer we visited complained about being unfairly restricted, prohibited from naming the grape variety of the wine on the bottle's label.

We met winemakers and watched them work in old, new, small, and large wineries, tasting as we went until our mouths had that familiar acid burn from swishing too much wine before spitting. On a tour like this, you only remember the places that stand out, either because of some winemaking innovation, a high-quality wine, a low-quality wine, or the personality of the winemaker. I can recall one small winery where the oak casks of ageing wine were stored in a wonderfully cool cellar, barrels stacked on white gravel, and the entire building sparkling clean. The wines, made from local grape varieties like Grenache and Mourvèdre, were just as clean as their surroundings, and were obviously made with loving care. Contrast that with a large winery we visited in Fitou, where unwashed workers in stained blue working dress, cigarettes dangling from their lips, shovelled grapes into a fermenter, caring not a whit if cigarette ashes fell into the wine. There were even several cats about, making you wonder what else might find its way into the wine. In fairness, the wine didn't taste bad, and local people were lined up with their jugs to buy from the huge vats at the retail store.

Our wine tasting took us to Limoux, famous for sparkling wines, where it is said that Dom Perignon stopped on his way home to Champagne from Rome and showed the locals how to capture bubbles in their wine. Quite close by is the mediaeval town of Carcassonne, one of the most spectacular sites in all of Southern France. A modern tourist town is built around the castle, which is one of the best-preserved castles in the world. People still live within its walls, almost as they did several centuries ago, only now they have electricity. Shops in the narrow, winding streets that sold the necessities of life to people 500 years ago now offer bargains to tourists such as souvenirs made in China. The castle and its village within the walls have been used in countless movie period epics. Carcassonne was the home of the Cathar religion, a heretical belief widespread in Europe in the twelfth and thirteenth centuries. We were invited into the home of an elderly woman who spent an interesting hour trying unsuccessfully to convert two of us.

After Carcassonne we drove south to the coast road, heading for the eastern limits of the Languedoc-Roussillon wine country. We followed the sand spit that divides a large inland lake from the Mediterranean, with small waves whipped up by the wind driving down from the mountains towards the sea. Without any notice, two or three sails appeared beside us on the lake. Windsurfers. They were going at least as fast as our minibus, some of them even faster. Speeds of more than eighty kilometres an hour have been clocked on this lake, according to our driver. This great inland lake is a favourite spot for windsurfers, who come from all over Europe because of the strong, almost constant wind.

On a trip like this, you have to change hotels frequently, sometimes every night. A wise tour conductor, like Christine, arranges at least a couple of nights in the same place for the group, a location that can be used as a central base for several days of winery inspections. Our target for the next base was the old Roman city of Nîmes, where we were also to be allowed most of a day free to attend a bullfight. It was my first and only trip to view a bullfight. I'm not sure I'd go again, but I would not have missed this one for anything.

Nîmes is part of Catalan country, and until recently, bullfights there were a regular thing. Now they take place only a few times a year, on special holidays. We were fortunate enough to be there for such an occasion. The whole town was wild, like Mardi Gras in New Orleans. There were sideshow tents, street food vendors, amusement rides, and small bands playing all over town. Street dancing was everywhere.

The bullring at Nîmes isn't really a ring. The arena is a huge oval, surrounded by the stone arches typical of a Roman arena. The only thing changed since Roman times are the wooden seats, which have been replaced as needed, probably when the stonework was repaired once a century. I don't know of any other Roman arena still in use like this. It's a building of real historical beauty, so that as you mix with the crowds entering, you take a giant step back in history.

There were six bulls on the program that afternoon, with three matadors, two bulls each. The star of the afternoon was to be a nineteen-year-old Spaniard said to be headed for the best bullrings of Madrid and Barcelona. The first bull of the afternoon was shocking slaughter. Picadors goaded the back of this big black animal until blood ran from his neck in gobbets. The role of the picadors is to weaken the neck muscles of the bull just enough, not too much, so that the bull's final stand against the matador will at least have the elements of a fight. This poor animal could hardly stand when the matador took centre stage to end the ordeal. The crowd was not pleased.

Conscious of their error, the picadors were less enthusiastic with their lances on the next bull, so the performance of the matador had some of the elements of bullfighting so praised by Hemingway. The next bull was slaughter again, the fourth was a little better, the fifth again dominated by overly enthusiastic picadors, which meant that they treated the last bull, to be fought by the young Spanish protegé, much more lightly. The bull was so feisty when the young matador approached that the young man, slightly injured, was chased from the ring, something that would probably spell the end of his career, or åt least mean a long learning stint for him back in the minor leagues.

One of the seasoned matadors, a greybeard of perhaps twenty-five, stepped out to finish the job. He played that bull magnificently back and forth, with his red cape swirling in the best style. The crowd, disappointed until now, came to life and chanted "Olé!" at every pass.

Finally the matador took his sword, hidden from the bull by the killing cape. He stood his ground as the animal lowered its head, then put the sword exactly where it should go for a clean kill. The bull stood there, sword protruding from its neck. The matador turned his back, and took off his hat to the crowd, accepting the cheers. Then he reached behind him with one arm. Without looking, he pointed at the bull, and in Catalan shouted, "Die, *Toro*!" The bull collapsed, dead. The crowd went absolutely wild. I left the Nîmes arena with something of an understanding of why people can be such ardent fans of bullfighting.

We fought through the excited departing crowd, and went back to a hotel to attend a reception for the bullfighters, mingling with several hundred invitees, to sip Pernod and watch the fans buzzing around these matadors like a New York crowd around the Pride of the Yankees. There may not be weekly bullfights at Nîmes any more, but the population certainly looks forward to the few occasions that still remain.

We had one more day of winery visits left on this trip, then we headed north to Dijon to catch the super-fast train for Paris and the plane that would take us home. The smog got thicker as we neared Dijon, so thick that our eyes began to sting. The atmosphere, I guess, was part of the price for living downwind of considerable economic activity. The acidic sting of our eyes stayed with us on the train, right up to the time when we reached the air-conditioned sanctuary of Charles de Gaulle Airport.

I haven't been back to the south of France since that trip. Friends who go there often tell me that we were unlucky to meet a rare pollution condition that does cause trouble with air quality from time to time. All I know is that it was great to be home again.

# GRENACHE

If you're sipping a blended wine from anywhere around the Mediterranean, chances are excellent that you've got some Grenache wine in your glass. Most growers prize Grenache, because when ripe it's a grape with a very high sugar content, which equates to high alcohol content in the fermented wine. Growers who take care to limit production per acre get both the high alcohol and some remarkable flavours. Grenache is one of the main building blocks of the great Châteauneuf-de-Pape wines of the Rhône, as well as many of the other high-quality Rhône wines. When they are well treated, Grenache vines can produce heavy, spicy, meaty red wines, like those of Gigondas and Vacqueyras. It does best in poor soil and in a hot climate. It's Spain's most planted black grape variety, used sometimes for a blending wine and sometimes by itself, where it can produce real quality wines.

The first time I tasted a Cannonau wine from Sardinia I was impressed with the body and concentrated flavour. Of course—Cannonau and Grenache are the same grape. Sardinians and the Spanish both claim the origins of Grenache, each maintaining that the other got the grape from them.

Many of the wines from Spain and southern France use Grenache in blends, although it's going slightly out of fashion in the stampede towards Merlot and Cabernet Sauvignon. Grenache grows on sturdy-trunked bushes, making it not the ideal vine for mechanical harvesting, a fact which goes against it with many growers. Grenache is also planted in Australia, New Zealand, South Africa, and California, but in declining amounts.

# COGNAC

It's rather strange that the Moors, who are Muslims and teetotallers, were responsible for one of the world's greatest liquid palate-pleasers. If it hadn't been for the Dark Ages, and the invasion by the Moors of Atlantic Europe right up to the Loire River on the Bay of Biscay coast, we might never have been able to stick our noses into the heavenly scent of a well-aged Cognac.

The Muslim Moors didn't drink alcohol, but they did have a passion for perfumes, and they had the scientific knowledge to make them through distillation. When the Moors were driven out of western France and Spain, they left behind them the huge onion-shaped copper kettles used for distilling rosewater and the like into perfume, so that Moorish nights would be less ripe.

From what we know of history, the worthy citizens of the Atlantic and Biscay coasts concerned themselves far less with the way they smelled than did their former Muslim masters, so the Moorish copper stills lay idle and oxidizing in their abandoned perfume plants, awaiting the call of destiny.

The Moors ate grapes and drank unfermented grape juice, but there are other things you can do with a vineyard. It didn't take the liberated west-coast peasantry—or the nouveau nobility, for that matter—very long to begin making the wine that had been prohibited under the Moors. Winemaking was so successful in some places that a thriving trade grew up, selling wine to foreigners who were not blessed with the climate of the Atlantic and Biscay coasts.

Wine was shipped off by the "tun," as the huge shipping barrels were called. Ships soon became rated in size by how many tuns of wine they could carry. Eventually all merchant shipping was graded into the number of "tuns burthen," something that still causes confusion today when landsmen try to understand the difference between displacement tonnage of ships, weight, and cargo capacity.

Those great early seamen-traders, the Dutch, provided the next necessary stepping stone along the path to the first Cognac. Shipping trade was attracted to the Charente River because of the considerable salt deposits in the area. Nobody is sharper in trading than the Dutch, and those sea captains of the Middle Ages noticed right off that the district between the mouth of the Loire and Gironde Rivers produced fairly cheap, but not very good, wines.

Captains with space available after loading salt took to shipping wine as deck cargo. A captain sharper than most with mental arithmetic is said to have conceived the idea of boiling off the water in the wines of the Charente, and shipping the stuff back home as concentrate, where water would be added again. Presto, you'd have the original volume of wine to sell, having used only a fraction of the number of tuns in shipping it to northern Europe.

After considerable experimenting with boiling off the water, the frustrated embryo brandy-makers discovered that when you boiled wine, the alcohol came off first, leaving the water behind. Then somebody remembered those old copper things that the Moors had used to make perfume out of rosewater. Why not apply the distilling science to wine?

It must have been quite an experience to taste the first result of putting wine through a Moorish perfume still. One would presume they washed the still before using it, but given some of the sharp practices with export wine that still persist today, one cannot be sure. Suffice it to say that there was some success in converting the perfume stills of the Moors into equipment for "concentrating" wine.

What came out of the still became known as "burned wine," or, as the Dutch would say, "Brandewijn." Trading captains discovered that there was a terrific market for their Brandewijn. Particularly in winter, most customers didn't bother adding water to their "concentrated" wine, preferring to knock it back straight because of the warm glow it could quickly induce. People were even willing to pay a premium for the burned wine, which must have been somewhere in the order of forty percent alcohol. For a year or so, no doubt, burned wine probably proved to be a pretty good dodge around the customs officers, too.

So here we have the Biscay coast chock-a-block with Dutch and English trading vessels, all hastening away with the wines and brandy of that blessed piece of real estate to sustain the frigid regions of the North Sea. In areas like Charente and Armagnac, where the wine wasn't top quality, people made a good living from the now-revived stills of the Moors, as they concentrated wine into brandy.

Now came the Crusades, which set the stage for the final phase in the birth of the first Cognac. A lonely and passionate young wife, caught in bed with a stay-at-home neighbour, provided the climax.

Here's the story the way it was told to me on my first visit to Cognac.

The Chevalier de la Croix Marrone came home unexpectedly to Cognac from crusading one year. When he flung open the doors of his castle and shouted, "I'm home!" he surprised his wife in bed with a neighbour. Being handy with a sword, and short of temper, he despatched them both. The townsfolk had male chauvinist ideas in those days, and they felt that the returning knight had delivered no less than justice to his unfaithful wife and her lover. He was exonerated on grounds of justifiable swording.

Having made quite a mess of the bedroom, the Chevalier was filled with remorse over his hasty deed. He discovered that whenever he slept, a strange dream pursued him, in which he would burn twice in Hell, over and over, every night. That's not conducive to a good night's sleep. The Chevalier, shrewdly guessing that the dream had something to do with his homecoming swordplay, went off to the local priest for advice on how to shake the nightmare. The priest listened, and then offered his advice, reputedly along these lines:

"You must go home and burn twice what you love most, O Chevalier de la Croix Marrone. This will rid you of the troublesome dream, because it will be penance for your hasty sword-work."

"Right," said the Chevalier to himself. "Now what do I love best?"

Being something of a toper, the Chevalier concluded that his favourite thing in life was his wine. Burn it? How would he do that?

Of course! Those Moorish copper stills that the Dutch sea captains keep hanging around. Let's take some wine from the estate and run it through the distilling pipes twice instead of just once.

And that's exactly what he did. Once through the still, and out came the usual liquid, fiery and clear. A second time through the still—burning the wine twice—there was probably a near-visible haze over the result, so powerful it would have been. Even today, when you taste raw Cognac straight from the second stilling, it's like putting a red-hot poker in your mouth. It truly burns. If the Chevalier de la Croix Marrone sampled this, the first Cognac, he must truly have believed he had paid penance for despatching his wife and her lover.

The story, as told in the town of Cognac, claims that the twice-burned wine of the Chevalier de la Croix Marrone was too strong for anyone to handle, so it was stored away in an oak barrel that happened to be around. The barrel got tucked away in some corner and forgotten—forgotten for ten years, until somebody saw it, remembered, and decided to have a look.

The oak had imparted a golden-brownish colour to the "twice-burned wine," and it smelled most delightfully of vanilla, with an overlay of toasted nuts. Who could resist a taste when it smelled like that and looked so inviting? Golly, not bad! Not nearly as raw as it was when we stored it away in this barrel.

So it was really two accidental discoveries that made Cognac what it is today. Double distilling concentrates the finest characteristics of rather undistinguished wines; oak imparts flavour to ageing Cognac, and allows the harshness to escape through the pores of the wood.

Raw Cognac is about eighty percent alcohol when it emerges from the still for the second time, and putting a drop or two on your tongue gives the same effect as eating lighted matches. Cognac's alcohol content diminishes steadily while it ages in oak casks. At one of the largest Cognac houses, Martell, they lose the equivalent of two million bottles a year in alcohol evaporation through the barrels. In Cognac, they call it "the Angels' share." That magical osmosis through the staves of French oak barrels makes the Cognac that remains into an extraordinary drink, justly prized by connoisseurs.

Cognac makers, who today "burn" their wines in copper stills, produce works of art, thanks to the perfume-making skills of the Moors in the Dark Ages, the profit motive in a bunch of sea captains, and an unfaithful wife.

The dominant building in downtown Cognac is a castle by the Charente River that used to be home base for King Francois I. He's the chap who married Maria de Medici, and through her talents, was consequently responsible for bringing Florentine cooking to France to form the basis of French cuisine. It's a beautiful castle with a delightful smell, and has more than the making of booze to commend it to the attention of tourists. Barrels of Cognac are trundled through the vaulted main guardroom of the old castle these days, but it pays to pause and examine the walls.

Carved pictures of sailing ships decorate the alcoves, along with dozens of carved names and Canadian addresses. These are the names of prisoners taken during Napoleonic times, shipped to Cognac, and held there in King Francois' castle. Tourists trek through the castle daily, enjoying the sights and delightful smells of Cognac. It's headquarters for Outard, the place where that company stores, blends, and bottles fine Cognacs.

In Cognac country they make the romantic parallel between a bouquet of flowers and a glass of their brandy. Red roses, they say, make a nice display for the nose and the eyes, but can be improved by the addition of some yellow and pink ones. Sprigs of fern, and the addition of other flowers that will complement the roses, make a more interesting bouquet. So it is with creating a Cognac.

Cognacs have a widely varied style. Some are light and ethereal; some are dark and heavy, tasting of caramel. Each Cognac producer guards the secrets that make possible his distinctive blend.

Virtually all Cognacs are blends, and that makes the cellar master the most important man on any Cognac producer's staff; he's the one responsible for blending. The job is usually handed down from generation to generation. A cellar master might begin work at twenty years old under his grandfather, and continue working with gradually increasing responsibilities until he eventually becomes cellar master at the age of forty-five or so, when his father retires.

Each Cognac company has a particular style, and each strives to maintain that style. The price of the product depends on the reputation of the producer, the age of the Cognacs in the blend, and the origin of the grapes.

There are six districts in Cognac, graded according to the amount of chalk in the soil. Grand Champagne, the district around the town of Cognac, has soil containing the most chalk, hence it produces the most prized Cognacs. In order of descending chalk content, the other districts are Petit Champagne, Borderies, Fins Bois, Bons Bois, and Bois Ordinaires. Each district produces Cognac of different characteristics, used for blending with others, to create distinctive styles.

Borderies, for example, produces heavy-bodied Cognacs ideal for blending with the more refined Cognacs of Grande Champagne.

A native of Cognac samples the good stuff; in the background is the main Cognac bridge over the Charente River

Cognac is classified in specific categories, according to rules of the Bureau du Cognac. VS Cognac, for example, must have an average age of five years, and contain no Cognac in the blend that is younger than three years old. VSOP Cognac must have an average age of seven years and contain no Cognac less than four years old. (VS and VSOP, by the way, stand for Very Superior and Very Superior Old Pale.) There are higher degrees of designation for Cognac, usually at the discretion of the bottler. You'll find XO, Napoleon, Reserve, Cordon Bleu, Extra, or Paradis used to describe special category Cognacs. There are even some companies that market Cognacs of a specific vintage, from a specific area in the Cognac district. The best Cognac I ever tasted was a Fine Champagne 1940 vintage from that superb house, Delamain. I still have the empty bottle, because just a trace of the Cognac's wonderful bouquet lingers. Remember, Cognac only ages while it's in the cask, and there's not much point in ageing a Cognac beyond forty years, because by then the alcoholic content has slipped down to forty percent or slightly less.

Once a Cognac is bottled, it doesn't change any more with age. Glass prevents evaporation, and there are no staves of an oak barrel to meld wood flavours into the taste. A 1930 Cognac, bottled in 1960, is still only thirty years old today, however good it may taste.

Every major Cognac house has its own special area for storing the oldest Cognacs, the ones dating back in some cases to the eighteenth century. These precious fluids will be stored in dusty glass demijohns, or, for the more rare samples, in individual bottles. These are for show, and for the occasional sniff accorded to special visitors.

The life of a Cognac begins with the harvest of the grapes—they are mostly Saint Emilion, known in Italy as Trebbiano—with a few Colombard and Folle Blanche. Fermentation takes place normally, to produce a rather thin wine quite low in alcoholic content. It has been said that the wine of Cognac is fit only for drinking with shellfish, and even then only if nothing else is available.

The new wine then goes through a pot still for the first time. These huge copper kettles sit on brick ovens that used to be fired with wood, but are now almost universally fuelled with gas, which makes the tricky control of temperature much easier. Fumes from the heating wine escape through the "swan-throat" tubes at the top of the copper kettles, where the alcohol is condensed out to form the "*brouillis,*" a liquid of roughly twenty-five to thirty percent alcohol.

In each distillation house in Cognac there is often a cot beside the still. Cognac requires close personal attention and great skill during the second distillation, something that is increasingly difficult to find in the present generation. An expert must be there continually through the second distillation process, because when raw Cognac begins appearing from the condensing tube, it must be sniffed carefully almost drop by drop. Only the centre or "heart" of the second distillation is kept. The "head" and the "tail," determined by the skilled nose of the distilling master, are discarded to make one more trip through the still with the next batch.

Raw Cognac is kept up to a year in new barrels made of oak from either Limousin or Tronçais forests. These days, it will almost certainly be Limousin oak, because Tronçais has become too expensive. That initial year of taming the raw spirit in raw oak is followed by periods in barrels of greater age, depending on the judgment of the cellar master. In a twenty-two (Imperial)-gallon cask of Cognac, aged in oak for twenty-five years, there would be one pound of oak extract. It's the barrel ageing that gives Cognac its colour and vanilla flavour. Flavour and colour are imparted more slowly in older casks, so one of the cellar master's major skills must be judging when to shift ageing Cognac from barrel to barrel. His happy task is to sample each batch of Cognac at least once every six months, keeping detailed notes on the characteristics he finds.

A Cognac cellar master poses atop his still

The cellar master must duplicate his company's brands of Cognac exactly on demand, using the Cognac in stock to achieve the trick. Hennessey VSOP bottled this week, for example, must be exactly the same in colour, bouquet, alcoholic content, and taste, as was the Hennessey VSOP bottled fifty years ago.

The cellar master must carry in his head or in his books a description of the Cognacs available for blending that will produce the exact result he requires. He must accomplish this within the regulations of the Bureau du Cognac, and he must do so as economically as possible. When the rules specify that VSOP must have an average age of no less than seven years, it would be uneconomical for the company to use a blend that averaged ten years old.

Each barrel of new Cognac is marked with specific information cataloguing where the grapes were grown, who grew them, and who distilled the Cognac and when, as well as the date it was put into the cask.

At some point during the ageing career of a cask of Cognac, it may get blended with another Cognac from another location and another year. Once the first blending takes place, the barrels are marked in code, so that only the cellar master, with his codebook, knows the exact proportions of the blend used to achieve a specific result.

It is a marvellous experience to watch stacks of huge barrels hoisted to the top floor of a five-storey building, then splashed into a trough, which empties to blending vats on a floor below, which in turn empty into filtering vats, and then to machines that fill new casks for further ageing. Then when a Cognac is ready for sale, it is piped directly to the bottling plant from the last stage, instead of being put into new casks.

The entire spectacle is made more attractive by the delightful perfume of Cognac, oak and vanilla that pervades everything. Mysterious men with guarded slips of paper appear occasionally, checking the blending proportions. At some stage before bottling, Cognac is blended with distilled water, to reduce it to the forty percent alcohol level at which it will be sold. After blending with water, it has to rest to get over the shock. Quite understandable.

Cognac is aged above ground in airy stone buildings that are sometimes not much more than converted barns. You can drive down a country road and spot a Cognac ageing "*chais*" with ease. The walls and roofs are blackened with vapours of the escaping essences, which encourage a sort of fungus growth. Usually there are a number of spiders about, too, because they discourage pests that could ruin valuable barrels.

Production of Cognac depends on the producer maintaining a great variety of stock of different ages for blending. Imagine the trauma that Cognac producers suffered during the German occupation in World War II when the conquerors began celebrating with irreplaceable vintage stuff. There was no hiding the best Cognac, because German searchers began taking to the air with Storch spotter planes, looking for the blackened roofs that indicated a Cognac storage *chais*. Finally the Bureau du Cognac went to the occupation authorities with a proposition.

"Look," said the Cognac consortium, "obviously Germany is going to win the war, and will benefit from international sales of Cognac.

"When you allow your troops to drink their way through the best stuff, you are letting them ruin the future of the trade. It must be stopped, if you want Cognac to be a healthy foreign-exchange earner to help pay for the New Order."

"You're right," said the Germans. And they appointed a Col. Klaebisck, a native of Cognac who had moved to Germany long before the war, as the man in charge of all Cognac. No one could liberate a bottle of Cognac from any of the ageing *chais* buildings without approval from Col. Klaebisck.

Producers in Champagne, who also depend on aged stock for blending, faced the same problem with occupation forces during World War II, and they solved it in the same way. The brother of Col. Klaebisck was appointed overseer of the stocks of Champagne.

The next time you hold a snifter of Cognac in your hand, warm it lovingly as you swirl your glass gently. Lift the Cognac to your nose and sniff lightly. The bouquet of aromas can tell you the history of what's in your glass. It suggests the tastes and personality of the cellar master who made it, and concentrates the finer qualities of French oak, together with the character of the chalky, flinty soil of the Cognac region.

The Moors, the canny Dutch sea captains, and the cuckold Chevalier de la Croix Marrone unconsciously combined to do the world a great service with their collective contributions to the creation of Cognac. Here's to them.

# PINOT GRIS

This mutation of Pinot Noir reaches its best in the vineyards of Alsace, making the deep-flavoured substantial white wines that used to be called Tokay until the Hungarians won their case that the name Tokay was too close to that of their great dessert wine, Tokaji. Pinot Gris, like so many other grapes, can produce excellent wines, loaded with pear or peach perfumes, set off by a lively acid. Over-cropped, Pinot Gris produces lots of acid and not much flavour. It's harvested early in many places to make relatively inexpensive sparkling wines. If it's allowed to mature too much, acidity drops like a stone, leaving the wine flabby in your mouth, and hot with too much alcohol.

The vine looks very much like Pinot Noir. The berries can be everything from light green to almost black in colour, shades of colour often varying in the same bunch of grapes. It used to grow right in amongst the Pinot Noir in some Burgundian vineyards.

Pinot Gris is Pinot Grigio in Italy, where it is responsible for an ocean of mid-to-low-priced wine, some of which can be good value.

It makes a perfect sipping wine of a hot summer afternoon, usually not very complex, reasonably acidic, and refreshing.

One of the best adaptations of Pinot Gris has taken place in Canada, in both Ontario's Niagara region and British Columbia. The best Canadian Pinot Gris wine I've tasted comes from the Tinhorn Creek winery in British Columbia's Okanagan district. We will undoubtedly see much more of Pinot Gris in Canada, and hopefully more of such high quality.

# ITALY

In 1979 Canada was in the process of deciding whether to buy new frigates for the navy from offshore sources, or build them in Canada. I was a member of the Parliamentary Press Gallery, specializing in defence and foreign affairs reporting, so it was no surprise that a representative of the Italian Embassy came to me with an extensive presentation on the Maestrale class frigates, developed for the Italian navy, but available for sale to allies anywhere. I told him that in my opinion, the Maestrale, a wonderful warship, was designed for the Mediterranean, not the North Atlantic, and chances that Canada would choose such a vessel were non-existent. Mind you, my opinion was based on crediting Canadian politicians responsible for buying defence hardware with some common sense. In the light of the helicopter fiascos, ongoing since 1993, and the used submarine scam, maybe the common sense factor should be rethought.

The Italians were keen enough that they wanted to send me to Italy to spend a couple of weeks visiting all the companies that made parts for the Maestrale frigates, from the company that made the hulls to the designers of radar, weapons, engines, and fire control systems. They said they knew I also wrote a weekly wine column, and the trip could be larded with visits to various Italian wine producers. I told them the offer was extremely tempting, but I had just returned from a fairly lengthy overseas trip and my wife would kill me if I took off again so soon.

"Bring her along," offered the Italians. "She can sightsee while you study the ship industry. We'll provide her with a car and driver."

You can't say no to an offer like that. I accepted, subject to ratification with Jane. She was excited when I told her, but raised a sobering thought. Our children Tim and Wendy were off on their own for the summer, but younger son Mark, at seventeen, should not be left alone in the house for two weeks. I asked if we could take Mark along, provided we paid his airfare. He'd be good company for Jane while I was off looking at frigates and gun makers. That posed no problem, so we set to work to prepare for departure in a couple of weeks.

We flew via London to Milan without a hitch. Tired, but excited, we were met by a driver at Milan who loaded us into a car for our first experience on an Italian superhighway, where every car is driven exactly as fast as the driver wants. In those days, every car wore a number—80, 100, 120, or more—beside the licence plate. The number depended on the size and power of the car, and described the speed limit in kilometres for that particular make and model of car. Well, you know how well Italians take to being regimented into rules. Imagine a small Fiat thundering along at 120, when its speed signs clearly said 80. Very few drivers paid any attention to the theoretical speed limit for their individual cars.

We did not sleep on the lengthy drive to Genoa. I remember we had a delightful chicken dish with a bottle of Antinori's Santa Cristina for dinner, and turned in rather early. The lead company in the consortium building Maestrale class frigates was picking us up next morning, when we would get our itinerary for the two weeks. Promptly at nine a.m. we were picked up and driven to headquarters. Jane and Mark waited only a few minutes before a driver collected them for a tour of Genoa. They'd meet me for lunch with some senior company executives.

I was shown all manner of organization charts, told about the history of Maestrale Frigate design, and received a presentation on other warships the Italians had sold to foreign governments, including Israel and Libya. It was a terrific morning, which included an explanation of how the Maestrale syndicate was organized. It seemed that each company in the consortium would be responsible for us in each particular territory. In between, we'd be visiting wineries.

Lunch was wonderful. Great wines, and the best *carpaccio* I've ever tasted. Our seventeen-year-old Mark was used to having the occasional glass of wine with dinner at home, and he seemed to be handling things pretty well, not emptying his glass every time a waiter came by. He was discreetly passing up second glasses. After lunch Mark and Jane retired to rest up for dinner that evening. I went back to the office for more briefings.

Dinner is a vague memory, because of jet lag, but we soldiered through half a dozen courses, each with the appropriate wine, and discussed Canadian naval needs in the North Atlantic—things like hull insulation and heating requirements, not to mention the need for equipment to function when the temperatures hit minus twenty Celsius—and the difference between the seas in a Mediterranean storm and a full-blown howler in March off St. John's.

We were collected next morning at nine a.m. and set off for La Spezia, the shipyard where Italian frigates were being built. The road from Genoa down the coast of the Ligurian Sea is one of the most spectacular in the world. It hangs from the steep hills as though pegged in place on the cliffs, with houses clinging to ledges above and below. The road alternately climbs and dips, passing through delightful little seaports like Rapallo, the yacht haven made world famous when the Bolsheviks signed the treaty with Germany there, taking Russia out of World War One.

La Spezia is a marvellous harbour, famous since early history, and a traditional shipbuilding town. There were three or four frigates in various stages of completion in sheds or on slipways at the water's edge. Jane and Mark went off to see the sights. I scrambled through the construction maze with senior executives, all of us in hard hats. The Italians were doing something in shipbuilding that was not common in those days. Each section of a ship would be built separately, complete with piping and electrical wiring, and then the sections were welded together to form the complete ship. The technique made it possible to complete fine work on each section under shelter with easy access. It also made installation of heavy machinery and diesel engines more convenient. The downside might well be the strength of the welding once a ship went to sea, but I was assured the welds and joins made these frigates even stronger than ships built the conventional way.

It was a wonderful morning, and I learned a lot. Lunch was to be late, and I was warned it would be the main meal of the day.

We went to a place called Wall of the Angels, and they had a private dining room for our group—three senior executives from the consortium, an Italian admiral, a four-ring American captain, an Italian naval captain, Jane and I, and Mark, stuck down there at the end of the table with the two captains. We talked ships, building techniques, food, and Italian wines—wines that kept coming at a frightening rate with each course, each one suited to the food like a kid glove to a lady's hand. Needless to say the conversation became more animated as one course followed another. I remember once looking down to the end of the table to see how Mark was doing. He smiled with a silly grin, and lifted his glass. As I recall, we dined and talked from two-thirty p.m. to about five p.m. I was taken down two storeys underground to look over the restaurant's truly extensive and diverse wine cellar. When I came back up, there was Mark with Jane. He was asleep and Jane not far from it. Jane and Mark went on a driving tour of the coast, probably zizzing in the back seat, and I was taken to watch a company slide show in a darkened room. Not much came across to me from that slide show . . .

We drove back to Genoa for a light dinner and bed, because the next day, wine was going to happen. We drove north through Piedmonte to Alba, and to Barolo, where we stopped at Fontanafredda's huge establishment. The centrepiece of the winery is an old three-storey building that used to be the home of King Victor Emmanuel's lover, the Contessa Rosa. Outside, peacocks roamed through the greenery and around the tables set for luncheon alfresco. It was the perfect place to show off fine wines, and that's exactly what Fontanafredda did. We learned a lot, ate considerably, tasted a lot, and left with two or three bottles of excellent Barolo, at least one from the fabulous 1974 vintage.

That evening we met executives from Fiat in Turin, part of the Maestrale syndicate by virtue of the fact that this company made much of the internal shipboard machinery, excluding the huge main diesel engines. Fiat, too, had heard that I was a wine columnist as well as a defence/economics journalist, so for dinner we went to a restaurant called Le Tastevin. I've never been to a place like it before or since.

Waiters rolled a huge cart loaded with different wines from table to table. If they wished, diners could order glasses of wine from three or four bottles, and management would serve you the right food to accompany the wines you selected. You could, if you wished, go the conventional route and order food first, then either select your wines, or let the waiter do it for you. Often there would be three or four wines possible with a dish, and, if you wished, you could have a taste of each to decide which you preferred. It made for an extremely interesting dinner, although we had to watch Mark carefully. He was really getting into this wine thing.

The following day Mark and Jane were scheduled to explore Turin, including a visit to the famous cathedral that houses the Shroud of Turin. At Fiat's engine plant, I was impressed with the assembly line, where delicate parts were robotically machined, assembled, and tested. This was 1979, remember, and we hadn't seen much of robotics in Canada yet.

It was at Fiat that I was first told about the Italian umbrella corporation called IRE, which seamlessly blends government and private industry into a powerful bureaucratic tool. Virtually all companies in Italy are part of IRE. Some companies are totally privately held, others jointly held by private enterprise and government, and others are owned totally by government. The economy is divided into various sectors: communications, heavy industry, light industry, electronics, transportation, chemical, energy, financial, etc. Managers of IRE companies can switch within a division, or, at senior levels, cross from one division to another. For example, an executive in a heavy manufacturing company like Fiat could be asked to transfer to another company within the division. A vice-president could be shifted to the presidency of a smaller company, and eventually he might rise to be in charge of a division of IRE. The system allows wonderful coordination between companies, and excellent selection of management talent, but both of these come at the expense of competition, which is certainly seen as a consumer's best friend.

Later on this trip, in Rome, I got to speak with a senior IRE executive and told him how impressed I was with what I had seen of Italian industry. I did say that I was amazed at how Italy had managed to make such huge strides economically, despite the fact that the government changed at least once a year.

"Oh," he said, "those are just the politicians. WE are the government!"

I got the impression that if some elected Italian government reached the stage where it wanted to start tinkering with the operation of IRE, why then the senior bureaucrats might discover some problems that would present difficulties severe enough to require dissolving a ruling coalition, probably leading to formation of another government and new ministers, or maybe even an election. One thing about the system, at least in my experience: the trains run on time.

We left Turin on a Friday afternoon. The way this trip was working, we were being passed from company to company, and we were scheduled to spend the weekend in Venice, on our own, as guests of the company that made the main diesel engines for Maestrale class frigates. As we boarded the train in Turin for Venice, the Fiat executive saying goodbye gave me a slip of paper with the name of our hotel in Venice written on it. I glanced at the paper, tucked it in my wallet, said our thank-yous for a very interesting visit, and found our compartment.

We were sharing with a young Italian and an American man of about sixty, who was very engaging and knew a great deal about Italy. He said he was in plastics. It was warm in the compartment, so I took off my jacket and put it on an empty seat. Our American friend got talking families, and was very interested in ours. Did we have any pictures? We did, and I got them out of my wallet to show him. We chatted on as the train rolled towards Milan, which was his destination. I noticed that he had put his briefcase down on top of my coat, I guessed because there wasn't room anywhere else.

It takes only about an hour to go from Turin to Milan, and we were sorry to see our companion leave. Our compartment filled up, and as we started to move, I had to retrieve my coat to make room for one of the three Italian ladies who had moved in to fill the compartment. My wallet was gone. Surely, I thought, it must have fallen out onto the floor, so I made myself unpopular by getting down on my hands and knees to look under the seats for that wallet, through the skirts of some outraged ladies.

No wallet. It was gone, with about $600 US in cash, plus all my credit cards—Visa, American Express—and the slip of paper telling us what hotel we were to find in Venice. Thank heavens I had about $500 in travellers' cheques and Jane had her credit card for my Visa account. But how would we find our hotel? We worried for the rest of the way to Venice.

There was a soft drizzle when the train pulled into the Venice station. We corralled a baggage cart and lugged everything to the local railway police station. A frowning desk sergeant listened to our story of the lost wallet. His face lit with pleased surprise when I told him the most likely thief was an American who got off in Milan. At least we weren't blaming an Italian. He gave us a caring, but disinterested Italian shrug when we presented our dilemma about losing the name of our hotel with the wallet. Mark caught my eye, and with surprising insight for a seventeen-year-old, suggested in sign language that our policeman might be interested in wine. We gave him a bottle of '74 Barolo. What a difference in cooperation that made! He produced a list of hotels, and we began to thumb through, hoping to recognize the name.

I'd shown Jane the name on the slip of paper before tucking it into my wallet, and she was sure the name was a musical term, something like Allegro.

Running through the list, it seemed to me that the name Europa Britannica was familiar, and I said so to the sergeant.

"Are you sure? That's a pretty expensive hotel," he said skeptically.

I said I was pretty sure, and the sergeant reluctantly telephoned the Europa Britannica to see if we were expected. We were, and the sergeant's attitude brightened considerably. The hotel had been concerned about our failure to appear, and would send a launch to the train station for us immediately.

Our first view of Venice was at about eleven p.m., with a soft rain, and the reflected lights bouncing off canals and wet roadways alike. When we came out of the station entrance to the edge of the first canal, Mark, amazed, dropped the two suitcases he'd been carrying and said simply: "Wow!" The launch came, complete with bellhop to load and unload baggage, and whisked us down the Grand Canal to the Europa Britannica, which sits on the water a few hundred feet from the great lagoon and landing place for Piazza San Marco.

A desk clerk told us we were the weekend guests of Grande Motore Trieste, makers of Maestrale frigates' main engines, and we were to do whatever we liked—rent a gondola or hire a launch, or eat at any of Venice's restaurants and have the bill sent to the hotel for inclusion on the account. We were shown into a third-floor suite overlooking the canal, and after a quick unpacking, we decided to have a cappuccino on the floating terrace. The rain had stopped and the midnight air was soft and magically attractive, enhanced by the occasional launch sliding past and the flotillas of gondolas tied up nearby awaiting the morning rush of tourists.

Just before one a.m. we decided on a brief walk before bed. Over a small bridge we went, through a stone archway, and then we stopped, breathless in awe, on the edge of a deserted Piazza San Marco. The square was illumined by lights around the edge that were reflected on the stone pavement. The huge column with its Lion of Venice rose from the centre, and the distant loom of San Marco cathedral came through the light mist. Jane said she could practically see the gentlemen of Venice, with their capes, hats, and swords, heading home from some party of 300 years ago.

The first thing I had to do in the morning was report my lost credit cards, hoping that our American friend hadn't gotten too deeply into the business of my plastics. There was a lineup of people reporting lost or stolen cards at American Express, none of them, as far as I could determine, victims of the same American smoothie that conned us.

We had a glorious two days in Venice doing all the usual touristy things: have a gondola ride, visit the glass works, climb five storeys to see where the clock was struck, and tour the Doge's palace. We even had a lovely dinner overlooking the Grand Canal while gondoliers sang "Santa Lucia," staying relatively well on pitch. It truly is a wonderful city, particularly when all you have to do is sign for everything.

Monday morning we took the train to Trieste for two days while I investigated the mysteries of manufacturing large diesel engines. Jane and Mark got to tour another city, and this one, too, is quite remarkable. There's a huge, attractive paved square right at the waterfront, and cruise ships are usually anchored offshore. Everything seemed to be freshly washed. The food was a cross between Italian and Slavic, which is quite natural, considering the way Trieste has traded nationalities in history. The port actually faces west, because Trieste sits on the end of a hook of land protruding into Slovenia on the Adriatic Sea. It's almost due east of Venice. I could have stayed there a week, but the relentless tour's schedule called for us to leave Trieste by train for Rome with a two-day stop in Florence to explore Tuscan wine.

We checked into the opulent Excelsior Hotel, on the north side of the Arno River and perhaps 100 metres from the Pontevecchio. We walked until dark, enjoyed a street pizza, and bedded down early to be ready for the next day's wine tour. We left early for the vineyards of Ruffino, east and slightly south of the city. Vineyards, delivery docks, crushing machinery, fermenting tanks, pumps, and barrels make most wineries similar and very like a refinery. Ruffino is a very large operation with widespread vineyards, and a central winemaking, bottling, and warehousing establishment at Pontassieve, where the owners, the Folonari brothers, have a living suite.

We were invited for lunch to the family quarters by Ambrogio Folonari. Jane, Mark, and I sat with our host in a lovely second-storey room, probably the family dining room. We were warm from tramping the vineyards, and dusty, too, so a chilled glass of white wine went down extremely well. Lunch was a production of five courses, with the right Ruffino wine in the right glass gracing each course. Conversation became animated by the time the main course arrived, matched by big balloon glasses full of Ruffino's flagship Chianti, Riserva Ducale.

I made a conversational point in the Italian manner, with a sweeping arm gesture, and knocked about eight ounces of deep red wine right into the crotch of our host's grey silk suit. There are no words to describe the embarrassment. I spluttered over an apology, but Ambrogio was grace itself as he wrung out his pants.

He smiled, and said, "That's all right, Mr. Ward. In our country when a guest spills wine on you it's regarded as good luck."

Maybe, but not good luck for him. I've met him several times since, and notice that as soon as he remembers who I am, he takes a careful step backwards, whether I'm holding a glass of wine or not!

There was a minor panic as we checked out of the Excelsior Hotel, where I had assumed the bill was being picked up by Ruffino. Thanks to a lifted wallet, I didn't have the necessary funds, and I had reported all our credit cards stolen. I remember going to Jane and telling her to give me her Visa card without asking any questions. I was mortally afraid that she would tell me in a loud voice that I'd reported this card stolen, or that the hotel, when I gave them the card, would discover the card's number on the stolen list. Neither calamity occurred, and next day Ruffino was in touch to say that a representative had been to the hotel and straightened everything out.

Meanwhile, we were picked up by Betty Ann Scavetti, a wonderful American woman then married to a Tuscan, who was going to take us to Antinori's establishment.

Our destination was San Casciano, perhaps twenty kilometres south of Florence, where the company's Tuscan production is centred. That's where Antinori first made, and still makes, Tignanello, the first of the Tuscan super red wines that swept the world. I'd met Piero Antinori before in Ottawa, where I was a director of the Italian wine society Amici dell'Enotria (friends of the land of wine), and he had visited several times. He greeted us at San Sasciano and personally showed us the winemaking facilities, the cellars, and the vineyards. He then led us through a tasting that included his 1971 Tignanello, the first year he made this marvellous wine; the 1975; and then a barrel sample of the 1977.

His particular blend of red grapes from well-pruned Cabernet Sauvignon, Canaiolo, and Sangiovese vines, then aged eighteen months in 225-litre French oak barrels, produced a wine of great depth and staying power, ready to last in your cellar for thirty years under the right conditions. So exalted is Tignanello's reputation that when a shipment of the latest release arrives at Canadian wine stores, there are always lineups of people ready to pay the price, which now flirts with $100 a bottle. When Amici dell'Enotria first ordered the 1971, it was priced at $11 a bottle, and I bought three cases. I know a man who bought nine cases and still has a few bottles left. After more than thirty years, you can tell by the taste that this is an elderly wine, and there's still something special about it.

Antinori posed for photos at San Casciano with some bottles of Tignanello, and we had a wonderful lunch with him, at which I carefully avoided dramatic gestures in the vicinity of any wineglasses. He talked at some length about his dreams for winemaking in Italy. There's no doubt he became the inspiration for a new wave of Italian wines, both red and white, which now compete on a level playing field with the best wines of the world. Last time I spoke with Antinori, his enthusiasm was for the new vineyards planted near his Castello de Sala estate in Umbria with Pinot Noir. In Italy you can now find Antinori Pinot Nero, and it's damn good.

After the day with Antinori, Betty Ann Scavetti drove us to the station, where we boarded the train for Rome, and the next scheduled stop on the Maestrale frigate industrial tour. I investigated the design and manufacture of radar sets, while Jane and Mark toured the old city, the new city, and many points in between. They got to tour the Vatican while I looked at weaponry; they went to the Coliseum while I checked out the electronic marvels of battle computers.

I do remember one exquisite dinner at a small restaurant on the banks of the Tiber, where we sat outside on the edge of a small square and enjoyed a variety of seafood cooked to perfection. The wines were white and from quite close to Rome. The shellfish and squid mix was delicately fried to a delicious crispiness and the poached sea bass sauced to perfection in a liquid that probably had Bardilino wine as the base. Dessert? By this stage of the trip we were opting for chunks of Parmegiano cheese and a glass of red wine, with coffee later.

We drove the next leg of our trip to Naples, where we had several industrial plants on the visiting list, plus the delight of staying with friends, John and Shirley Campbell. He had been the British High Commission information officer and was now the British Consul in Naples. John had always been a larger-than-life character, known when he was in Ottawa for his love of wine—he was the first diplomat, in the mid 1970s, to regularly serve Canadian wines at his receptions. He could often be spotted jogging through the streets of Ottawa, even in a February blizzard. His hardiness may well have come from his World War II days with Popsky's Private Army, a group of mixed nationality irregulars under command of a Polish colonel that operated behind Germany's lines, first in North Africa, and then in Italy. John was no stranger to adventure.

John and Shirley billeted Jane and me in a huge bedroom with twenty-foot ceilings and a luxurious king-sized bed in a room where Princess Margaret stayed when she visited Naples. Mark had his own, less grand, room, which suited him very well.

Most people remember Naples for a visit to Capri, or something equally romantic. I remember it for an electronics plant that turned out printed circuit boards for radar installations, and for a visit to the company that made the main armament gun for Maestrale frigates, as well as turning out the latest model of German-designed Leopard tanks. There they were, rolling off the assembly line for a test drive, complete with clanking treads and bristling machine guns.

The electronics plant was fascinating. Circuitry was laid down on thin metal sheets by photography, then panels of metal went through a series of acid and fixing baths, to etch away all but the desired circuits. The whole plant was run by a handful of people, because once the metal sheet was on an assembly line, it was dipped into each solution automatically from an overhead track, allowed to stay in the acid or fix bath for precisely the right length of time, then lifted and moved on to the next dipping. Raw metal with photographic images went on the line at one end and the finished product came off the other, without being touched by any worker's hand.

We also had some fun. John said there was an employee of the consulate who was a real expert on the ruins of Pompeii, so it was arranged for us to go there with him for the day. From the city's impressive entrance to the memorials and houses within, he showed us the lot, usually with some insight that only an expert could offer. At one point he stopped us in the road and pointed down at a design carved in the stone.

"What's that?" he asked. Well, you could easily tell when you looked that it was a carved erect penis, pointing down the road.

"Let's follow and see what we can find," suggested our expert. A block farther on, there was another aroused penis, pointing onward. One more pointing penis, and then there was one pointing down a side street. By following the pointing penises, just as sailors or out of town merchants must have done, we came to the remains of an easily recognizable whorehouse, with the tiny action cubicles in remarkable repair, right down to the stone couch in each one, which used up almost all the space in each room. Either those things had been well padded, or the customers would not have lingered very long.

We prowled through Pompeii's houses, in remarkably good repair after centuries under the ashes, many with surviving murals still adorning the walls. There were shop stalls, and one bakery with milling stones still in place, close to the ovens. We gaped with other tourists at the shapes of some of Pompeii's citizens, caught by the killing ash in touching poses of sudden death, as the debris from erupting Vesuvius surrounded them, now restored to three dimensions by plaster poured into the hollows left by their decayed bodies.

After two short days in Naples, we had to return to Rome for the trip home. By this time we were burdened with the impedimenta of baggage, souvenirs, bottles of wine, and a couple of precious bottles of Tuscan olive oil. The breakables went into carry-on baggage, which made the bags heavier and the breakables safer. It's a long flight across the Atlantic to JFK Airport in New York, and it was a long wait on a very hot June day to get through customs and immigration. Our flight was late, and consequently the connection with our onward flight to Ottawa would be very close. Jane said we couldn't make it. I said we should try.

Mark and I took the checked baggage, leaving Jane to carry two carry-on bags, with the wine and olive oil. At one stage Jane put the two bags down dramatically, perhaps with more force than she meant. The olive oil broke and began to seep out of the bag and onto the terrazzo floor of the terminal. As we headed towards the bus stop for the Air Canada terminal, we could see behind us a thin film of olive oil, with the potential for turning smooth stone into a skating rink. By the time we reached the Air Canada terminal, the air was decidedly frosty between Jane and me, despite the external heat wave.

With ten minutes to spare, we arrived with baggage at the check-in counter and presented our tickets.

"Oh you're not on that flight," the agent said. "We knew the Alitalia flight was late so we've booked you on a flight leaving in two hours."

I'm not sure how we managed to check our baggage without speaking to each other, but we did. Boarding passes in hand we went our separate ways, me to the bar, and Jane off somewhere with Mark. A quick drink cooled me off nicely, and I went to the newsvendor's to buy a paper. There was Jane, buying paper to sop up olive oil from the bottom of Mark's carry-on bag, and from various items of clothing that now had a distinctive Italian oily look. We glanced at each other, the way strangers do, then went our separate ways, me to the bar, Jane to an area of the transit lounge that Mark was protecting from lunging masses of Japanese tourists.

We did speak again on the plane back to Canada, and by the time we got home, things were quite civil. It's remarkable after that trip to think that we willingly went to Italy together on three subsequent occasions and very much enjoyed ourselves each time. Mind you, Jane refuses ever again to pack wine or olive oil in her carry-on baggage.

# SANGIOVESE

A good Sangiovese wine can offer the complexities of black plums, raspberries, saddle leather, and even traces of the farmyard smells that make wine lovers smack their lips over old Burgundies. It's the most planted red grape in Italy, where it forms the backbone of Chianti and of the new super Tuscan wines. It's also the red grape of Vino Nobile di Montalcino, of Brunello, and that great Umbrian wine, Rubesco. Sangiovese may be one of our oldest red grapes, too, because there are suggestions that it was made into wine by the Etruscans, long before the Roman Empire. Sangiovese means "blood of Jove."

There's a lovely spicy, meaty flip to a good Chianti, a character that comes from Sangiovese grapes in the blend. You'll notice that quality in a Brunello, too. That depth makes Sangiovese wines good company for red meats, and in some lighter versions they are a good match for fowl. The vines bud late and ripen late, so it's not a variety to be grown in cold climates. Italian immigrants have taken cuttings to most wine-producing areas of the new world, with very spotty success. Sangiovese thrives in Argentina and it's a growing popular success in California.

Well-made Sangiovese wines, like Brunello and Rubesco Riserva, can improve for decades in your cellar, developing complexities to rival the best of Cabernet. As with most grape varieties, it makes the best wine when harvest volumes are kept low; but in less expensive versions it can be a good quaffing wine, provided you drink it when it's youthful.

# BANCO

In late autumn of each year there's a gathering of wine people from around the world at Torgiano, just south of Perugia in Italy's Umbrian region. The occasion is Banco di Assaggio, the annual judging of Italian wines. The late Giorgio Lungarotti can take credit for instituting Banco. He was the first in Umbria to spend big money developing and promoting the new wave of quality Italian wines; and Banco was one of the building blocks to create that upscale image for Umbrian wines, and for all Italian wines. Giorgio married Maria Grazia, and while he promoted the wines, she took over converting an old Torgiano warehouse into a classy hotel. She also built and opened an excellent wine museum next to the hotel. The Lungarotti hotel, winery, and museum became the centrepiece of this small Italian town.

David Campbell, Teresa Lungarotti, and Dick Singer at a rooftop party at the Tre Vaselle, Lungarotti's super hotel

Within a few years of the first Banco competition, wine entries were coming from all parts of Italy. A medal won at Banco became a ticket to fame, with all the market benefits. Most of those invited to judge the various classes of wine at Banco are very knowledgeable Italian wine experts, with a sprinkling of foreign wine people, some expert, some aspiring so to be. Banco paid expenses for these foreign judges, because Lungarotti and those who administered Banco wanted to have extensive foreign coverage for this judging of quality Italian wines. I remember one year Robert Mondavi arrived by private helicopter to be a celebrity judge.

Judging lasts for three days, and it is a real marathon. Each judge is given a complex marking sheet to value each wine out of 100 points. There are fourteen categories to be marked for each wine, ranging from limpidity and hue, through refinement and harmony in bouquet, to intensity, harmony, and persistence in taste. You're also required to note any defects you find in each wine. Judges are seated at tables of four or five and the same wines are delivered to each judge at the table. You might judge thirty or so sparkling wines, for example, and then move on to off-dry whites, where there could be sixty or more entries. The wines arrive in flights of up to twelve at a time. You carefully examine the colour and clarity of each, then assess the bouquet, the taste, and the aftertaste.

The exercise requires concentration and the ability to spit without dribbling on your marking sheet or down your shirt. There is plenty of water and plain bread to cleanse your palate between samples, and each judge has a spit bucket. Although it's difficult to spit the good stuff, if you swallow, your judgement is shot within an hour.

One year I was one of three Canadians invited to judge at Banco, with Dick Singer and David Campbell. Dick is an old-time newsman like me, who writes about wine and holds wine courses in Toronto. David is more the next generation wine person, who has now moved from writing about wine to being a successful wine agent; in San Francisco, the last I heard. We three managed to get through the judging without disgracing ourselves and were looking forward to the closing banquet thrown by Banco at the Lungarotti Tre Vaselle Hotel, that delightful establishment built inside an old warehouse, where every room has been customized with period furniture to retain atmosphere, and the plumbing is designed for comfort, not period accuracy. Dick, David, and I were in rooms on the top floor, with windows opening onto small, charming, spaces on the roof. During the Banco competition, we had hosted a couple of evening parties up there under the stars. There are few finer places for an after-dinner Cognac than an Umbrian rooftop on a clear autumn evening.

There were other things arranged to entertain all these judges with weary palates. One afternoon we were all loaded into a bus after the morning's judging and driven eastward to the mountainous boundaries of Umbria. We were being taken for lunch to visit the largest truffle shipper in Umbria. This company buys truffles wholesale from the area farmers who search with dogs beneath oak trees for those delicious nuggets of fungus so prized by gourmets around the world. (They use dogs for truffle hunting in Umbria, not pigs as they do in France.) You can pay several hundred dollars a kilo for black truffles, which are more common, and almost twice as much for white truffles. One of the most memorable meals I ever had was in a restaurant in Rome that served a plain dish of pasta with fresh truffles grated on top.

We were led into the truffle shipper's building through the washing and sorting area, where bins of black and white truffles sat waiting for packaging. The entire building smelled marvellously of truffles. Upstairs, we sat down to a lunch that featured truffles in every dish, from soup, fish course, entree, and dessert. As this great experience drew to a close, the manager asked if any of us would be interested in buying some truffles at a good price.

We sure would, but how would we preserve them for the trip home, and avoid having all our luggage smell like a truffle farm? We were not to worry about that, because he had the answer. We each took a sturdy paper bag and went to the truffle bins to select our purchases. I piled in half a dozen black truffles and went to the weighing station.

"You've got 750 grams there. Give me $16 American and that will be enough."

What an unbelievable bargain! Now to follow the directions we'd been given. First find a grocery store and buy some of those large jars of fruit juice, and some raw Italian rice. Drink the fruit juice, or throw it out, then ensure the inside of the jar is totally dry. Next step—slide the truffles into the jar, filling it as much as possible. The raw rice then gets poured into jar over the truffles. You have to shake the jar to make sure it is completely filled with rice and truffles. The lid has to be screwed down tightly so the fit is as air tight as possible.

No matter what precautions we took, the truffle smell still seeped out of our jars. I got my truffles home safely, and transferred them to jars filled with Port. We took a truffle out occasionally for a treat, and sometimes poured a drop or two of the Port into a special gravy. Yum. The rice was immediately made into the best-tasting risotto you ever had.

We wine writers gather around huge bins of black truffles at a truffle packing plant where we were allowed to buy wholesale

Back at Tre Vasele, the dominant bouquet for the last day of judging was certainly tinged with truffles. As the supervisors of the judging checked the final scores, the judges changed into dinner jackets for the closing banquet. As we three Canadians headed downstairs, Dick Singer gloated over the fact that he was already packed and ready to leave at our scheduled eight-thirty a.m. departure for Florence, while David and I would either have to get up very early with fuzzy heads for the packing chore, or do it before we collapsed into bed.

David and I left the banquet early, grumbling because we had to pack. Then a strange thing happened. There's a touch of the child in every newsman, which gets exaggerated by a few drinks. We were hit by the muse of devilment. David went out onto the roof from his window, along to Dick's room, and in through the window. There was Dick's bag lying packed on his bed. David took the bag, locking Dick's door behind him, and took it to his room. Then we waited. In less than half an hour Dick appeared, looking into our rooms to gloat over us doing late night packing. We heard him open his door, then a howl of outrage.

"My bag's gone! How in hell did that happen?"

"Gosh, Dick," I said. "You know, that bunch of Americans who came with Mondavi are leaving tonight. You don't suppose somebody saw your packed bag and took it by mistake, do you?"

Panic. Singer tore down the stairs to investigate. As soon as Dick left, David went back onto the roof, through Dick's window, and opened the door. We restored Dick's packed bag to his bed, locking the door again as we left.

Dick dragged the manager upstairs while the poor man was still putting on his pants. He'd obviously been in bed, and he was very concerned that a guest had lost his luggage. Dick flung open his room door and pointed to the bed without looking. A stunned look from the manager, replaced by an expression of weary understanding.

Dick was speechless.

"Did you enjoy the wines at the banquet?" asked the manager. "I think I'll go back to bed, unless there is something else."

Next morning a limousine collected the three of us for a drive to Florence, where we were scheduled to meet with the Frescobaldi family. Dick Singer was worried about the trip, because he was taking some prescription diuretic pills that caused him to make frequent visits to the restroom. As we approached Florence, the traffic became very congested, because this was October 31, and All Hallow's Day is a big holiday in Florence. Dick began looking urgently for a restroom. We stopped at a couple of bars, but none of them would let a stray

Canadian use their facilities. Dick's urgency had reached the frantic stage by the time we arrived at the Frescobaldi palace.

This is one of Italy's most aristocratic families, described in some detail in Robert Lacey's book *The Aristrocrats*. The family made its fortune in the Middle Ages through the invention of money. It was the Frescobaldi and families like them who discovered how to convert grain, hides, livestock, and wine into money, making wealth internationally portable. They were part of the original banking fraternity. Wine was merely a sideline. The Frescobaldi empire stretched across Europe to such an extent, according to Lacey in his book, that they could face down the British royal family. The claim is that at one time in the fourteenth century the British royals had trouble honouring loans from the Frescobaldi and the family virtually took over England's taxation system and, in effect, became the Bank of England.

We approached this august family with some sense of reverence, combined with Dick's eager interest in their facilities. Our car arrived at the Via Santo Spirito palace, and we were surprised to find it rather ordinary, at least on the outside. There was a huge dingy archway with entrances leading off from either side once one went through the arch. You could see sunlight, lawn, flowers, and a fountain straight ahead, obviously a garden courtyard. The gatekeeper had no intention of letting some stranger use the Frescobaldi powder room, so Dick simply fled towards the courtyard, a hundred feet or more down the passageway. I followed to make sure he didn't get into trouble. By the time I reached the courtyard, there were rustlings in the bushes against one of the walls, and I swear Dick's relieved "ahhh!" could have been heard a block away.

The left-hand door at the entrance led to an elevator, and four or five floors of offices. That's where we went for conversations with Vittorio, Ferdinando, and Leonardo. Vittorio, the eldest, was sort of chairman of the board and CEO. Ferdinando handled domestic sales, because he was married at the time responsibilities were delegated, and Leonardo, single when the jobs were decided, handled export sales. A fourth brother, Dino, avoided the wine business and stuck to the original Frescobaldi line of influence. He was, at the time, senior diplomatic correspondent for Rome's leading daily newspaper, *Corriere della Sera*.

At meetings with the three other brothers Dick was much more relaxed, so we mapped out a program to look at Frescobaldi properties and winemaking establishments over the next few days. It was quite an opportunity, because the Frescobaldi firm is one of the few large wine producers in the world that uses only grapes from its own properties to make its wine. It was agreed that Ferdinando would be our guide, provided we could be finished by Thursday evening, his regular poker night.

We were invited to luncheon with the family, after we had checked into a nearby hotel—a beautiful place where we had a two-floor suite overlooking the Arno River, about a block west of the Pontevecchio, of which we had a super view.

Back we went for luncheon, this time turning right after entering the archway, into the family quarters. Up we went in an elevator to a wonderful, old-world opulence. The walls of the huge drawing room were crowded with ancestral portraits in all manner of poses, most of them military. Vittorio and his wife greeted us with Ferdinando and Vittorio's son Lamberto. The only other guest was a charming woman who was chief lady-in-waiting to Queen Elizabeth. There were tall, sweating flute glasses of Frescobaldi Spumante making the rounds on silver trays, just to slake the pre-luncheon thirsts.

Conversation was vivacious at luncheon, with the table set in a room with windows overlooking the courtyard. The food was superb and the wines even better. There was one waiter for every two guests and the service was impeccable. I forget what we ate, but we had some elegant Pomino white, and some rich Montesodi red, the aristocrat of Chiantis, both wines from estates we would visit in the next two days.

As we left the dining room, Dick whispered in my ear and pointed out the window: "See that wall there? That's where I had my leak." So much for aristocratic elegance.

# NEBBIOLO

If ever there was a grape fussy about soil and climate it's Nebbiolo. It does best in the calcium-rich marl of Italy's Piedmont region, in the districts of Barolo and Barbaresco, where weather conditions usually allow this late-ripening grape to wait until mid-October for harvesting from the south-facing vineyards. In most places you can see the Alps from the vineyards of Barolo and Barbaresco. Nebbiolo at its best produces a wine rich in tannin from fermenting with its deeply coloured skins, with enough fruit and acid to create perfect balance with the wine's high alcohol levels. You'll pay at least $50 for a good bottle of Barolo.

Expect a wine with heavy body, rich in tannin, which offers the aromas of roses or violets. Barolo bottles especially benefit from being opened the day before you drink them. The best Nebbiolo wines, my kind of B&B—Barolo and Barbaresco—can age for decades, and need at least ten years to reach the beginnings of drinkability. Our first son, Tim, was born in 1958, one of the best years of the decade for Barolo. We were fortunate enough to be able to bring a bottle home from Italy one year, and to share this treasure with Tim and two of his friends also born in that great vintage year.

Nebbiolo wines are not for sissies. In its two best forms, B&B, Nebbiolo makes a wonderful choice to serve with red meats, lamb in particular, or with a sharp old cheese at the end of dinner.

Elsewhere in the Piedmont, Nebbiolo is used to make Spanna, Ghemme, Gattinara, and Sizzano. There are continuing attempts to grow Nebbiolo in California and Argentina, with varying degrees of success.

# CYPRUS CAPERS

In early March 1964, United Nations troops began arriving in Cyprus to stop the horrific bloodletting taking place between Greek and Turkish Cypriots. At that time eighty percent of the island's population were Greek, seventeen percent Turkish, and the rest were the usual polyglot mixtures of Mediterranean people, from Lebanese to Armenian, and everything in between. Greek and Turkish Cypriots were fairly well divided geographically, but both populations had families and even villages that were isolated; Greek Cypriot families were surrounded in some Turkish enclaves, and even more Turkish Cypriot families were surrounded by Greeks in Greek areas of the island. Those isolated minorities that didn't immediately flee to safer areas were either chased out or killed, often in very brutal ways. Turkish Cypriots in a small village south of the Kyrenia Mountains had a house of horrors preserved to show visiting journalists. Dried blood was spattered everywhere: walls, ceilings, floors, and even a bathtub, which was coated with blood. There were photographs of how and where the bodies were found.

You might ask what a story about the Cyprus civil war more than forty years ago has to do with wine. Let me tell you, Cyprus produces some super wines and some deadly brandies. In fact, without alcoholic fuel some of the bitterest fighting might never have taken place.

Once I joined a United Nations foot patrol into the Kyrenia Mountains, where the Turkish and Greek Cypriots were shooting at each other. We climbed down a rope from a hovering helicopter. Turks and Greeks stopped shooting as we came up a ravine into range. The Turks promised to stop shooting, but resumed fire the moment we went back down the ravine. Both sides stopped again as we climbed the other side.

Visiting the Greek lines we discovered that the irregular troops were being supplied by donkey. There was as much wine and brandy carried up by the pack animals as there was food. If the UN had been able to cut off the brandy supply, fighting in the mountains would likely have tapered away to nothing.

The British had a couple of major sovereign military bases on Cyprus, so they were the first of the United Nations peacekeepers. The troops Britain had readily available were the "paras"—particularly tough paratroopers who were well trained in the skills of all-out combat, but completely unschooled in the more subtle arts of peacekeeping. They began operations still wearing their red parachute regiment berets, and handling their weapons like the combat troops they were. Denmark, Sweden, Ireland, Finland, and of course Canada contributed troops to the Cyprus peacekeeping force—UNFICYP—but it took time for these UN troops to arrive, to get settled, and bring their blue berets to wedge between the warring Greeks and Turks.

Blue berets were known as "no-shoot-'em hats," but that didn't always work. The first Canadian troops, mostly the Royal 22nd Regiment, the "Van Doos," were airlifted to Cyprus. The Royal Canadian Dragoons, their armoured cars, and heavy trucks for the Canadian contingent came later, by sea. I was with them when they left Halifax on HMCS *Bonaventure* in an early springtime North Atlantic storm. Seas were so high that half *Bonaventure*'s sea boats were smashed to kindling by the waves. The carrier's hangars were packed with Ferret scout cars and trucks. That meant the Navy's anti-submarine tracker aircraft were tied down on the exposed flight deck.

I was assigned by the old *Toronto Telegram* to travel with the *Bonaventure*, then write about how the Canadians were making out as peacekeepers. On board ship there were live firing exercises with machine guns into the sea, peacekeeping lectures, and drills wherever there was room and once the ocean settled down. We made a rapid passage because orders were to get there quickly. We stopped for refuelling at Gibraltar, then pushed on through rough weather in the Med. Off the north coast of Africa we ran into a sandstorm, which left the aircraft on deck badly covered in muck. Seas were heavy enough for us to see the exposed sonar dome under the pitching escorting destroyer, HMCS *Restigouche*.

At Famagusta, on the east coast of Cyprus, we unloaded armoured cars, trucks, troops, and a hitchhiking journalist, right onto the line dividing Greek and Turkish Cypriots. Everything looked peaceful, although it certainly was strange for a North American to see civilian policemen carrying submachine guns. Canadian troops arranged for a ride into Nicosia for me, where finding a hotel room wasn't easy, with a couple of hundred foreign journalists already in town, not to mention a large gaggle of United Nations civilians.

In the early stages of any international story like the Cyprus situation, the people back home who are paying your considerable expenses expect lots of copy quickly, and there's always competition between Canadian news organizations, but you're also competing with some pretty professional wire services: Canadian Press, Associated Press, Reuters, and, in those days, United Press International. The usual tactic for someone representing one newspaper, one radio station, or one TV station is to leave stories dealing with the overall picture to the wire services, and to seek out stories of separate incidents. If it's possible to get a Canadian involved in your story, particularly one from the city where your newspaper is published, that's jam on the cake.

I was a reporter/photographer in those days, and the *Telegram* wanted some colour pictures from Cyprus quickly. That wasn't difficult, because our troops moving into positions in Nicosia and Kyrenia were responsible for some pretty hot areas and quite eager to be photographed doing their jobs. I also managed to get into the Turkish Cypriot stronghold of St. Hilarion's castle, a Crusader vintage fortification in the mountains, once used by Disney as a model for his fantasy castles. St. Hilarion was built by Richard the Lion-Heart, right into the side and top of a mountain, complete with a tower on top, from which previous lords of the castle used to push their enemies.

St. Hilarion was occupied by the Turkish Cypriots, with some Turks in residence as expert advisors/commanders. When I arrived, the Greek-Turkish competition for the hearts of the media was running hot, so there wasn't much difficulty convincing the Turks to have troops pose for me in defensive positions.

Once you got used to people running around with guns, Cyprus wasn't really a war. It was very dangerous, simply because most of the people with weapons didn't know how to use them. Teenaged Greek Cypriot boys had Sten guns of the old variety, which, when dropped accidentally, would usually fire a whole clip of ammunition, bouncing around and spraying bullets everywhere. The younger lads of twelve and thirteen often had nine-mm Browning automatics. I remember being in a Nicosia restaurant when a disgruntled customer pulled out an automatic to settle his argument over the bill and put several holes in the ceiling.

On weekends the militant Greek Cypriots would recruit "fighters" until they had a couple of busloads, then would head out into the countryside to surround a Turkish Cypriot village, taking potshots at anyone who appeared. There were suspicions that aggressiveness was directly proportional to the amount of cheap brandy carried on the buses. The British paras, first troops to keep the peace on Cyprus, would station half a dozen troops in each of these isolated villages to protect the inhabitants. In late March such a weekend attack by about 200 Greek Cypriots was broken up by a platoon of paras. Something like 1,500 rounds of ammunition were fired by the attackers with no British casualties resulting. The paras fired less than 100 rounds, wounding six and killing two of the attackers.

We journalists would chase down such incidents in our rented cars, usually convertible sports cars, and often we ran into trouble. It was quite usual to get stopped by some fifteen-year-old with a Sten gun who wanted to see your papers whether he could read or not. It was advisable not to argue, and to keep both hands in sight as you reached slowly for the documents. A friend of mine once had a youngster rap the barrel of his Sten gun against the doorpost of the car. Old Sten guns—and almost all of those being used in Cyprus were old—are held on the cock by a slot in the breech, which holds back the firing hammer. Jarring the gun can release the hammer, which will then will fire a round, with the recoil setting off the next round, and so on, until the entire clip is fired. Sten guns are dangerous even in experienced hands.

We journalists quickly fell into a routine. We'd gather for breakfast at the Ledra Palace Hotel, attend the morning UN briefing, then head off to investigate some area or incident we'd learned about either from the briefing or from one of the special sources we had all developed. The doorman at the Ledra Palace seemed to know far more about what was happening than even senior UN commanders. For the right price, he could even arrange an interview with Archbishop Makarios, the Greek Cypriot president.

We would cover the war until about two p.m.; then a group usually met at the Harbour Club, overlooking beautiful Kyrenia Harbour, where we would lunch on the patio, with the mountains of Turkey looming in the distance over the Mediterranean coast. We got to know Aphrodite white wine and Othello red very well. We also appreciated a wonderful liqueur called Filfar, made in Cyprus from oranges, and tasting like a Grand Marnier on steroids. It's still the best orange-flavoured liqueur I've ever tasted. Try it mixed with sparkling white wine and orange juice. Wow.

The Harbour Club was run by Judy and Roy Findlay. In her younger days Judy was on the London stage, appearing in Noel Coward musicals. Roy had been a British Army major fighting communists in Greece. His establishment was totally safe from the right-wing Greek Cypriot nationalists, because when he was fighting the communists in Greece, one of his officers had been George Grivas, leader of the Greek Cypriot Enosis (union with Greece) movement. We always enjoyed our Harbour Club lunches, particularly when Roy joined us, because he really knew what was going on in Cyprus. We could combine lunch with research.

About four-ish we'd do a bit more war reporting, then head for the Ledra Palace for showers, prior to joining the gang for drinks. The idea seemed to be: let's get the other reporters smashed so we can find out what they've been doing all day. Needless to say there were always stories made up to worry opposing reporters. Sometimes the more careless reporters actually wrote a story that had been made up to fool them.

We'd move the party to a couple of restaurants at about nine p.m., eat well, then get back to the hotel about midnight. We'd then get up at about five a.m. to write, and put a story on the wire back to Canada by nine a.m., which was plenty early enough for our papers (because of the eight-hour time difference). Then we would join the guys for breakfast and the morning briefing, and start the whole process over again.

I got to know some very interesting characters: Janos Pistos, for example, who was in charge of Kyrenia castle for the department of antiquities. The castle, another one started during Crusader times, was a thick-walled complex that the Turks claimed was used by Greeks as an inhumane jail. Janos was primarily occupied with making sure that valuable antiquities were not sold illegally to be spirited out of the country. There were archaeological sites all over the island. Turkish Cypriots, strapped for cash because of the fighting, would quite often offer pieces of 4,000-year-old pottery for sale at very low prices. Even some large, old amphorae were sold and smuggled out of Cyprus. One day Janos took me to a room full of valuable artefacts in the castle, where there was also a shelf full of skulls taken from tombs. He picked up one lovely miniature sculpture, small enough to fit in the palm of one's hand. White and red paint were still visible on the comical face, which portrayed a clown.

"Hold this in your hand," said Janos. "Feel the warmth. In those days they couldn't write, so when a man loved a woman, he made something like this and gave it to her. This might have been a funny love letter."

I also got to know Costas Collis, the guardian of Bellapais Abbey, on the north slope of the Kyrenia Mountains, overlooking the sea—one of the most beautiful places on Cyprus, in fact one of the most beautiful places in the world. The abbey—again a Crusader relic—was mostly in ruins, but the church still operated for the local community. Costas, a character who features strongly in Lawrence Durrell's book *Bitter Lemons*, took people on tours of the ruins and tended his garden with great skill. He had a tree that, thanks to his grafting abilities, produced thirteen different kinds of fruit—several varieties of oranges, lemons, limes, plums, and apricots.

Bellapais climate and Bellapais soil did wonders for plants, particularly roses. I was curious about what would happen to Canadian seeds given such advantages, so I got some Canadian zinnia seeds for Costas. They grew to the size of sunflowers. Costas established a Canadian section for his garden, to which other Canadians contributed different seed varieties.

I saw Costas many times on subsequent visits to Cyprus. He always greeted me with, "Yasoo, Peter. Come and have a glass of wine." No wonder I kept going back. When Jane visited in 1967, Costas asked us both to his home for a traditional Greek Cypriot dinner, cooked all day in a clay oven, cracked open only when everyone was ready to eat. We sat at a table out of doors, in soft starlight, eating *dolma,* roast lamb, and a delightful sort of cabbage roll, washed down with a delicate white wine Costas had made himself.

When the Turks invaded Cyprus in 1974, Costas was taken prisoner and removed to Turkey, his health not very good. According to friends, it became obvious that he was dying, and he asked his captors to allow him to die in Bellapais. The Turks returned him there, installed him in a stretcher on a balcony at the abbey, where every evening the swallows would swoop at him, swerving away at the last minute. Costas died there. I'm told that these days the church part of Bellapais Abbey has been made into a casino. No Greek Cypriots now live in the village.

Sometimes there was a break in the routine, even for swimming. We had a favourite beach a few miles west of Kyrenia, and when our editors had tired of daily stories, we would go there to swim, because there was a lovely hotel nearby, with a bartender who would listen for telephone calls from our editors, and bring us messages and cooling drinks when needed. We used to call such afternoons "watching for the Turkish invasion."

South of the Kyrenia Mountains, just east of the road that snaked through the pass from Nicosia, was a cooperative pig farm, run by a group of Greek communal farmers. Onassia Farm was in the no man's land between Greek and Turkish Cypriots.

Very early in the emergency, Turkish irregulars began taking shots at the Greek farmers as they went about the business of feeding their pigs. The farmers promptly left their dangerous farm and agitated for UN troops to occupy it— and take over care of the animals. The first UN troops into the farm were a platoon of British infantry and a troop of the Royal Canadian Dragoons, led by a character named J.J. Gallant, a young lieutenant from Prince Edward Island that I had become friendly with on the *Bonaventure* as we sailed from Canada to Cyprus. I visited J.J. and his troops, and we came up with the idea of a mess dinner at the farm. We agreed that next evening would be ideal, and I went shopping for some liquid refreshment.

Next day I drove my rented light blue Triumph Herald through the Turkish checkpoint in the late afternoon, and parked beside a Ferret scout car in the dusty yard of Onassia farm. J.J. came out to help unload a few bottles of wine and two bottles of Keo One Star brandy. One of the guys in J.J.'s troop didn't drink, so he was appointed cook. Somebody else had liberated a couple of chickens, and cleaned and plucked them, ready for the oven.

The only table large enough for our party was the former pig-slaughtering table. The blood had been scrubbed off, so with the table covered with a lovely white bed sheet, it was quite respectable. From somewhere, the industrious RCD soldiers had found candlesticks and candles—the final touches for a perfect mess dinner.

Pre-dinner cocktails were the commercial wine that I'd brought, served up with some bits of sausage discovered in the basement. The chicken was fabulous; so was the wine we had with it, also liberated from the basement. There were even some potatoes, discovered growing in the garden, and roasted with the chickens.

Sometime during the evening we heard gunshots and noticed a pattering sound on the roof.

"Don't concern yourself," said J.J. "They're using old .303 rifles. The barrels are so worn that the bullets are going end over end after the first fifty yards. That's expended rounds bouncing off the roof."

We didn't let that harmless exchange of fire dampen the party. Both sides must have wondered at some of the songs we sang, and when I drove my car back through the checkpoint at midnight, the Turkish Cypriot guards had big grins on their faces.

Three years later I was at another mess dinner at Onassia farm. As a reservist I was serving with the UN force in Cyprus. When my duty was over, Jane flew out to Cyprus for our tenth anniversary second honeymoon. We rented a house in Kyrenia from Roy Findlay, where Jane claimed we frequently entertained the entire Canadian contingent. Only partly true, although I must say those soldiers far from home were very keen to spend time with my wife. Jane wore red and white outfits when we visited Turkish Cypriots, and blue and white when we were seeing Greek Cypriots.

The colonel commanding Canada's PPCLI insisted that Jane should join him in an inspection tour of the isolated outposts, each manned by half a dozen soldiers under command of a corporal. I was allowed to go along as one of the aides to Jane, the star of the show. Our cavalcade of vehicles would climb over some of the steepest and dustiest roads on the island, often newly made by the UN between Greek and Turkish Cypriot lines. The troops at these outposts took shifts to be on duty round the clock, watching for hostile activity from either side. They were part of the network put in place by the UN across the island, separating Greek and Turkish Cypriots. Since 1964, most Turkish and Greek Cypriots have only known each other through the sights of a rifle, or by insults shouted across no man's land. Each year of such separation created added problems for peacemaking.

At each outpost we were greeted by smartly dressed troops whose boots were glistening, despite all the dust. There could not have been more ceremony for royalty.

By 1967, a full company of Canadian troops from the PPCLI had been stationed at Onassia Pig Farm, which had become headquarters for soldiers doing rotational duty at a dozen of those isolated outposts between the Greek and Turkish Cypriot sectors. The Onassia Farm guys were taking a severe ribbing from their buddies about farming life in the UN, so to counter the teasing, Canadian soldier pig farmers created a mess dress uniform for themselves consisting of a white shirt with rank worn on shoulder boards, a special black badge bearing the golden outline of a saddled pig, black trousers, and knee-length rubber boots. Pig farm soldiers wore this getup in all seriousness at regimental affairs.

When they saw Jane, they said they simply must hold a mess dinner for her at the farm, to entertain, and to bestow a special honour on her for the inspection tour.

There was a guard of honour when we arrived, and the "mess" was certainly much tidier than it had been when J.J. and I had staged the farm's first mess dinner three years earlier. The wine was better, too, and so were the smells that came surging from the kitchen. No pig slaughter tables for dinner, either, but proper folding tables rented from the British, like most other UN equipment.

Dinner was delightful, both the food and the company. The officers of Pig Company presented Jane with a regimental plaque that included PPCLI shoulder flashes, badges of ranks, and the crest of Onassia Pig Farm. They gave her a fancy badge in black with a golden pig wearing a saddle. Then they absolutely took her breath away—by naming her "Queen Pig."

"I don't talk about that very much," said Jane. "Are you sure it should be in this story?"

# MERLOT

Merlot has become such a fashion statement red wine that it is now the red grape with the world's fastest growing planted area. Consumers can't get enough Merlot wine; their thirsts are amplified by the French Connection health dictum that so praises the virtues of red wine in lowering the risks of heart attack and stroke.

For years Merlot has been more heavily planted in France than either Cabernet Sauvignon or Cabernet Franc. Many of the greatest Bordeaux wines are 100 percent Merlot, or at least made with a majority of this popular grape. Fastest increases in planting are in California and South America's biggest wine producing countries. There's also a growing volume of Merlot vineyards in Ontario.

A good Merlot will have deep, rich, red colour; and a bouquet of blackberries, black currants, and perhaps plums or cherries, plus the complexities wood ageing can add. It should offer good tannin in balance with the fruit, and, for my taste, be aged in oak barrels to add complexity. A good Merlot will improve for five to twenty years in your wine cellar, providing the vintage year was a good one, and the wine was carefully made. It becomes brick red in old age.

It costs money to make a good Merlot wine. The vines must be heavily pruned to limit production, and the fruit must be handled with great care because the grape skins are tender and easily damaged by weather extremes or by roughness in picking. The vines bud early, which can expose tender shoots to late spring frosts. The grapes mature about a week before those of Cabernet Sauvignon, which makes the two grape types a natural fit in a winery for labour and equipment efficiency.

To get colour in the wine, the grapes must be allowed to ferment on the skins for a considerable length of time—often for three weeks—and that in itself can create problems of too much tannin. In Ontario, watch for Merlots from Henry of Pelham or Stony Ridge.

Merlot wines range in price from around $10 all the way up to $100 and more, for the great Bordeaux wines like Chateau Petrus. Drink them happily with red meats, lamb or beef, or with strong cheeses. Some of the less expensive Merlots, for example those from the north of Italy, are thinner and higher in acidity and will go better with stews or red-sauced pasta dishes.

# ASSESSING WINE

"I don't know much about wine, but I sure know what I like."

That's by far the most common comment you'll hear at neighbourhood wine tastings, and it's invariably uttered with a tone of defensive truculence. By all means drink what you like, and there are some simple steps you can take to add to that pleasure by discovering *why* you like a wine.

There's more than sip and swallow to tasting a wine properly. Tasting and assessing a wine can be fun, it can be informative, and you don't have to become a wine snob. Watch your friendly local wine expert carefully at the next opportunity, and count the steps involved in the wine assessment ritual. There really is a purpose to those rude slurping noises and furrowed eyebrows. Subjective assessment of wines will teach you the quirks of your personal palate, then gradually help you get better value for your wine shopping dollar at wine stores and restaurants.

Wine is a combination of chemicals. The art of assessing any particular wine depends upon the development of an individual's ability to play detective with the evidence collected through his or her natural human senses: sight, smell, touch, hearing, and taste. Wine, after all, is designed to appeal to all those human senses.

Treat a bottle of wine gently while you're preparing to open it, particularly an old bottle of red. If you shake it about, you'll stir up the deposit and give the entire bottle a bitter taste.

Heavy-bodied red wines are bound to need decanting when they've reached the right age for drinking. Medium weight red wines, like a Chianti Riserva, are likely to have thrown some deposit if they are more than five years old; they should be decanted if there's any deposit visible in the bottle. If you're doubtful, hold the bottle close to a light bulb before you open it to check for precipitation.

Glance at the seal on a bottle of wine before you open it. When there's evidence of some leakage through the tiny holes in the foil covering the cork, you could have a flawed cork, although it's not cast iron evidence.

Remove the seal (or watch the waiter do it) by scoring it with a knife around that ridge of glass just below the lip of the bottle; then lift off the part you've cut to expose the top of the cork. The winemaker designed that colourful sleeve seal on the bottle to look attractive, so leave it around the barrel of the neck of the bottle, peeling back just enough so that it won't interfere with pouring the wine.

Sometimes that colourful foil on the neck of the bottle can be invaluable. I remember a dinner party once when one of the guests produced a bottle of red wine masked by a paper bag. He wanted to see if Mister smartie wine writer could identify the wine. The wine gods were with me. That morning I'd been at a wine store checking new arrivals and one of the wines was a Chianti that wore a distinctive design on the foil around the neck of the bottle. I'd tasted the wine, checked the producer, and made note of where it came from, because the wine was really quite impressive.

That unique design on the foil was exactly the same as the foil on the neck of the barrel I was supposed to identify. Probably a gentleman would have owned up to advance knowledge, but this guy was a real creep. I poured a glass and sniffed. Obviously Chianti Riserva, I said, and it probably came from about ten kilometres north of Greve. It smelled like a wine from (and I named the producer without even glancing at my notes from the morning tasting). I took a small sip, then a larger one, and correctly gave the year. Boy, were people impressed! There was no more trouble from that smartass.

On the way home my wife turned to me and said: "How did you do that? You sure impressed me." I told her about the morning tasting and the case of the unique foil on the neck of the bottle. We laughed most the rest of the way home.

There are lots of wines with screw caps. These days some of them are even pretty good drinking. For most bottles, you still need a corkscrew. You can pay anywhere from fifty cents to $500 for a corkscrew. You should use your favourite kind, provided it is capable of removing the cork from a bottle of wine without tearing the stopper to shreds. Nothing so frustrates a wine lover as a cork that comes out of a bottle in crumbles and by stages. For minimal difficulties, use a corkscrew with good breadth to the twisted business end. In some bottles of old wine the cork may have become stuck to the inside of the neck of the bottle. When you spot such a condition, it sometimes helps to press gently with your thumb on the cork, thumbnail against the glass of the bottle, to loosen it slightly. Be careful. If you press too hard while performing this stunt, you could push the cork into the bottle and get a shirt full of wine for your lack of care.

Once you've pulled it, examine the cork. It should be moist and flexible, evidence that the wine has been stored lying down, to keep the cork wet and the bottle well sealed. You may find some crystals on the end of the cork. Don't be concerned. Those are tartaric acid crystals, precipitated out of the wine after bottling. They have no flavour, and no effect on the wine, except perhaps to make it look less pleasant. Some producers deliberately put their wines through a period of refrigeration before bottling to force out as much tartaric acid as possible.

Smell the cork. If there's anything wrong with the wine in the bottle, the cork will usually offer you evidence. There's no mistaking a "corked" wine, one that has an "off" smell because of a bad cork. It's a musty, oxidized, old-clothing odour, created by an irregularity in the cork that may have allowed a leak, or possibly by an improperly cleaned cork. The whole bottle can taste like that bad smell. No decent restaurant should argue with you when you send back a bottle of "corked" wine, and any reputable wine merchant, including government monopoly shops, will refund your money if you return the wine. Mind you, most places frown on customers who drink three-quarters of the bottle before they determine that it's bad. Most stores want the bulk of the wine still in the bottle before they'll give a refund. In thirty-five years of regular wine drinking, I've run across less than half a dozen "corked" wines. Either I've been lucky, or "corked" wines are not very common.

It can pay handsome dividends to take a careful look at the cork. More than once a host has kept a wine label hidden, then challenged me to name the wine by sniffing and tasting. There's no problem if I get a look at the cork.

Most corks name the wine producer, and some even give the vintage date of the wine. A quick glance at the cork and you're equipped to be impressively expert, by naming the producer, the wine, and even the year. A little acting ability helps.

If the wine you've just opened is one that must be decanted, because you've spotted some sediment, then prepare a carafe or decanter. Either decant the wine over a light-coloured counter, or use a candle to check the clarity of the wine as you pour. I keep a small glass handy, too. With the side of the bottle that has been "down" in the cellar held down, hold the bottle in one hand and the decanter in the other, so that you'll be able to see the candle or the light-coloured counter through the neck of the bottle.

Gently and slowly, pour the wine, watching it glisten in the light, so that you can tell the moment any sediment begins to flow into the decanter. Stop pouring when the crud appears. I carefully switch the bottle from decanter to glass, and try to pour another ounce or so of wine that is relatively free of sediment. It makes an advance sip for the host, if you're careful. If this is a dinner party, you should serve the wine in its decanter, along with the cork and bottle, complete with wine and sediment, displayed on the sideboard. Your guests might be interested in seeing how much sediment the wine had collected.

Avoid those cute little wine baskets like the plague. They are only useful for holding a wine bottle before you decant the wine. If you try to actually serve an old wine from a wine bottle basket, it will rock back and forth each time you pour a glass, thoroughly mixing the sediment with the good wine, and spoiling all but the first glass.

A wine should be tested by the host, whether at home or in a restaurant, and there's a particular routine that produces the best results. A small amount of wine should be poured into the host's glass. He or she can then make a critical examination. If you are the designated tester, tilt your glass with a small quantity of wine in it, and hold it close to a white napkin or tablecloth so you can look through the wine at a source of light. The wine should be clear, with no cloudiness or suspended solids. White wines should be light to dark yellow, with green tinges in some young wines.

If a wine has been properly filtered by the producer, it should look brilliant, even polished. When red wines are young, there is often a purple tone to them. When they begin to show their age, you'll find orange-brown tints, particularly at the point where the wine meets the glass.

Your eyes can collect considerable evidence about the care a winemaker has taken, about the age of the wine, and the body. Sharp eyes in a knowledgeable head can even come up with a good idea about the type of grape that made the wine.

Your nose is the best wine detective on your team. Smell is the least developed sense in most people, yet it can provide the most information. Once it starts to work for you, a whole new world unfolds. Your mouth and tongue can detect sweet, sour, bitter, and salt—and something called *yomami*, a Japanese term for the meaty flavour you get from consommé in your mouth. The olfactory bulb, tucked at the back of the nose above the entrance to the throat, can be trained to collect and identify more than 5,000 sensations of smell. With potential like that, it's important that we give the old schnozz as much help as possible.

Okay. Take that small amount of wine in your glass and swirl it around, wetting the entire inside surface of the glass. What you've done is provide the maximum possible evaporation of the esters in the wine. Now stick your nose in one side of the glass and sniff gently, drawing air across the wetted surface and collecting all those smell molecules. Think about what your nose is saying. Odds are you'll smell acid. You might smell fruit, like tart apples, or peaches, strawberries, raspberries, or apricots. The perfume of flowers is also something you could find. In some wines you'll sense sweetness through your nose; in others you might detect saltiness, fresh-cut grass, almonds, or the suggestion of herbs.

A good wine will present an interesting combination of smells that come together in harmony, like an orchestra striking a chord. When the mixture of smells from a wine is a pleasing combination—a harmonious chord for the nostrils—we say *the bouquet is in balance*. That means the acid, alcohol, fruit, sugar, and body suit each other, the way notes in a fine piece of music make an artistic blend.

When you inhale and drag air across the wet inner surface of a wineglass, you can find evidence for anything from a wine aristocrat to vinegar. Smell any sulphur there? That would indicate a winemaker who sterilized his product with too much enthusiasm, either because he had to, or because he was careless. The hint of something musty could mean wine made in a dirty cellar, or stoppered with a tainted cork. Too much acid would indicate a cheaper wine; something flabby in the smell would suggest not enough acid; and caramel hints in a red wine would tell you it's getting on in years.

The more facets of bouquet there are enhancing the harmony of a wine, the more expensive the wine is likely to be. Some wines are like a trumpet solo—pleasant, but not very complicated. Others can be like a symphony, with dozens of themes blended artfully together. Those are the wines that can cost a lot. You pay for complexities. See how many smells you can identify in your next glass of wine.

If your nose tells you the balance is off in a wine, ask yourself questions about the dominant smell, and try to guess what would correct the imbalance. It can be interesting to dissect the aspects of a flawed bouquet, because sometimes you can learn a great deal from a bad wine. Usually your nose can give you sufficient information about a wine for you to pass judgment on its soundness. In restaurants, when the waiter pours you a tasting sample, swirling and sniffing is generally enough for you to tell if the wine is okay. When you decide about a wine simply on the basis of its bouquet, any waiter will realize that you know what you are doing.

If you wish to taste-sample a wine thoroughly, either at home or in a restaurant, some impolite noises may be involved. Make those noises as unobtrusive as possible. The technique used by wine judges combines the talents of the palate and the olfactory bulbs, and involves some slight risk for neophytes. Sip a small amount of the wine, and hold it in your mouth, rolling it around the tongue and gums as it warms to body temperature. Warmth reveals more of a wine's character. Next bring the warmed wine forward in your mouth, with your head canted slightly downward. Breathe in gently through the wine, making a faint burbling sound.

Some hostesses I know might object to this performance, but with practice, the noise can be held down to something akin to the soothing chuckle of a small creek. By dragging air through the wine in your mouth, you are sending air saturated with the wine's esters back over the olfactory bulb, drawing information from the combined senses of taste and smell. The technique will intensify both senses and make it possible to spot characteristics of a wine that would otherwise remain undetected.

Be careful with this "chewing" of a wine. If you don't breathe in through the wine with enough vigour, you'll dribble wine down your front. If you breathe in with too much enthusiasm, you'll inhale the wine and drown. Best to practise somewhere in private before trotting out your new talents for public inspection. And don't wear a white shirt when assessing red wine.

Correct use of the wine tasting ritual can ensure that you'll get some extra attention from the staff of a good restaurant, particularly if you are courteous. Nothing stamps a person as being a boor quicker than impoliteness to waiters and waitresses.

That's not to say you should let wine waiters bully you, as they have been known to try and do. Picture dinner for five journalists on an expense account in the dining room of the Horse Guards Hotel, a classy establishment close to Whitehall in London. We enjoyed rack of lamb, with several bottles of 1974 Barolo, and when it came time for dessert, the waiter pushed over a trolley full of selections. Included in the offering was a particularly nice-looking round of Stilton cheese, and a decanter of Port. Yes, we all agreed, Stilton and Port would make the ideal ending to a marvellous dinner. The waiter suggested we could each have a glass of Port and he would leave the decanter so we could have a second glass. Great idea, we agreed.

The Stilton was ripe and as good as it looked. The Port was good but not excellent; improved, perhaps, by being partnered with the Stilton.

Then came the bill. It was 69 pounds 10 shillings for the Port alone!

"Waiter," we asked, "what was that Port?"

"It was Dow '53, sir," he said.

"I doubt that. It tasted more like a late bottled vintage, and at any rate, it certainly wasn't a 69 pound, 10 shilling a bottle Port."

"Yes, sir. Dow '53."

"Please can we see the bottle?"

We had him there. The wine had been in a decanter, and if it was indeed the Dow 1953 Port, as the waiter claimed, he should be able to show us the bottle. I'd like to be able to report that we triumphed and made him cut the price of the Port at least in half because he couldn't produce the bottle. In fact, he told us that the bottle had been thrown out, and stuck to his guns about price. He faced us down. We should have called the manager, but we didn't. Like most people, we decided that a fuss in the dining room is bad form. Trouble is, when people avoid unpleasantness by giving in to bad treatment, it means service suffers for everybody.

Next time, I vowed, I wouldn't be such a patsy in a wine disagreement with a waiter.

# CAVA, FINO AND SPIDERS

It's easy to become prejudiced in favour of the Spanish sparkling wine industry. Quality for the dollars you spend is unmatched when you buy Spanish sparkling wine, which is known the world over as Cava, because the Spanish don't even flirt with that dreadful practice of calling their sparkling wine Champagne. Only sparkling wines made in the official French district of Champagne are really entitled to use that name.

Several trips to Spanish Cava country taught me a great deal about the making of sparkling wines, not to mention the experience of side trips to a sparkling casino, with a visit to the surreal castle of Salvador Dali at his hometown of Figueras, on the Mediterranean coast near the French border. The first time we passed Dali's castle-like home, with its walls looking like a wedding cake that somebody had flung jam at, the master artist was in residence, dying, we were told. Despite pleadings from our group, we were not allowed time to stop. Next time I was in Figueras, Dali had been dead for several years. The castle—now a museum—was closed, but we did have the opportunity to wander through the forecourt, which is filled with Dali's dream-like art, sculptures and pictures of liquid clocks. No question, the man's art makes you think.

We visited almost a dozen Cava producers on that second trip, some of them quite small, and others of gigantic proportions, like Freixenet, where we tasted some exquisite wines. These far exceeded the very good quality of the Carta Nevada and Negra Brut we see on Canadian store shelves.

At several stops we were walked through the entire process of making sparkling wines, learning some interesting lessons. We were there at harvest time. Our guide had already explained that grapes were picked, then put into relatively small boxes to avoid having the weight of grapes in large containers break the berries. Loose juice can begin fermenting on its own, which creates serious problems. At one winery, boxes of grapes were arriving faster than they could be fed into the de-stemmer/crusher, so several tons of the grapes sat waiting in the sun while a virtual fog of wasps had a field day with the sweet juice. No question about it, an hour or two of sitting in the sun would damage the quality of the wine—wild yeast would start fermentation and the wine could suffer a slight oxidation, or worse if the wasps had dirty feet.

Grapes for sparkling wine are usually picked slightly underripe, so that their acid content is higher, a requirement for making sparkling wine. Ideally the grapes are picked in the cool of the early morning and taken to the winery, where they are de-stemmed and crushed immediately. Not only does this cut down on oxidation, it also leaves as little room as possible for impurities to get into the juice.

Another major lesson we learned was that the quality of a sparkling wine depends very much on the amount of juice that is taken from the grapes. First-run juice comes from the grapes easily as the grapes are gently pressed inside one of those huge bladder presses. It's possible to press grapes down to almost dry pulp, but the cut-off point for making quality sparkling wine is using only fifty percent of the juice that it's possible to extract from the grapes. Take more than that, and the end product wine will have a bitter aftertaste. The more juice you take after the first fifty percent, the more that bitter aftertaste will spoil the wine. The best quality sparkling wine is made from juice taken early in the pressing process; lesser quality wines result from more thorough pressing. Next time you sip a sparkling wine, look for a slightly bitter flavour in the aftertaste. If you find it, you're drinking cheaper stuff.

Once the juice for winemaking has been extracted, the presses keep working to squeeze the last possible ounces from the grapes. Imagine the amount of juice left over in the process of making sparkling wine in Spain. It's a virtual ocean. Some of it gets made into rough local wine, some is destined for industrial alcohol, and a large percentage gets shipped away in tankers. As I described earlier, years ago on a visit to Georgia in the old Soviet Union, we were shown through a "Kognac" factory, which used imported Spanish white grape juice, arriving in huge tankers, to make a fiery Georgian version of Cognac, which they carefully spelled with a "K."

The Spanish Cava industry relies chiefly on the Methode Champenoise to make sparkling wine, in a very mechanized way. As in the French Champagne district, Cava making begins with the fermentation of good white juice from quality grapes; then a second fermentation takes place inside the bottle. The wine is sweetened with an exactly measured dose of sugar designed to produce exactly the right amount of carbon dioxide. As that secondary fermentation takes place, the carbon dioxide gas produced remains in solution under pressure, and a yeast deposit is thrown off by the process. If that yeast deposit is allowed to stay in the bottle, the wine will become cloudy when the bottle is opened. Problem: how do you get rid of the yeast deposit and keep the carbon dioxide under pressure in solution?

First, get the yeast deposit to the neck of the bottle. In Champagne the best wines are "riddled" by hand—stored resting in holes in slanted wooden panels, and shaken regularly to send any yeast deposit to the neck of the bottle. As the weeks go by, each bottle is gradually tilted more, until all are standing upside down, with the yeast deposits from secondary fermentation resting on the crimped cork and metal stoppers. Today virtually all the world's Methode Champenoise sparkling wines, except those of the very top quality, are riddled by machine and stacked in huge metal cubes where they are shaken just the right amount at just the right time by computer-controlled motors.

After riddling, Methode Champenoise sparkling wine spends up to several years standing on its head in crates, ageing on the lees—that's what they call the bits of yeast deposit left by fermentation. It's that time spent ageing with the yeast deposit which gives sparkling wine some of its sought-after characteristics: the smell of fresh rolls, a nutty, creamy flavour, and attributes that meld well with the fruit and floral properties contributed by the grapes.

Then comes *dégorgement*, the act of getting rid of the yeast sediment that has been collected on the cork while the bottle was upside down. In older times, skilled workmen eased out the cork just enough for the internal pressure to force out the deposit. This was a messy, imperfect process at best. These days the neck of the bottle is frozen so that the cork cap—looking exactly like a soft drink cap—can be removed, together with a plug of ice containing the yeast deposit. The bottle is then dosed with a small amount of wine, containing some sweetness if the end result is to be a slightly sweet wine. Then, before much gas escapes, the final cork is rammed home and wired tight to the neck of the bottle, and it's ready for labelling.

In one Spanish Cava winery we watched the final stages take place in a totally automated manner. I'm a sucker for bottling lines, but I'd never seen anything like this. A block of 144 bottles standing on their heads was hoisted into an icy brine bath, immersing four inches of the neck of each bottle. One set of 144 bottles followed the other as they advanced in rows of twelve bottles through the icy brine, each spending perhaps ten minutes to have its top frozen before hitting the bottling line. At the end of the brine bath, each row of twelve bottles was turned right side up and fed into a machine that pried off each cap. Each bottle's internal pressure popped out the frozen plug at the neck, getting rid of the yeast deposit. Next on the line each bottle was topped up with wine, then stoppered with those bulbous sparkling wine corks, which were wired tight to the neck of the bottle. From there on, it was a regular bottling line—rinsing, labelling, and packaging in cartons. I could have watched the process all day. There's something very compelling about lines of wine-filled bottles clinking their way through this progression from winery to consumer-ready. Bottling lines make me thirsty.

One evening we had dinner in a private dining room at a luxury casino near the French border, with plenty of time allotted to try the gaming tables. Baccarat, 21, and roulette are too much for me, especially for the stakes that were moving across those tables, so I just watched the big players. Drinks of Cava were free. Slot machines were more my speed. In less than an hour, the one-armed bandits took care of the modest funds I'd allowed for the evening's fun. Thankfully there was no gamble on the Cava I was sipping.

There's a wonderful custom in Spain's Jerez district, the home of Sherry. When you sit down at a restaurant for dinner, the waiter brings a small bottle of Fino

Sherry in an ice bucket so you can sip while you choose your food. I suppose it's possible that this custom is only for groups of touring wine writers, but we did notice that the same thing happened at the next table.

Fino gets its flavour not only from the grapes, but also from the "*flor*" that forms on top of the fermenting wine. Sherry is fermented in casks that are only partly filled, so that the fermenting wine is exposed to air. A white protective film of dead yeast cells forms on the top of the wine, protecting it from oxygen contamination, and imparting that characteristic Fino flavour. It makes ice-cold Fino the perfect tipple to perk up your taste buds, particularly after a tough day in the vineyards and wine cellars.

We had toured the great vineyards of Palomino grapes, vines poking up from their crust-like soil, baking in the sun, and ready for the pickers' shears. We'd sampled grapes warm from the heat with sweetness so concentrated they were sticky. We'd sampled antique Amontillado Sherries from the great reserve casks of Gonzales Byass, called the Twelve Apostles, and gloried in the complex depth of flavours chasing round our mouths; and we'd watched cellar masters pull samples from the great ageing casks with that little silver cup on the end of a bamboo wand. The wand flicks the cup through the *flor* in a cask of Fino so the cup can bring back a clean sample of the wine, which a skilled cellar master can pour into your glass from a couple of yards away without spilling a drop.

We had the opportunity to sample a variety of Fino Sherries of varying ages, so we could follow the development of the wines. Sherries are aged in a *criadera* (which means nursery) with rows of barrels stacked five deep, the youngest Sherries on the top, oldest Sherries on the bottom. Aged Sherry has the happy ability to pass on its characteristics to younger wines. In the *criadera* system, Sherry for sale is taken from casks at the bottom of the stack, which are then filled from the cask above, which is also filled from the cask above, until the top row cask is used, at which point it is refilled with fresh wine. There may be only a few suggestions of the wine that was originally in the bottom row of casks, but its glories of age will be passed on to the new wines each time the *criadera* is used.

We made a very interesting side trip from Jerez to Sanlucar de Barrameda, to the west, on the seacoast. The trip was arranged to show us the difference between Sherries from there and Sherries from Jerez. It is claimed there's a slightly salty tang to the Sherries of Sanlucar de Barrameda, because of ageing in the salty sea air. A Sherry made there and aged in Jerez supposedly will not have that salty touch, while one made in Jerez and aged in Sanlucar de Barrameda will have it. We toured a major Sanlucar de Barrameda Sherry producer's facility where the cellar master claimed there was another major difference. He pulled the bungs on several barrels of ageing Sherry and showed us something on the inside of the bung stopper that looked like a smudge of rust. "Look closely," he advised. We did, and the smudge was wriggling. In fact the smudge was composed of hundreds of tiny red spiders, which the cellar master claimed were unique to Sanlucar de Barrameda cellars. The spiders ate even tinier organisms in the barrel wood, helping to produce the Sanlucar de Barrameda Fino taste, he said. We certainly couldn't argue, but I've never heard that story anywhere else.

I'll always remember our visit to the *bodega* of Emilio Lustau, one of Spain's most famous Sherry blenders and bottlers. Blending, after all, is a demanding and necessary part of making Sherry. We entered a cellar half the size of a football field, stacked to the fifteen-foot-high ceiling with casks of Sherry in ordered rows. The whole was dimly lit from ceiling lights above the corridors between the rows of casks. The air was filled with the most exquisite Sherry smells. A brighter light shone at the end of one of these corridors, leading us to a tasting table, set on planks in an open space, surrounded by tiers of barrels.

There were about thirty bottles lined up in a crescent, and lots of glasses for tasting, flanked by small dishes of olives, slivers of cheese, and chunks of Spanish bread. The Sherries ranged from the driest Finos on Emilio Lustau's list, through to several kinds of Palo Cortado, down to a group of Amontillados of varying ages, and finally to a small group of rich, sweet wines made with Pedro Ximenez grapes, wines normally used to sweeten drier Sherries into styles like Bristol Cream or Santa Maria Cream—Sherries that Jane likes before dinner over ice. Had she been at this tasting, she would have sipped exclusively from the right-hand side of the table. Ever since that Emilio Lustau tasting, I've looked for their wines on the shelves of wine stores, and bought them, realizing that although they were sometimes more expensive, you would never get a bad bottle or an unfair value.

# TEMPRANILLO

If you like those great Spanish Rioja wines, you're a fan of Tempranillo. Rich, deep colour and flavour, with smells of leather, spice, and tobacco leaves are what you get when Tempranillo wines are at their best. It's the grape most used in the Rioja, where it is often blended with Garnacha (Grenache), and sometimes it flirts with a touch of Cabernet in a blend.

There's a growing international taste for the red wines of the Ribera del Duero region: that part of Spain north of Madrid, near the upper corner of Portugal. Here Tempranillo makes those red wines what they are, although locally it's called Tinto Fino. Some people have called Tempranillo the Spanish version of Italy's great Nebbiolo grape. There certainly are some similarities in taste.

Across the Spanish border in Portugal, Tempranillo becomes Tinta Roriz, one of the chief grapes for the blend in making Port wines. It's also a major player in the wines of the Dao, and the table wines now being produced in Portugal's Douro region. There's a slow growth in the spread of Tempranillo vines to other wine-producing areas, notably to southwestern France, Argentina, and even California. So far no winemaker has managed to make Tempranillo into wines as fine as those created in Spain or Portugal.

Tempranillo makes the kind of wine that goes very well with red meat or strong cheeses; but remember, Rioja red wines also suit a Spanish paella very well, a dish where seafood plays a major role.

# STOMPING AT SITGES

I'd always had a hankering to go to Barcelona for the weekend, so there was joy in the office one August when an invitation to do just that came from the Torres family, best known wine producers in Barcelona's Penedes wine region, just south and west of that city. Each year the Penedes region honours a different country at harvest time, and in 1996 it was Canada's turn. No doubt the countries to be honoured each year are chosen with something of an eye to export sales of wine, which, of course, is why the Spanish choose wine writers from the featured country to visit for the harvest. Write and ye shall travel. On this trip, there were also certain physical obligations that came close to producing heart attacks.

There were four of us on the trip: Michael Vaughan and Steven Drotos, both from Toronto, Memory Walsh, a petite and respected wine writer from Vancouver, and myself. We met in Toronto and flew business class SwissAir to Geneva, then transferred for the last leg to Barcelona, arriving on Friday morning. We were met at the Barcelona airport and bussed to a first-rate hotel in Sitges, a resort town on the Med, about twenty kilometres west of Barcelona. You're always a bit groggy after an overseas flight, but the sights of this lovely old city, the shops, the waterfront, and the beaches, some of them topless, banished the idea of sleep. A couple of us went for a swim after lunch, and a couple of us went strolling through the town.

By mid-afternoon we were at it, touring wine facilities at Torres, tasting, taking notes, and watching slide shows. They dine late in Spain, and by the time we got to that point we were all pretty bushed. It was a massive celebratory occasion that featured the choosing and crowning of that year's Miss Sitges Harvest Queen. Everybody who was anybody in Sitges was present, plus every winemaker in the region.

At that dinner we met David Wright, Canada's ambassador to Spain at the time, who was there to take part in the proceedings. He turned out to be an excellent dinner companion, and all-round good guy. He'd brought with him an RCMP sergeant in full scarlet dress to add some spice to the way we showed the flag. That certainly attracted interest.

The Penedes area of Spain is Catalan country, home to a race of people that are the majority inhabitants there, as they are all along the Mediterranean coast stretching nearly to Marseilles in France. Catalan is the second language in southeastern Spain and southwestern France; in some areas it's unofficially the first language. There was a time 200 years ago when Catalans were ready to fight for their own nation. There's still a pretty strong separatist feeling in some of the smaller towns. Catalans are super people with a devout interest in drinking wine, which is probably why I like them so much. I remember on a previous visit to Catalan country, in southwestern France, being introduced to the mysteries of drinking wine from one of those flasks with a long spout. You start squirting wine into your mouth with the flask held close, then gradually extend your arm to full length, theoretically keeping the stream of wine flowing into your mouth, not onto your shirt.

We spent next morning touring more vineyards and tasting more wine, before a late and sumptuous lunch. We were allowed the afternoon off to either swim or tour Sitges, and to get ready for the coming Saturday evening ceremonies. All four of us were to be inducted into the Cofradia de Caballeros de San Miquel de las Vinas, which would involve certain initiation procedures.

We bussed it to Vilafranca del Penedes, about twenty kilometres into the hills north of Sitges, where fifty or so members of the Cofradia were waiting for us at an old castle that had been converted to a large restaurant/hotel.

Dinner was a wonderful combination of Catalan food—lots of red meat and garlic—great wines, and conversation, mostly in Catalan, some in Spanish, and all translated for us by good-natured dinner companions. After a few glasses of red wine, you even had the impression that you could understand Catalan. After a brandy or so we retired with our glasses outside to the courtyard, where a huge bonfire had been built. Then a man came running out of the gloom, straight at the bonfire, and leapt over it. Another man followed, leaping high over the flames, and then another. There must have been a dozen fire leapers, whom we recognized as members of the restaurant staff.

In order to become members of the Cofradia of San Miquel, we were told, we had to leap over this fire. No wonder our hosts had been so generous with the brandy. Imagine anyone in his or her right mind, and over sixty, trying to leap those flames. You sure don't want to spill your brandy when you try that. Spanish brandy is pretty good stuff, and we'd all had our share, so we all gave it a try, even Ambassador Wright. What's more we made it and passed the first initiation hurdle: trial by brandy and fire.

Next, we all returned to the castle's main room, which had been transformed into a meeting room with raised dais and observer seats. We were front and centre, on the dais with the Gran Condestable, Canciller, and Gran Veguer of the Cofradia. We were each required to answer some rather taxing wine questions, and if we failed, then there were bumper glasses of Penedes wine which had to be tossed back in one continuous chug-a-lug. I can't for the life of me remember any of the questions, but I do recall having to chug-a-lug a penalty glass or two.

We each got a sommelier's *tastevin*, an impressive, gold-bordered scroll attesting to our status as Caballeros of the Cofradia, and a bus ride back to the hotel to rest up for Sunday's festivities.

Over breakfast we got word that Sunday afternoon would be the annual grape stomping competition at Sitges, with us four wearing Canadian colours, representing the red maple leaf. Any worries we had were waved away with Spanish aplomb, assurances that the host country's team was always well received by the crowd. (Crowd? What's this?) We were to have ironclad security, from the RCMP sergeant, and the best possible coach: David Wright, Canada's ambassador to Spain.

Meanwhile, we were ushered out to a hill in the countryside to inaugurate a vineyard planted by Torres in honour of Canada as guest country. Naturally there were a few glasses of wine involved. Then came lunch, which is always late and very liquid. We sipped our way through the usual bottle of ice-cold Fino while making our luncheon choices. Appetites enhanced by Fino. Very civilized.

We were all much more enthusiastic about the grape stomping competition after lunch. We four were issued with rather garish bathing suits and oversized white T-shirts emblazoned with the Canadian flag. There were rope sandals, too, but we were advised that they would merely get in the way of our stomping. In these getups we walked through the tourist-heavy seaside streets of Sitges to the mediaeval town square, large enough to hold the more than 5,000 people gathered to see the competition. At centre stage was a raised dais about thirty metres long, a huge open tank in front, and a regiment of large wicker panniers full of grapes. On the dais were sixteen cut-down 300-litre casks, each mounted on a frame to leave half a metre below the cask. There was a hole in the bottom of each cask.

The idea was that two people would stomp grapes while the other two collected juice from the hole in the bottom of the cask.

Grape stomping teams at Sitges, with Memory Walsh and Peter Ward stomping in the barrel closest to the end, and Ambassador David Wright, then Canada's man in Spain

We knew we were in trouble when the Catalan teams appeared, with huge feet, sashes to keep themselves tidy, and skills that were obviously the result of lengthy Olympic grape stomping experience. There were fifteen teams of these Olympic grape stompers, flexing their bulging calf muscles, each team assessing the competition, and offering smiles of patronage to this guest team of competing Canadians. Certainly it was the imposing scarlet tunic of our RCMP security guard that drew the most attention to us.

Rules dictated that two members of the team would crush grapes from the first thirty-kilogram pannier of grapes for ten minutes, while the other two team members would use buckets to collect the juice. As each bucket was filled, a team member would rush to the measuring station, get the juice measured, and then dump it into the big vat, where the product of every team's stomping would be mingled, for eventual use in making some of this year's Penedes wines.

Memory Walsh and I stripped off our sandals and made ready for action. At the signal, every team's first thirty-kilo batch of grapes was dumped into the vats, so the first pair of stompers could have at it. We rapidly discovered that grape stems tended to plug the hole through which juice was being collected. The answer was a pause every minute or so to clear away stems with our toes. Tromping grapes is heavy, messy work, especially when speed stomping is an important factor. It was like living in a grape storm. Juice and grape skins were flying everywhere. Memory and I were spattered to the chest with grape stains in a very few minutes.

It became clear that a scarlet coat for our security guard was a pretty good idea, because the grape spatterings that he collected from standing too close were hardly noticeable at all. Our team's coach, Ambassador Wright, carefully stood a little further from the action when he saw how far the juice was spattering. With a minute or so to go in our ten minutes in the barrel, Memory and I were seriously out of breath.

When the half-time bell rang, ending our turn in the barrel, we were both purple to the waist, and very sticky all over. Sadly, the measuring score showed our Canadian team at the bottom of the pack, but we had half a bucket of juice left over, which could be used to our credit in the second half. In the handicap department, we'd be better off, too. Memory Walsh, petite and not much more than 100 pounds, had been paired with 210-pound Peter Ward, overweight and out of condition. Canada's anchor team of Michael Vaughan and Steven Drotos were both in better shape, and fairly matched at just under 200 pounds each; and they had big feet.

Boy did they make the grape pulp fly at the start of their ten minutes in the barrel! Memory and I now had workstations below the stomping action, so we got sprayed even worse with juice and flying pulp. Memory and I rushed buckets of juice and pulp to the weighing station, elbowing aside competitors. We'd also discovered that when the barrel's drain hole got plugged with grape stalks, the thing to do was to pull them through. That brought pulp through into the bucket to be measured and allowed the stompers to keep treading, without the need to pause and clear the hole from the inside. Vaughan and Drotos were so heroic they even had some Catalan competing teams worried.

Ambassador Wright watched over Canadian interests as the scores were counted, then joyfully reported that we had managed to press almost 200 litres from our sixty kilos of grapes, enough to give us seventh place. It may not sound like much, but that, we were told, was the best finish ever for a team of foreign grape stompers. Our RCMP security guard and the ambassador were generous with their compliments, but we noticed they didn't want to get too close to our sticky foursome. We were all dripping with grape goo.

Miquel Torres awarded prizes—cases of wine and bottles of brandy in varying numbers, depending on where each team finished. We each got a couple of bottles of wine for our efforts.

As a finale, Miss Sitges Harvest Queen came to the platform to be weighed in one of those huge balance scales. Her prize was the number of bottles of wine it took to balance the scales against her weight. The total came to about five cases.

Then the crowd pressed forward, undeterred by a bit of grape juice and all slightly hoarse from cheering on each person's favourite team. Everybody got a glass, and officials opened the taps on a couple of huge vats of wine so everybody could slake the thirsts of competition. I tell you, it was difficult to get your bare purple toes out of the way of the well-shod, thirsty mob.

After a drink or two from the common vat, we escaped for showers to change out of sodden, grape-stained briefs and tops. No way you could get the purple from your feet. Covered with socks and faint respectability, we Canadians retired to a glassed-in restaurant near one of Sitges' golden beaches, and had a glorious celebratory seafood dinner—of course with plenty of wine.

We were happy to get to bed, and sad to realize that next day would be Monday, with a morning flight back to Canada and the end of a stomping good time, at Sitges, not far from Barcelona.

# PINOT BLANC

Sometime in the late nineteenth century, a few Pinot Gris vines in Alsace took on a different look. They were mutating into Pinot Blanc, which has a leaf so similar to Chardonnay that even some experts can be fooled. They won't be fooled by the taste, however, because Pinot Blanc tastes like crisp Granny Smith apples and doesn't take very kindly to the heavy wood treatment many Chardonnay wines get. Pinot Blanc has some plantings in Burgundy, but it's in Alsace where this variety really shines, although it's rated as a lesser variety alongside Riesling, Gewurztraminer, and Sylvaner. It makes an ideal blending wine.

If you find a German white wine labelled Weissburgunder, that's Pinot Blanc. You might get something of excellent quality, too, because in German hands this grape can produce wines that will actually improve with some cellar ageing. It's used to make some of those special quality German wines, like Beerenauslese.

Any Italian wine called Pinot Bianco is also Pinot Blanc, a serious contributor to the wine lake. Pinot Blanc is fairly heavily planted in North America, including Canada. I have seen instances where North American Pinot Blanc was labelled as Chablis. Many of the ubiquitous white wines from Eastern Europe come from Pinot Blanc, as well as many blended low-priced white wines from around the world.

Generally, Pinot Blanc is a refreshing summer drink, for which you should not pay a great deal.

# BIRTH YEAR WINES

Nothing matches the thrill of drinking a bottle of wine that was made in the year you were born, particularly if you were born in a good vintage year. I was born in 1930, and you don't have to check many wine books to discover that 1930 was a rotten year for wine in most places. Happily, in most bad years you can find someplace from the world's diverse vineyards where it was a good vintage year. If weather was bad in Bordeaux, it might have been super in Tuscany or California; or South Africa, or New Zealand.

I remember running across a bin full of 1930 Chianti in a Tuscan cellar. Gosh, I said to our host, that's the year of my birth and it's the first time I've ever seen a bottle of that vintage. Being Italian and an excellent host, he picked up a couple of bottles and announced we'd be having them with lunch. What a sensation to drink that birth year wine; not a bad wine, either.

One year my wife and I came home from Italy with a bottle of 1958 Barolo—an excellent vintage year and the birth year of our eldest son. We'd been visiting Fontanafredda, and at lunch they actually served a 1958 Barolo. Wow, said Jane, that's the year our eldest son Tim was born. When we left, there was a package for Jane containing a 1958 Barolo. It came home with us, treated like the fragile crown jewel it was. We shared that wine with Tim and two of his friends also born in 1958 on a truly memorable evening. I wish we'd had a case. Laying your hands on a birth year vintage becomes more difficult the older you get.

Think about the emotional investment of laying down a case or two of birth year wine for your children or grandchildren, while the wines are still available. You may or may not get to attend the parties, but I guarantee you'll be remembered . . .

It's vital to buy wines that will have the staying power to last at least twenty years (longer if possible), and that means checking the vintage charts carefully in the two or three years after the birth you'll be remembering. It will also be important to ensure there's a good cellar available to store the wine so it will last those necessary twenty years. That means a cool, dark place where the temperature stays reasonably constant, a place that's free of vibration and has some ventilation. If you volunteer to store birth year wines for your kids in your own cellar, be careful temptation doesn't lead you to some early sampling. The best defence, I suppose, is to tell the recipients of the wine about their coming gifts so they can police the donor's thirst!

Bordeaux reds and Italian reds from Piedmont like Barolo and Barbaresco, or super Tuscan wines like Brunello di Montalcino, Tignanello, or Sassicaia are certain bets to last the required several decades in good vintage years. Expect to pay $40 and more a bottle. Some of the better California Cabernets and

Merlots will last the two decades. Vintage Champagne is wonderful, if you can afford it. Vintage Ports are perhaps the best wines for birth year gifts.

It used to be a tradition in England that a wealthy father would always buy a few cases of Port for each son. These days you'd better include daughters, too, because women are proving they have palates at least as good as men, often better. I know our daughter appreciated it when I brought home a couple of bottles of her birth year Port.

Peter with a bottle of 1930 Chianti—his birth year

It's delightful that Ontario now produces wines that will stay the course for twenty years or more, and thus are appropriate for birth year wine purchases. Look for heavy-bodied red wines with lashings of both fruit and tannin, and with good acid balance. The premium grade of Henry of Pelham's Baco Noir will last that long when the vintage year is good; so will the premium grade of Pillitteri's Cabernet Franc, the premium Cabernet Sauvignon of Inniskillin, Chateau des Charmes, or Lakeview Cellars. You may have to telephone the winery you choose to order premium brands. Tell them why you want the wine and ask if it will keep for the necessary years. Ice wine is another good choice for laying down a birth year vintage for children or grandchildren. Choose an ice wine made with Riesling grapes, or Gewurztraminer, because they'll last longer than ice wines made with Vidal. Riesling and Gewurztraminer ice wines will also improve in the bottle as they age.

I've done the birth wine thing for my grandchildren, and I'm hoping that when they are old enough to sample their wine, I'll still be around to sample at least the first bottle with them. I'd hate to see youthful palates attack such august wines without some expert advice, particularly when it comes to vintage Ports.

# TREBBIANO

Under various aliases, this is probably the most planted white grape in the world. It's certainly the most planted grape in Italy—and in France (as Ugni Blanc)—and these are the world's two largest wine-producing nations. Trebbiano is a popular grape because it's easy to grow, produces a prolific crop, is easy to make into wine, and is a grape that readily distils into brandy. In the Cognac district, where it's known as St. Emilion, it makes up ninety-five percent of the vineyards. You're an Armagnac fan? That's distilled Ugni Blanc you're drinking. A good deal of the production gets converted to brandy.

Trebbiano is grown in South Africa, Australia, Argentina, Brazil, and Mexico, where the wines are thirst quenchers of dubious quality, but it does makes a good blending wine. At their best, Trebbiano wines can offer a slightly lemonish bouquet, fresh fruit flavours when young, and with acidity fit to match food like shellfish, or light fish like sole or orange roughy.

Perhaps the best performance of Trebbiano comes in Italy's Soave wine, which can have its fresh acidity laced with the flavour of almonds. Trebbiano makes a wine that is often thin, invariably acidic, and spoiled if you keep it much more than two years. Unless it's at a high summer party, I prefer my Trebbiano/Ugni Blanc after it's been converted into something more solid by the stills of either Cognac or Armagnac.

# CALIFORNIA CHARACTERS

Your first trip to Napa-Sonoma will make you a California wine lover, whilst simultaneously stretching your liver, and offering a graduate course in human nature. My favourite wineries involve interesting people. If it's true that the better you know the people who make the wine, the better it tastes, then it's also true that the more interesting the characters, the more complexities you can find in the wine.

For example, take Saintsbury Winery, at Carneros, south end of Napa-Sonoma, just north of San Francisco Bay. A couple of Chicago businessmen who loved Burgundy, David Graves and Richard Ward, decided in 1981 to make wine with Pinot Noir and Chardonnay. So they hired a winemaker, William Knuttel, and established their winery. They're still having fun making wines, which get better each year.

The first time I visited, David Graves poured me a glass of their Vincent Van Gris, which sported a Van Gogh-style picture of their barn on the label. Lovely, refreshing white wine, tinged slightly pink, with considerable character. It was made, said Graves, because there was lack of colour in the previous year's Pinot Noir, so they ran off some of the early juice to make their blush wine, allowing the rest of the crush to macerate with skins so it could develop a decent deep red colour.

As we knocked back a glass or two of Vincent Van Gris, Graves remembered aloud how a San Francisco artist friend had volunteered to paint a picture of their main winery barn in the Van Gogh style for the label.

It worked so well that Graves claims some visitors to the winery were convinced the label painting had really come from Van Gogh's brush. One customer, Graves said, had even claimed that he'd seen the original painting at the Louvre!

We walked the vineyards that warm late summer afternoon, and saw workers slashing off bunches of grapes that were left lying on the ground. How come? Well, said Graves, we're just a couple of weeks from harvest, and there are too many grapes on the vines to ripen properly, so we're cutting off the excess to make sure everything we harvest is really ripe.

When you buy wine made with that kind of care, it costs a bit more. Taste a Saintsbury Pinot Noir to see if it's worth the extra price. It's one of my favourites. I can't take a drink without remembering a warm afternoon tasting with David Graves and watching his workforce discard excess grapes.

I hate to go to California without stopping to see the folks at Arrowood—Richard Arrowood and his charming wife Alis. Arrive at Arrowood and right away you can tell there's a strong Canadian connection, because of that Canadian flag flying out front. Alis, you see, is from Montreal. She was an Air Canada flight attendant, and sometimes worked at California wine tastings on layovers, helping to pour wine. At just such a tasting she met Richard, and their chemistry was exactly in balance, just like a fine wine. Richard was working as the winemaker for Chateau St. Jean, and thinking about his own winery. Alis and Richard established Arrowood in 1986, just a few miles south of Chateau St. Jean, and, until 1990, Richard remained the winemaker for Chateau St. Jean as well as running his new winery.

Alis Arrowood with a prize bottle made by husband
Richard Arrowood

Alis was the one who promoted Arrowood successfully in Canada by her regular appearances at the annual California wine fairs across the country. When she's in Ottawa, she makes a point of visiting her mom and family in Montreal. She's got rich auburn hair with a flawless complexion, sparkling eyes, a great figure, and a formidable intellect. Richard Arrowood is a great winemaker. Alis has excellent business sense and superb promotion abilities, so they make a great team.

On one visit to Arrowood I remember Alis being quite distracted because she was entertaining a couple of bankers, and angling for a necessary loan. She talked later about how nervous she had been, but you never would have known it, the way she mixed poise and confidence with charm and business ability as she locked up the loan.

The last time I saw Alis was in Ottawa in 2000. She was the usual bubbly enthusiast, with an added carefree note. She and Richard had just sold Arrowood to Mondavi, but with the proviso that they'd stay on to run things, just the way they were, for a number of years. No more worries about financing, said Alis.

Richard Arrowood does indeed produce wines worthy of world attention, albeit in reasonably limited quantity. His Cabernet Sauvignon wines, his Chardonnays, and his Merlots are among the best in the business. His Riesling and Viognier aren't too shabby, either. I've got a few treasured bottles of Arrowood Cabernets and Merlots in the cellar waiting for a special occasion.

I remember back in the 1980s discovering a truly excellent California sparking wine—in Ottawa. Friends with an interest in wine arranged a great winter afternoon of Champagne tasting. At least fifteen couples came, each bringing one or two bottles of Champagne or sparking wine. The wines included all the big names from France, from Krug to Moet et Chandon, with a few ringers thrown in to add interest. Each bottle was masked and numbered and the guests provided with scorecards. Each person was asked to name his/her first, second, third, and fourth choice. Points were given on the basis of five, three, two, or one, depending on where each wine ranked in each individual's preference.

Peter sampling some Krug wine at the north end of the Napa Valley

The big surprise was that Schramsberg Vineyards' bubbly was the runaway winner. It had only one or two first-place choices, but almost everybody else gave it second place, so in total score Schramsberg waltzed home comfortably ahead of giants like Krug, Dom Perignon or Veuve Clicquot. The downside of this is that I can never remember seeing Schramsberg on a Canadian wine store list. You have to be in the US to get it.

Naturally, that meant Schramsberg Vineyards was my top priority for a visit the next time I went to California. Schramsberg is near Calistoga, just west of the Napa Valley wine highway. I telephoned ahead for an appointment, so proprietors Jack and Jamie Davis were waiting for me with samples cooling in ice buckets. Before we tasted, we strolled through ageing cellars that looked as though they'd come straight from the real Champagne district.

Schramsberg was founded in 1862 by an itinerant barber, Jacob Schramm, who had been saving to buy a wine property. He came to the US from Germany at fourteen, and never lost his family's love of the wine business. He kept cutting hair to make ends meet until the wine business began to pay enough. His big break came in 1880 when Robert Louis Stevenson visited the winery on his honeymoon and was smitten by the Schramm wines to such an extent that he wrote about it at great length—"the wine is bottled poetry," wrote Stevenson.

Schramm's sons couldn't keep the business going when Dad died in 1905, and the winery closed in 1911. Several other owners tried unsuccessfully to revive the winery, and things were in pretty much of a mess when Jack and Jamie Davies gave up their business careers in Los Angeles to follow their winemaking dreams. For their first vintage, Jack had to search frantically for Chardonnay grapes. The best he could manage was five tons of Johannesburg Riesling. Robert Mondavi said he would trade Jack for five tons of Chardonnay, and did, although he was in the process of leaving the family business at Krug to start his own winery.

Jack and Jamie got their own vines planted, and set to work restoring the Schramm property. They rebuilt the homestead and moved in. They restored the cellars and extended them further into the volcanic rock. They rebuilt the stables, outbuildings, and winery, and then proceeded to make the best sparkling wines California had ever seen. Schramsberg makes only sparking wines, using Champagne grape varieties, the traditional Methode Champenoise, and ageing the wines thoroughly before sale.

At the tasting he held for me, Jack offered five different styles of his "Champagne," and if ever sparkling wines produced outside the legal French geographic limits for that Champagne deserved to borrow the title, these were the ones. Not only did Jack adhere strictly to Champagne production methods, he also had the good sense to limit the amount of juice taken from each load of pressed grapes. He and Jamie were meticulous in the vineyards, winery, ageing cellars, and bottling process. No wonder their wine did so well at our small Ottawa tasting.

Sadly, Jack Davies died in 1998, leaving the business in the able hands of his wife Jamie and their kids. I haven't been back there since.

Another of my favourite California wine characters is Orville Magoon, a Hawaiian native, who is now very much a part of California. Orville's family in Hawaii owned property near the Honolulu airport, which the University of Hawaii wanted for expansion. The university had extensive California property, donated by alumni, so in 1963 they proposed a swap—twenty-three acres of Magoon land near the Honolulu airport for 23,000 acres in California's Lake County, property that included five decent-sized lakes, and the former estate of famous Edwardian beauty Lillie Langtry. Jersey Lillie had made some excellent wine there from 1888 to 1906, built a beautiful house, and loved her estate. The swap offer was too good for the Magoon family to refuse.

Orville and his brother Eaton studied winemaking, planted vines, and with the help of established winery owners Roy and Walt Raymond, they got into the wine business. For the first few years, wines were produced at the Raymond winery. Roy and Walt helped with the design of the Magoon Guenoc Winery, and by the late '70s, the Magoons were in business, their wines sporting a cameo picture of Lillie Langtry on the label.

Orville Magoon of Guenoc Winery watches a load of his grapes head for the de-stemmer.

Over the years I must have visited Orville a half dozen times and seen him at California wine fairs in Canada at least that many times. I've tramped the vineyards with him, even examining the last few still producing vines that Lillie Langtry had planted a hundred years earlier. Not only is Orville's property beautiful, it affords him unlimited land for winery expansion, and it represents the main drainage basin feeding that scarce resource—water—to the Napa Valley.

Talk about environmentally friendly, Orville is the only one I know to get rid of pesky grape-eating birds around harvest time without using nets or those automated bangers designed to frighten the pests off with simulated shotgun blasts. He discovered that birds hate human conversation, so he bought several hundred cheap transistor radios, tuned them to a talk show, and scattered them through his vineyards. If the radios play music, it doesn't scare the birds away. Public radio talk shows they can't stand. I wonder if the CBC would work in Canadian vineyards.

Orville holds dinners sometimes for visitors in the restored Lillie Langtry house, and, if you're lucky, he even offers a night's stay in Lillie's restored bedroom. I've had that opportunity, but no matter how I taxed my imagination, it was impossible to conjure up the ghost of the beautiful Miss Langtry.

One year I visited Orville in the late summer, just before harvest, to spend a day or so tasting his wines and touring his expanded facilities. As it happened, there was a formal dinner scheduled in Sonoma, a good hour's drive away, for the wine industry—the Knights of the California Vines, or some such organization. Orville said he planned to taste a lot, so I was to drive. He and his wife Karen—a great classical singer—piled into my rental car, and away we went. Both of them were smart in formal clothes. The best I could muster was a business suit. I did notice, however, that Orville was wearing his scuffed and muddy field boots with his dinner jacket.

We arrived in plenty of time for the outdoor pre-dinner drink, which consisted of wines from every conceivable Napa-Sonoma winery, and conversation with some of the best-known people in the industry.

At dinner I was at a table that included Mike Grgich, wearing his trademark black tam, and Stag's Leap owner/winemaker Warren Winiarski. Both these illustrious winemakers had made the wines that were stars at the 1976 Paris tasting, where French judges in a blind tasting placed Winiarski's 1973 Cabernet first, ahead of French Bordeaux first growths, and Grgich's 1973 Chardonnay ahead of Grand Cru white Burgundies.

Grgich is a stocky, intense individual who speaks with a pronounced accent from his Croatian homeland. He came to California in 1958 with a degree in wine science from Zagreb University. After working with some of California's most illustrious wine people—Robert Mondavi, Andre Tchelistcheff and Lee Stewart—he established Grgich Hills in partnership with Austin Hills in 1977. He went back to Croatia when it became independent.

It was while Mike was working for Chateau Montelena that he made the 1973 Chardonnay that beat out France's best white Burgundies in that 1976 tasting. By any measure, Mike Grgich is a master of Chardonnay, not only because of his winemaking skill, but also because of the emphasis he puts on viticulture.

Warren Winiarski, Stag's Leap Cellars, is even more careful with his viticulture. He and his wife Barbara left Chicago for California wine country in the early 1960s. He left his job as a lecturer in Greek classics at the University of Chicago and set out to learn winemaking, also working with Lee Stewart and Robert Mondavi. Where Mike Grgich concentrated on Chardonnay, Warren Winiarski focused his attention on Cabernet Sauvignon. In 1972 Warren succeeded in putting together a syndicate of investors to found Stag's Leap Cellars. There was quite a legal battle over the name Stag's Leap Cellars, because at about the same time another group founded Stags' Leap Winery. The courts decided that both could use the name because they were established at the same time.

When Warren's 1973 Cabernet Sauvignon beat out wines like Mouton Rothschild, Haut Brion, and Montrose, at the 1976 Paris tasting, his newly established winery became instantly famous. So did he. He's quite an austere man; at least he was at that dinner I attended, so it was with some hesitancy that I asked him a question about viticulture.

"If you're really interested, come to the winery at two o'clock tomorrow," he said.

You don't refuse an offer like that, so I promised to be there. The thought of the next day—and the fact that I had to drive Orville and his wife back home—kept my drinking at very reasonable levels for the rest of the evening. The drive back to Guenoc was filled with sparkling conversation, and once there, I bedded down in Lillie Langtry's room for the night.

After a late breakfast, I headed off to Napa. Winiarski's Stag's Leap Cellars is a few kilometres north of the town of Napa, off Silverado Trail. His vineyards are spread out on the rolling hills that begin the range of modest mountains that form the east side of Napa Valley. Stag's Leap Cellars is a popular spot for tourists on the Napa wine trail, so the reception building was crowded when I got there. Just as I asked for Warren Winiarski, on the tick of two p.m., he came bounding into the room. He quickly showed me the tourist stuff, then led the way outside to a four-wheel-drive vehicle for a tour of the vineyards.

"First, you have to remember that the grapevine is a perennial plant," he said. "Its prime task in life is to store as much energy as possible so that it can survive the winter. Any energy left over goes into developing seeds. Our task is to give the vine a sense of security so it will divert more energy into making seeds—the grapes."

We looked at a variety of vineyards, just two days before harvest, and I noticed that there was quite a difference in the way different vines were pruned.

"Experiments," explained Warren.

He stopped the Jeep and we walked into the vineyard where vines on either side were heavy with almost ripe grapes. We came to a spot where there was a row of Cabernet Sauvignon grapes pruned in an upright fashion, beside a row pruned in the harp method, which is designed to have the leaves catch more sun.

"Taste the grapes," said Warren. "First this vine and then that one."

There was quite difference in flavour, and yet the vines were growing in the same soil, with the same angle of exposure to the sun, and Warren had assured me that they were the same clone. There was a touch more sweetness in the grapes from the harp-pruned vine, but the grapes from the vine with upright pruning seemed to have more of the essence of Cabernet Sauvignon about them.

Now Warren took hold of a branch of leaves, his hands gentle, almost in a caress.

"You'll notice that there are no new shoots on this branch, or on the vine," he said. "That's because the grapevine is very clever. It will continue to put out new green shoots in the stage we call verdant, until there are enough leaves on the plant to mature the grapes on the vine. Once there are enough leaves, the vine will go lignant—form a bark around the existing shoots and stop producing new leaves.

"You can look at a vineyard a week or so before harvest and tell whether or not you have a greedy grower. If the vines are still verdant a week or so before harvest, there are too many grapes and you should go through the vineyard to cut off perhaps a third of the fruit. When you do that, the vine will go lignant overnight."

I thought back to my visit with David Graves at Saintsbury, Carneros, and remembered how he had workmen cutting grapes from his vines.

Warren looked thoughtful for a minute, and then added, "Our data shows that with this clone of Cabernet Sauvignon, with this exposure to sunlight and in this soil, it requires fifteen leaves to ripen a bunch of grapes."

That seems to be cutting things pretty fine; but I have to say, I learned more about viticulture in that afternoon with Warren Winiarski than I had during dozens of previous visits to vineyards in a dozen or more countries. Not only must the grapes be pruned so the vine can give its best, but the harvest must be timed exactly. The longer the grapes stay on the vine, the sweeter they will be, thus producing higher alcohol in the finished wine. The longer the grapes stay on the vine, the lower will be the acid content, which is so essential for production of a balanced wine. For the best wines you need good vines planted in appropriate soil with good drainage. You need rigid pruning to control production from the vines, and you must have the right timing for the harvest, so that fruit, alcohol, and acid will be in good balance in the finished wine.

# GEWURZTRAMINER

When good Gewurztraminer grapes are properly made into wine, the result can be a luscious combination of honey, lychee nuts, and pungent tropical fruit, all wrapped in a perfect acid-fruit balance. These wines can be sweet, dry, or in between. Some wineries even make Gewurztraminer ice wine, which is worth the extra bucks it costs. Save that for dessert. The table wines can be an excellent choice to accompany Asian dishes or curries. Beware, though, of some Gewurztraminer wines, which can be plain, short on flavour, and very out of balance. You can usually spot such bummers by their low price, although experience is a better guide.

Cool climate, the right clone, and limited grape production from each vine are the keys to making a good Gewurztraminer. The vines need a soft spring so the early budding fruit doesn't get frozen; careful viticulture in the right soil to concentrate flavour; and choice of the best clone to suit climate and soil. It's quite possible to concentrate the distinctive Gewurztraminer flavour too much, resulting in a strong bitterness rather than a complexity that will become subtler with ageing.

Wine expert Jancis Robinson is convinced that the only great Gewurztraminer wines come from France's Alsace region, where the first mutation of Traminer grapes took place more than 100 years ago. Without question some of the Gewurztraminer wines from Alsace are rich in flavour concentration with a balance worthy of a Cirque du Soleil high-wire act—the right standard against which to judge any other pretenders. But I'd love Jancis Robinson to taste some of my Ontario favourites, like Herbert Konzelmann's Gewurztraminer in both dry style or ice wine, and the more readily available Jackson-Triggs variety, which is such an excellent dollar value. It's obviously a grape that can do well in Niagara's climate, and we'll be seeing more Ontario Gewurztraminer wines.

# CHAMPAGNE

The enduring success of Champagne in the world of wine is graphic proof of the wisdom of the old marketeering adage that you have to "sell the sizzle, not the steak." Champagne, that frothing, golden elixir of France's Marne Valley, has become synonymous with celebrations, special occasions, party time, and being wealthy—precisely the image Champagne makers have been promoting for their product over more than two and a half centuries.

The mystique of Champagne began because winemakers around the Mountain of Reims in northeastern France lost out to the boys of Burgundy in a vital seventeenth-century conflict over which area produced the better wines. In those days, the wines of Champagne, made just like Burgundian wines, with Pinot Noir and Chardonnay grapes, were "still" wines, sometimes unavoidably spangled with the carbon dioxide bubbles that later became the hallmark of Champagne.

Champagne winemakers work in France's most northern wine-production zone, where climate is not nearly as kind to the grapes as it is in Burgundy. They were left with the choice of being number two in terms of reputation and financial reward, or developing a unique, distinctive characteristic. Froth, sparkle, and salesmanship turned out to be the answer. The road to making Champagne internationally renowned as a special-occasion drink involved turning the problem of secondary fermentation into an asset, and creating a mystique that would stretch backwards to before recorded history.

Viticulture in the history of the Champagne district, as is the case with most other French or German wine regions, goes back to Roman times, although there's a volume of literature detailing how fossilized grape leaves from six million years ago have been found. There's no concrete evidence that the uncivilized tribes of Gaul were making wine before the Romans came. It is a historical fact that the land around the site of Reims proved extremely fertile for vines. The chalky marl subsoil of the region, left over from a prehistoric lake bed, did marvellous things to the flavour of grapes, and the climate was tough enough to make the vines struggle for life, a circumstance that produces the best fruit for wine.

The Gauls took to winemaking—and drinking—so enthusiastically that Emperor Domitian, in AD 92, feared his subject peasants would neglect the job of producing grain for the Empire in order to make wine for themselves. He ordered all vines in Gaul uprooted, and although it's doubtful that the order was universally obeyed, it certainly did add an interesting degree of risk to making your own wine. That imperial order may have been the first effort in Europe to impose a form of prohibition. On the books, it certainly lasted longer than the 1930s version of anti-drinking legislation in the in the US—190 years, to be exact.

By the year 280 there were unofficial plots of grapes all over Gaul, and undercover wineries were churning out wine aplenty, probably with the cooperation of thirsty Roman garrison troops. Emperor Probus, the son of a gardener, was a realist as well as an enthusiast for vineyards. When he came to power in 282, he officially revoked the order banning grape growing in Gaul. Winemaking became legal again.

The first French Christian ruler was King Clovis (465–511), a warrior who succeeded in unifying what is now France. He ditched his old Norse gods in favour of Christianity, trading his religious beliefs on the strength of a battle victory that he won after praying to Jesus. Clovis was a man of his word. Right after winning the battle he became Christian, and by an amazing coincidence, all his followers saw the light at the same time. Clovis won victory after victory, including a decisive one against the Romans, and all those he defeated keenly embraced Christianity, too. That made France Christian, because Clovis conquered virtually all the territory in present-day France, making Christianity the official religion.

Wine became particularly important as Christianity spread, because of the vital role it plays in celebrating the communion, and in maintaining health. Churches and monasteries discovered that when the questionable sanitary habits of the day made people sick, the best chance for recovery in most cases involved dosing people with wine, which was a damn sight cleaner than the drinking water. In Champagne, as in most other places, churches and monasteries became the experts in growing grapes and making wine.

Reims, about 145 kilometres east of Paris, was a centre of Christianity, so much so that a huge cathedral was built there in the thirteenth century, which became the traditional site for the crowning of all the French kings. Coronations require celebration, and celebration requires wine. The local wines of Champagne got their start in the social big leagues as refreshment for the guests at the coronations of French kings. The guest list would usually include leading members of the international royal set, who enjoyed the wines and often carted a case or two of their favourites home with them. Orders for more wine usually followed, giving Champagne the early basis of an international market.

One of the biggest coronation parties at Reims, for example, saw Charles V crowned in 1364, with royalty from all over Europe there as guests. The Champagne wines that Charles served at the coronation party were so highly regarded by his guests that many foreign courts sent permanent representatives to Reims, assigned to buy the best wines of the crop each year. Imagine what such competition did to the price of the best wines.

The popularity of Champagne wines—"still" wines without bubbles, remember—created considerable political difficulties with powerful Burgundy. So severe was competition between the two that duels were fought over the merits of Champagne and Burgundy. The noble grapes of Burgundy are Pinot Noir and Chardonnay, as are the noble grapes of Champagne. In some places, the soils of Burgundy and Champagne are similar, and indeed, in those days, the wines were often similar, too. Climate was a major difference, with Champagne's weather often being too severe for a grape crop to ripen properly. Still, the Champenois claimed their best wines were better than Burgundy's best.

Doctors at the court of Louis XIV settled the argument in favour of the Burgundians by declaring that Burgundy was better for your health than Champagne. The devastated Champenois then set about developing a wine with unique characteristics. If they couldn't win by playing the same game as the Burgundians, then they'd invent their own. By 1670 growers in Champagne had succeeded in producing an almost white wine from Pinot Noir grapes. They would harvest early in the morning, being careful not to break the skins of the grapes; then they would press the grapes immediately, so that no colour from the skins would invade the juice.

Sometimes a rose tint from the skins did appear, and then the wine was called "*oeil de perdrix*" (partridge's eye). The wines went into barrels for their fermentation, and when the cool winter air stopped fermentation, the wines would be stored in barrels or bottles, awaiting the pleasure of the thirsty.

Corks were in use in England by the mid-1600s, but were then only beginning to appear in France. French wines were stored in casks stoppered with wooden plugs, which were often wrapped in an oil-soaked cloth to keep air from getting at the wine. Experience had shown that air gave wine a funny taste—a result of oxidation. As wine was emptied from a cask for drinking, the wine that remained was liable to spoilage from the air. To better preserve them, some of the quality wines were stored in bottles, stoppered like the casks with cloth-wrapped wooden plugs, or sometimes with wads of oakum. Sometimes wine stewards dropped stones in the casks to replace the volume of wine used and keep air exposure to a minimum.

Champagne's new white wine showed a tendency to go into a second fermentation when spring arrived, following the year of the wine's growth, and it made quite a mess. Whether the new fizzy wine was stored in casks or bottles, it popped a lot of stoppers and soaked a lot of cellars. No wonder the stuff was called "*saute bouchon*" (jumping stopper), or sometimes, "*vin du diable*" (devil's wine).

# Dom Pierre Pérignon

Fortunately for those who were losing wine and money, getting regularly doused with *saute bouchon* wine, a monk named Dom Pierre Pérignon came along to solve the problem.

Dom Pierre was born in January 1639, and died in 1715, the year of Louis XIV's death. In 1658, about the time all that spilled wine was driving Champagne winemakers to distraction, Dom Pierre, at the age of nineteen, was appointed cellar master at the winery of Hautvillers, an institution founded a thousand years earlier by the Benedictine monks. Dom Pierre also became financial controller for the abbey and was to retain those two posts until his death.

The major concern of any respectable director of finance in Dom Pierre's position would have been the enormous losses of wine—and lost revenue—caused by *saute bouchon*. Dom Pierre was very concerned about the losses, and also extremely curious about the phenomenon of the second ferment in the monastery's wine, so he focused his considerable intellectual powers on the problem.

After many experiments and tests, Dom Pierre succeeded in controlling the second fermentation, by varying the sugar content and the temperature of the wine. Controlling sugar content enabled him to control the force of the gases in the bottle, and thus reduce the wastage of wine. There is some historical dispute as to whether Dom Pierre introduced the use of the cork to the Champagne district, or whether his contemporary and neighbour, Frère Jean Oudart, of the cellars of the Abbey of Pierry, should get the credit.

He was the first to use the old Roman caverns of Champagne for storage of the wines. The chalky soil offers perfect temperature control for Champagnes in the second fermentation, and ideal conditions for ageing the wine. During World War I, when all but a handful of homes in Reims were destroyed by bombs and shells, thousands of people lived in the wine caves, safe from the madness above, probably embracing some of the liquid joys to keep their sanity.

Dom Pierre is most famous for his experiments of blending the wines of grapes grown in different fields around the monastery property. By marrying these raw materials, he could produce the same distinctive "Champagne" taste, year after year. Dom Pierre's abbey had access to more vineyards, and probably more wine through tithes from faithful grape growers, than any other organization of the day, so he had plenty of different stock to choose from when he blended his wines. He also blended new wines with old wines to improve quality in a poor vintage year.

His development of blending techniques is rated by the industry as the single greatest contribution to Champagne production ever made, and the process today is relatively unchanged.

One of the great monk's most important discoveries was considered so secret, so valuable to the economic health of the abbey that it died with him. He had discovered a way to remove from Champagne the yeast deposit left by the second fermentation. That deposit, unless removed, makes the wine muddy and spoils the fine taste. Earlier attempts to remove the yeast deposit always resulted in loss of much of the gas that created the bubbles. Dom Pierre was able to make a clear wine, still with plenty of sparkling bubbles. It was the first Champagne ever to be produced as we know it, but the secret disappeared when he died.

## Methode Champenoise

For almost 100 years after Dom Pierre's death, Champagne was crudely clarified by decanting, at the expense of losing a lot of the captured gases that gave the wine its sparkle. Each bottle would be held erect, right side up, then rapped smartly several times on the bottom to bring down the solid particles clinging to the side of the bottle. The bottle then would be opened, and the clear wine decanted into another bottle, usually taking at least some of the muddying deposits along with it, and losing much of its fizz in the process.

*Veuve Clicquot*

In 1805, the newly widowed Madame Clicquot, twenty-seven years old, took over her husband's winery business, complete with the problems of trying to produce a clear wine that still had lots of sparkle. She developed the *"remuage"* process, known as "Methode Champenoise," which is now universally used in the making of Champagne and many other non-Champagne quality sparkling wines. Methode Champenoise has already been described in the chapter where we sampled Spanish Cava wines. Veuve Cliquot's work has benefited sparkling winemakers the world over, and sparkling wine lovers who can enjoy crystal clear bubbly of a near-infinite variety from producers in every winemaking nation of the world.

When she assumed control of her late husband's winery, *"Veuve* Cliquot"— the widow Cliquot—faced more than the problem of cloudy wines. Breakage was seldom less than ten percent, and sometimes reached eighty percent. Quality of glass was inconsistent, and so was the pressure that built up in the bottles during secondary fermentation. With such high breakage, Champagne was terribly expensive. One is tempted to speculate that increased demand brought sloppier methods into vogue with some wineries, increasing breakage as winemakers hurried to maximize profit.

A druggist named François from Châlons discovered that the bubbles of the secondary fermentation could be exactly determined by precision control of the sugar content. He based his work on the earlier studies of Napoleon's Minister of the Interior, Jean Chaptal. As a result of François' contributions to controlling sugar content, Champagne breakage went down to five percent. His new techniques didn't reduce the price of the wine, but they sure boosted profits. Modern manufacturing eventually made possible stronger bottles that reduced breakage to one percent.

## Selling the Sizzle

Producers of Champagne were among the first to recognize the social changes of the late nineteenth and early twentieth centuries, which created a middle class with a large disposable income. For the first time in history, a wealthy middle class, outside the aristocracy, had lots of money. People began going out to dinner, and spending their money on status symbols to impress their friends.

A solid-based reputation of Champagne as the wine of the aristocracy already existed, thanks to tastes acquired by royal guests at French coronations in Reims. Fortunately for makers of Champagne, the richest of the new European middle class, the English, already had a partiality for their wines. Champagne wines had been popularized throughout the English aristocracy years earlier by a Frenchman named Saint-Evremont, who was exiled from the court of Louis XIV, perhaps because of his philosophical bent and his biting wit. In London, he made himself the social arbiter of society, and soon every fashionable aristocratic table was serving the wines of Champagne.

If dukes and duchesses drank Champagne, why then that's what the newly rich mill owners of Manchester had to have, too. A river of Champagne began flowing to England to answer the demand. The first international advertising campaign started, promoting Champagne as the tipple of prestige. Next thing you knew, corks were popping in every major city of Europe, and the mystique of Champagne was thoroughly launched. The English still drink more Champagne per person than any other nation outside France, although North American sales are increasing steadily.

## Champagne Country

Strict French laws set out the precise boundaries of Champagne, 150 kilometres northeast of Paris. It's the special requirements for soil to grow the grapes that go into Champagne wines that determine the geographic limits for the vineyards. Champagne country was once the bed of a huge prehistoric lake, 220 million to 70 million years ago. Marine fossil deposits have enriched the subsoil.

Only where six to twenty inches of surface soil covers the chalky gravel of the lakebeds can Champagne grapes be grown. The roots of the vines probe deeply into the gravel, pulling all manner of interesting mineral tastes from the ground.

Originally there were four departments of Champagne: Aisne and Haute-Marne in the north; Marne in the centre; and Aube in the south. Today's Champagne district covers 24,200 hectares—18,700 in the Marne department, 3,700 in the Aube, and 1,800 in the Aisne. Champagnes of the Marne are most important. Those of the Aube and Aisne are of cheaper quality and usually get sloshed down parched throats at local grog shops, or hoisted by revellers at Paris nightclubs with a better eye to profit than quality. The better vineyards of the Marne have been classified by law.

Only Pinot Noir, Pinot Meunier, and Chardonnay grapes can be used in the making of Champagne. Today's districts are Montagne de Reims, Vallée de la Marne, and the Côtes des Blanc. The average size of a holding in eighty-eight percent of the legal Champagne district is a mere two acres; so growing Champagne grapes is largely the enterprise of small growers. The other twelve percent of delineated Champagne-growing property is owned by 146 Champagne companies, which use their own crops combined with purchases from independent growers to make their product.

Just prior to each harvest, the grape growers and the winemakers get together and decide on a price for the crop. Grapes that are judged to be 100 percent quality go to the Grand Cru houses, and those that are less than perfect go to other producers. The price gets lower as the rating of the grapes becomes lower.

Check the label of a Champagne to determine its category. There are only seventeen Grand Crus, the areas producing the best quality, rated at 100 percent; forty Premiers Crus, rated at between ninety-nine and ninety percent; and a number of lesser-production vineyards classified as *deuxième* and *troisième catégorie*, which are progressively rated at less than ninety percent.

## Making the Wine

The grapes for Champagne are picked, and then carefully sorted, with underripe or overripe berries being discarded. The grapes are then taken quickly to the presses, with great care to avoid damaging the skins. Four thousand kilograms of grapes are allowed to produce 2,666 litres of juice, or thirteen casks, for Champagne. By law, only the first ten casks are allowed for "*vins de cuvée*" (wines for blending), and the next three casks are called "*tailles*" and are used for "*vins du suite*" (wines that follow)—lesser wines, which are still allowed the Champagne label. The rest of the juice, the "*rebêche*," is not allowed to wear the Champagne name. It is used to make local table wines with no appellation, or used for distillation.

In good vintage years, Champagne houses produce Vintage Champagne, which sits on the top of the quality scale—and the price scale, too. It truly is special stuff to be savoured on special occasions.

A good litmus test for sparkling wines is the quality of the aftertaste. If there's a trace of bitterness, it means the winemaker has pressed more than fifty percent of the juice from the grapes. Up to a point, the less juice extracted from the grapes, the better the quality of the wine will be. Once juice for sparkling wine—particularly Champagne—has been pressed, the rest of the juice is squeezed out for use in distilleries or to be made into industrial alcohol.

In Champagne, each cask of the better wine is marked with the name of the grower, and the field where the grapes were grown. Traditionally, casks were stacked for the first fermentation, and the onslaught of cold weather would halt the yeast's work. Today, most producers use temperature-controlled stainless steel or glass tanks for that first ferment. They stop fermentation when they please, regardless of what the weather does.

During winter, cellar masters sample casks, and blend wines, usually employing older wines from previous excellent vintages to improve the quality of a new vintage. The operation is similar to that in a Cognac cellar, where Cognacs from different years and different qualities are blended together so the producer can achieve the same colour, the same bouquet, and the same taste, year after year.

The Champagne cellar master uses new wines and old wines together, carefully blending them to create a product that is the same each year, and stamped with the characteristics of the house involved.

Mixing is done these days with automated pumps, but the cellar master's nose and palate still determine the blends. In former days, Champagne makers depended on the sugar remaining in their wine after the autumn fermentation to create the bubbles of spring in the bottled wine. Today, Champagne is analyzed chemically to determine how much sweet "*liqueur de tirage*" should be added to each batch before it is bottled. *Liqueur de tirage* is plain sugar candy, dissolved into some Champagne. By controlling the sugar and yeast content, producers know exactly how much carbon dioxide gas will be produced, and exactly how much strain will be placed on each bottle during secondary fermentation.

These days Champagne bottles being prepared for their secondary fermentation are sealed with a cork-lined crown stopper, like the cap on a bottle of beer. It's considerably cheaper than the solid corks of the old method, and many consider it does a better job. The financial side of Dom Pierre would have approved of the savings in cost; his artistic side would have delighted in getting better quality. The infant Champagne is then stored deep in the chalky caves for two or three years. It takes eight weeks for the secondary fermentation to create the bubbles that make Champagne the celebratory drink that it is.

When it has aged a sufficient length of time, each bottle of Champagne must undergo preliminary treatment for extracting the deposit of dead yeast, tartaric acid, and mucilage produced inside the bottle during secondary fermentation. The process is called *"remuage,"* or "riddling," and in many places it is still done by hand.

Bottles are placed at a forty-five-degree angle in the holes of an A-shaped rack called a *"pupitre."* Riddlers shake and twist each bottle of Champagne every day, gradually increasing the slope of the bottle in the *pupitre*, so that eventually, over a period of six to twelve weeks, all the bottles are standing on their heads, and all sediment inside them rests on the cork. A skilled riddler can handle 30,000 bottles each day, but the process is very manpower intensive. Not many young people want to make a career of spending their working hours in Champagne caves, twisting bottles, so the skill is rapidly disappearing. Today most companies use machines for riddling. Machines are less time-consuming, and cheaper, although not necessarily more effective than manpower. In some cellars, huge metal containers of bottles line the walls of the cellar, each basket container mounted on a set of mechanical arms, which vibrate on the command of a computer. The machine gradually changes the angle of the container of wine bottles, until all are upright, with sediment resting on the corks. Some of the big Champagne houses keep this process out of the public view, because they don't like visitors to see they've gone modern.

When the bottles are standing on their heads—*"sur points"*—they are stored that way for the remaining portion of their "resting" time, which could bring their total time in cellar to three, four, five years, or even longer, if deemed necessary by the cellar master. One year of rest in the cellars after second ferment is the law, and most large houses give their Champagne three years. The best Champagnes have four years "on the lees" of the yeast before they face *"dégorgement."* The longer a Champagne rests "on the lees" of its second ferment, the finer and longer-lasting will be the bubbles of gas.

When the process of *dégorgement* first came into use, it required that skilled technicians perform the operation by hand on each bottle. The process required that the cork be eased out just enough for the internal pressure to drive out the deposit gathered on the bottle's cork. The technician would then quickly ram the cork home again, before all the gas was lost. Considerable wine was lost in training workers.

As I described in the chapter on Cava, a major advance in *dégorgement* came when Champagne houses began freezing the necks of their bottles, so that an ice plug would form to enclose the unwanted yeast deposits. These days, ranks of upside down Champagne bottles are moved down a bottling line, their necks immersed in a strong brine and ice solution, which freezes an ice plug of wine at the bottle neck—enclosing any yeast deposit. With that deposit safely contained, the bottle is returned to an upright position on the bottling line, the cork is popped off and the plug of ice is expelled, taking with it the dead yeast, deposited there by the careful riddling of the wine.

Most Champagnes now undergo this assembly line treatment. A few wines are handled individually, with experts checking the contents of each bottle to ensure high standards are maintained. In some Champagne houses, a *dégorgeur* is awarded a bonus for any substandard bottle he detects. Each bottle of Champagne is then injected with a *"dosage"*—a liqueur composed of Champagne and sugar—which determines the degree of sweetness the wine will have. Champagnes can be *brut* (extra dry), *sec* (dry), *demi-sec* (semi-dry), or sweet. Adding a small amount of liqueur results in *brut* Champagne; a large amount produces a sweet Champagne. The degree of sugar dosage depends on the market, because tastes in Champagne differ. North America and Britain, for example, prefer dry Champagne, while Latin nations seem to like it sweeter.

The final step before corking involves squirting a small amount of wine into each bottle, to restore each bottle to the same volume it contained before the yeast deposit and ice plug were removed. Corks are rammed home by machine, and under considerable pressure, because the cork must be squeezed to about half its normal volume to ensure a tight fit. Each cork is immediately wired down tightly, and the bottles sent to storage, to be recovered as needed for final labelling and shipping to thirsty customers.

## Corks and Removing Them

Corks on Champagne bottles are under unusually high stress, because the wine is at six atmospheres of pressure. Cremant, from Champagne, is made at three atmospheres, for people who feel that regular Champagne is too gassy. The extra importance of the cork for stoppering Champagne means that they must be of the best quality. Only those from trees in Spain or Portugal, which are at least fifty years old, are used. All corks are marked "Champagne" before they are wired into place. Corks on bottles of vintage Champagne are also marked with the year.

There's a real knack to removing those Champagne corks when the chilled bottle finally lands on your table. A cork that pops sounds delightful, but it also signals the fact that you're losing some of the bubbles the Champagne maker took so much trouble to create. Chances are that a popped cork will also mean some spilled wine.

Champagne gushes out of the bottle only when pressure is removed suddenly, or when the wine is warm. You'll often see a bottle of Champagne cooling in an ice bucket, for example, with the upper third of the bottle exposed to a warm room. Take the cork off a bottle like that and the warm glass of the upper bottle will make the wine foam with increasing vigour, until it's all over your hands, your table, your companion, and maybe even the ceiling.

Make sure the *neck* of a Champagne bottle is cool before you open it, even if it means you must turn the bottle upside down in the ice bucket for a few minutes before you open it. Take the foil off the top carefully, and, without disturbing the bottle too much, release the wires that hold the cork in place. Keep your hand on the cork and twist the bottle slowly to ensure that the cork doesn't get out of control. You'll hear a hiss of escaping gas when the cork comes free. If you're careful, there should be no spillage of wine, and maximum retention of the bubbles.

Please don't serve Champagne in those coupe-shaped glasses, which were invented, supposedly, when Henri II modelled in glass the left bust of his mistress, Diane de Poitiers. The rounded, shallow shape encourages Champagne bubbles to dissipate quickly. Champagne should be served in slender flute glasses, to conserve both the bubbles and the chill of the wine.

Champagne is more than a pretty wine in a pretty glass. The wine of kings is a favourite remedy for the onset of a cold or flu. Take one glass of *brut* Champagne every hour—a bottle a day—and either your flu bug will flit, or you won't really care. Marjorie Michaels, an enthusiast for Champagne therapy, wrote a book on the subject of self-dosing—*Stay Healthy With Wine*. She reports that one day her daughter brought a flu bug home from school to infect the entire family. Michaels is allergic to most medications, so her doctor suggested the Champagne treatment. She claimed that her fever broke in twelve hours, but she continued the treatment for two days anyway, probably because it helped her cope with the rest of the sick family. Her husband, on the traditional aspirin cure for flu, stayed sick several days longer than Michaels, and he didn't have nearly as much fun.

Treatment of the sick with wine in monasteries in the Middle Ages was of course a major factor in preserving and improving the skills of winemaking. Louis XIV's court may have decided that Burgundy was better for your health than Champagne, but Dom Pierre Pérignon would have been delighted with the fact that Marjorie Michaels, and millions of others, prefer Champagne.

# SEMILLON

That wonderful golden grape Semillon has a serious image problem. It's viewed by many people as a grape that makes an inexpensive blending wine, or as a grape to smooth down the power of some Australian Chardonnays.

Semillon is relatively easy to grow, resistant to many of the common vine diseases, and can produce a very hefty crop. It's also the source of great quality for the white wines of Bordeaux, including things like highly prized sweet Sauternes, Barsac, and Graves. Semillon is quite prone to develop something called noble rot, which only sounds like a plus if you're a wine grower or wine lover. Noble rot is the mould *botrytis cinerea*; it concentrates sugars and acids while diminishing the amount of juice you get from the grapes. It results in rich wines of enormous ageing potential, with complex honey and blossom flavours—dessert wines to die for.

Semillon is also responsible alone or in blends for the great dry white wines of Bordeaux, the dry whites of the south of France, and many of the wines of South Africa. South American producers use plenty of Semillon, and it's very popular in Australia, either as a single variety wine or blended with Chardonnay—once again, popular because the vine produces terrific volume. Semillon makes a pleasant but unremarkable wine when the cropping is heavy. It can make something exquisite with careful viniculture and plenty of bottle ageing.

# ONTARIO'S
# WINE REVOLUTION

One day in 1972 amateur winemaker Karl Kaiser bought some new grapevines from a young nurseryman named Don Ziraldo. Karl and Don met each other with growing frequency after that sale. A few weeks later they shared a bottle of Ontario wine and were mutually disgusted at the taste. We'll try and make a better wine together, they vowed. Their determination began the Ontario wine revolution.

Don Ziraldo is one of the most powerful salesmen Ontario has ever produced, so when he turned his attention to convincing the province that he and Karl should be issued a licence in a new category—cottage winery—it was no contest. The last winery licence issued in Ontario had been thirty years ago. Don aimed his salesman's skills at the then chairman of the LCBO, teetotaller Major-General George Kitching (Ret.), who was very impressed. Ziraldo and Kaiser were given their licence to start production in 1975.

"We made 500 bottles of Marechal Foch wine from the 1974 vintage," said Don, "and Inniskillin was in business."

I have a fond memory of tasting a bottle of that wine. A friend sampled it, too, with fairly dramatic results. He was John Campbell, Information Officer for the British High Commission. John decided on the spot that he would serve Inniskillin wines at all his Ottawa receptions, which meant that the smart set in Ottawa knew about Inniskillin much more quickly than did Toronto. Inniskillin's first bubble of sales success was in Ottawa.

What an experience it was to have been writing a wine column during the magic years that followed. Early experiments with Ontario wine had not been pleasant, particularly for a nationalist. Suddenly there were people in Ontario making wine that wasn't merely passable—it was actually good!

As other cottage and estate wineries followed Inniskillin, Ziraldo worked very hard to upgrade the image of Ontario's entire wine industry. His determined efforts established industry-wide standards for Ontario like those in the world's great wine-producing countries. Vintners Quality Alliance (VQA) was at first voluntary and for Ontario only, then for wineries in British Columbia and Nova Scotia, and finally became strict provincial legislation in Ontario. Ziraldo was the founding and first chairman of VQA, and all of Inniskillin's products wear the gold VQA letters on the bottle. Today Inniskillin produces 120,000 cases of wine a year, all of it quality wine under Ontario's strict wine laws.

Three years after Inniskillin's start in 1975, Paul Bosc left Château-Gai to establish Chateau des Charmes. Backed by lawyer Rodger Gordon, he bought sixty acres of land near the town of St. Davids, and established the first continuing vinifera vineyards in Ontario. Those three—Ziraldo, Kaiser, and Bosc—were the fathers of Ontario's wine revolution. There's a separate chapter on Paul Bosc, who can take credit for leading the wave of Ontario wineries moving to vinifera grapes.

Karl Kaiser, original partner with Don Ziraldo, in Inniskillin, Ontario's first "cottage" winery, which began the wine revolution

Shortly after World War II, Adhemar de Chaunac and George Hostetter, of Brights, brought some hybrid and vinifera vines to Ontario to experiment with growing them. Production levels from their new vinifera vines were so low that they turned instead to developing hybrids, one of which has provided reasonable red wine in Ontario for the past thirty years. This hybrid was later named after de Chaunac, and is still grown in Ontario.

Inniskillin and Chateau des Charmes were followed by more new cottage and estate wineries—Cave Spring, Hillebrand, Konzelmann, Lakeview Cellars, Marynissen, Stoney Ridge, Pelee Island on Lake Erie, Colio, Pillitteri, Henry of Pelham, Rief, and Vineland Estates. All were making vinifera grape wines, some on a real boutique basis.

Canada's Free Trade Agreement with the U.S. in 1988 was, in retrospect, the best thing that ever happened to Ontario's wine industry. At the time, executives from much of the industry, particularly from the older large wineries, were sure their businesses would be strangled by California's import wines, such as cheap jug wine from Gallo. How could they continue in business without their huge traditional markup edge over all foreign wines, and other Canadian wines from outside Ontario? They could see the end of what had been a very protected, profitable business. As well as preferential markup policies, profits were aided by benefits like the provincial government rule that allowed 1,022 litres of wine to be made from one tonne of grapes. To squeeze that amount from a tonne of grapes, the local water mains had to carry quite an extra load at harvest time, because there was no way you could get that amount of juice from a tonne of grapes without adding water. And that was after the grapevines had been squeezed to produce three times the volume that should be allowed for the production of quality wine.

In the days before free trade, many of the large wineries spent more money designing labels and marketing than they did on making wine. LCBO stores in those days had a "must list" policy, which required provincial monopoly stores to stock their shelves with any new brand of Ontario wine offered, to give new products a chance to sell. It was common practice, in at least one of Ontario's largest establishments, to get a sexy name and label for a new product, and then ship it off to the LCBO. When many of the bottles didn't sell, the winery would accept unsold stock back, have the marketing people brainstorm a new name, re-label the wine, and ship it back out to the LCBO as a new product for another "must list." They'd keep renaming leftovers until all the stock was sold.

So then came the free trade agreement with the U.S., coupled with a government ban on the use of labrusca grapes—traditional varieties like Concord and Niagara—and finally, later in 1988, an agreement under the then GATT (General Agreement on Tariffs and Trade) that the markup differential on all imported wines would be phased out over the next seven years.

To partly offset these changes, the Ontario government promised to spend money promoting Ontario wines, and also provided upwards of $50 million on a program to encourage farmers to rip out labrusca grapes. It was those labrusca varieties that gave the old Ontario wines their foxy aftertaste, which some people unflatteringly referred to as the taste of skunk tracks. The result was the downsizing of Ontario vineyards by about 7,000 acres, and smiles on the faces of many part-time farmers whose labrusca crop had been guaranteed a market for years under provincial legislation. Those part-time farmers collected most of the rip-out subsidies. It only takes a fraction of the effort to raise labrusca grapes as it does to rear vinifera grapes—the type that make the best wine. A guy with fifty acres could raise labrusca grapes with weekend work while pulling down a real salary during the week from the GM diesel plant in St. Catharines. Many did just that, so payment for them to rip out their labrusca grapes was a bonus.

The message to wineries and grape farmers in 1988 was to get out of the business, unless you were serious, and ready to take on foreign competition without protection. You had to make grape growing and/or winemaking a full-time job, or quit.

Today the LCBO still takes a healthy bite out of every dollar we spend on wine—fifty percent or more of the price on every bottle. Ontario wines are marked up fifty-eight percent on the landed base price, while wines from outside the province are marked up sixty-four percent, the difference being the LCBO's cost of storage and inventory. Then there's a federal excise tax of 51.22 cents a litre (not paid for U.S. or Canadian wines), plus LCBO charges of $1.80 a litre (a wine levy, a bottle levy, an environment fee), plus PST and GST. The end result today is that an Ontario winery gets $4.03 for a bottle that sells at the LCBO for $10, a U.S. winery gets $3.69 out of a $10 bottle, and a European shipper gets $3.36 for a $10 bottle.

Once the dust settled, existing Ontario wineries took up the challenge, and dozens of new wineries have been established over the past fourteen years. The older players in Ontario's wine game were best positioned to take advantage of some of the new rules. There was a huge merger rush.

When the Americans were bargaining over free trade, one of the aspects about protectionism for the Canadian wine industry that bothered them was the fact that Ontario wineries were allowed to operate their own stores, selling their own brands, albeit at prices that were the same as LCBO prices. Those stores made it possible for the wineries to pocket the LCBO markup and handling charge on all the wine they sold. Winery stores provide wine lovers with a smaller selection of select brands of wine not produced in sufficient volume for the LCBO to list.

The Free Trade Agreement grandfathered existing winery stores, and prohibited the establishment of any new stores. The law also provides that any private brand store can be moved to a different location. For example, should the Wine Rack chain want to open a new store in a growth area of Toronto, management could close a store in perhaps Cornwall, then open one in the new Toronto suburb.

Since the FTA there have been many mergers and buyouts in the Ontario wine industry. Private brand stores played a significant role in these buyouts. Inniskillin, Brights, and Cartier (the former Chateau Gai) merged to form Vincor, which also includes Jackson-Triggs, the old London Winery, and several others. All these companies had their own chain of wine stores. Each store in the chain—now called the Wine Rack—can sell all Vincor products, making those stores virtually a multi-brand private chain, circumventing LCBO markups. There are 164 Wine Rack stores in Ontario.

It soon became apparent that good vinifera grapes could be grown in Ontario and British Columbia, and first-class wines made by Canadian winemakers. It's one thing to make excellent wine; yet another to make a profit in the process. In order to become a world-class wine producer, a company has to make good wine to sell at a reasonable price in high volume. Ontario's best selling red wine, for example, is the Australian Wolf Blass Cabernet Yellow label, which currently sells for $16.95 a bottle. In Ontario alone that wine sells 50,000 cases a year.

So far, one Canadian company has shown the ability to make that leap to quality wines at an affordable price in high volume, and that's Vincor. Don Triggs, president of Vincor, said that in 2002 his company produced 8.5 million cases of wine, including coolers, 6.5 million cases of that in Canada. That makes Vincor the fifth largest wine company in the world.

Don Triggs learned the business from the ground up. In the 1970s he and Paul Bosc both worked for Château-Gai. Triggs says he still has some 1974 Pinot Noir that Bosc made. In 1978 Triggs went to California to run a bulk winery, where he met his future partner, winemaker Allan Jackson; in 1989, they bought Château-Gai-Cartier from Labatts.

Triggs's goal is to build a diversified premier wine business on the world stage. "There's no better argument for diversification than the terrible winter kill of vines that took place in Ontario over the winter of 2002-03," he says. "Vincor now has wineries and vineyards in Ontario, B.C., California, Australia, and New Zealand. That's diversification. It's highly unlikely that all those areas will be hit with bad weather at the same time.

"It's one thing to diversify growing. You also have to diversify access to markets. The top markets for new world wines are the U.S., the U.K., Australia, Canada, and New Zealand. We now have a distribution network in all of those markets."

Competition? Triggs loves it because a good competitor teaches him something every day.

"Our wines are sold around the world today, and Inniskillin ice wines are the company's flagships," he says.

The new Ontario wineries that in the late 1970s and '80s followed Inniskillin's 1975 opening were mostly established by people who previously had been growing grapes for the major wineries, or by amateurs who had proved their skills in amateur competitions. Karl Kaiser was a gifted amateur; so were John Marynissen, Jim Warren of Stoney Ridge, and Eddy Gurinskas of Lakeview Cellars. The Pennachetti family, of Cave Spring, and the Pillitteri family were long-time Niagara grape growers, as was the Speck family, of Henry of Pelham. As a wine writer, I found that the better you got to know the people who made the wine, the more interesting their wines became. Here's a brief profile of a few of the earlier players in the wine revolution.

# Cave Spring Cellars

There is a cave with a spring in it close to where the winery's first grapes were planted, on the Beamsville Bench of the Niagara escarpment. Here, there's a perfect mix of clay loam soil loaded with minerals washed down from the heights. In the 1980s, Len Pennachetti, Cave Spring's founder, came to Ottawa with samples of his Chardonnay and Riesling wines. They were both so good that you could hardly believe they were from Ontario. I thought the dry Riesling was by a whisker the better of the two, priced at just under $10.

Len, his winemaker Angelo Pavan—now a partner—and Len's brother, Tom, have travelled to most Ontario centres conducting Cave Spring tastings. Len and Angelo made just 5,000 cases in 1986, the year they established Cave Spring Cellars. Production by 2002 had reached 70,000 cases a year. Cave Spring was responsible for opening Niagara's first wine tour restaurant—On the Twenty—at Jordan, and they also run one of the area's finest hotels, the small, very elegant Vintners Inn, across the road from the restaurant and the winery. Cave Spring is a class act all the way. Len Pennachetti followed Don Ziraldo as chairman of VQA.

# Pelee Island Winery

Canada's most southerly vineyards are on Pelee Island, which juts south into Lake Erie to the extent that it's farther south than northern California. Canada's first commercial winery, Vin Villa, was established on Pelee Island in the 1860s. In Pelee Island's museum, they've even got a newspaper clipping to prove that Vin Villa's Catawba wines won French medals for quality before the turn of the century.

The modern era began in 1980 when Walter Strehn planted a selection of German vinifera grapes. He made Canada's first ice wine in 1983, and built a modern winery at Kingsville, on the mainland, which made it necessary to ship grapes from the island by ferry. German winemaker Walter Schmoranz took over the Pelee Island winery in 1986, and he made Ontario's first red ice wine—from Lemberger grapes—in 1989. Walter has been responsible for developing a huge public picnic ground and museum on the island. He's also planted a demonstration vineyard on the island with all the different grape types grown by Pelee Island, each variety labelled so the public can see the different vines. It's a joy to visit the vineyards—Ontario's largest vinifera planting of any estate vineyard. It's also a joy to take part in a tasting with Walter because he's always got a few experiments going.

# Reif Estate Winery

It's no wonder that Reif's wines are the most Germanic of Niagara's production. Klaus Reif trained in Germany, then brought German techniques and equipment to bear on the German varietals his uncle Ewald Reif had planted. Ewald, who runs the vineyards, ripped out the labrusca grapes on the property on the Niagara Parkway when he bought it in 1977. Klaus became winemaker in 1987. He's now assisted by Roberto Di Domenico, who is doing spectacular things with some red grape varieties—some bottles selling in the $50 range and worth the price. Ice wine is a particular Reif strength, with large sales in the U.S. and Asia.

## Konzelmann Winery

Canada's potential for growing wine grapes so impressed Herbert Konzelmann when he made a hunting trip to Canada in 1980, that he took back a number of soil samples for analysis in Germany. Four years later he was back to buy property right on Lake Ontario, just west of Niagara-on-the-Lake. Herbert brought with him a family winemaking tradition that went back to 1893 in Germany, and initially, his wines were very Germanic. He was one of the first to make Gewurztraminer wines, sweet, medium, dry, or even ice wine. His Chardonnay wines are elegant, his Rieslings crisp and filled with fruit, and his red wines in several varieties have also won international prizes. Herbert's ice wines are among the best produced in Canada.

Herbert Konzelmann shows off some of the vines that have made his Konzelmann Estate Winery a coveted label

Herbert is deeply Christian and carries with him a vibrant, smiling enthusiasm that shows in his wines, which he regards as close friends. Many of the vine clones he has brought back from Europe have been shared with other friends in the Ontario wine business. Herbert has recently bought more than 100 new acres slightly south of his original vineyards, but he has no plans to expand production beyond 100,000 cases a year.

## Marynissen Estates

John Marynissen started planting Chardonnay and Cabernet Sauvignon in the mid 1970s, which makes his vinifera vines some of the oldest in Ontario. He had been a very successful grape grower and amateur winemaker for years, selling grapes to the major wineries and racking up an impressive array of winemaking trophies. John and his family opened Ontario's first farm gate winery in 1990. I still have several bottles of John's 1991 vintage Cabernet Sauvignon, Cabernet Franc, Merlot, and Chardonnay in the cellar. Even after twelve years they were excellent drinking. John's daughter Sandra is gradually taking over more of the business as her father gives up increasing amounts of the workload. He has sold his farm to Sandra and her husband, Glen Muir, and as of this writing (2003) Sandra is doing virtually all the winemaking. In 2000, she made a Riesling that took honours as the best Riesling in Canada that year. She's now using some Canadian oak barrels to age Chardonnay wines. Marynissen sells eighty percent of its small production at the winery, or directly to restaurant customers.

John Marynissen and daughter Sandra,
of Marynissen Estates

# Stoney Ridge

Jim Warren taught high school in Hamilton, but his genius lay in making wine out of almost anything. Jim won every prize on the amateur winemakers' wish list before he took the plunge as a professional with a couple of partners in 1985. In 1990 he went into partnership with Murray Puddicombe, a grower of quality grapes near Winona, where together they established a large modern winery. It's a lucky wine lover who still has a few bottles of Jim's earlier red wines in the cellar. Jim makes wine that's fruit driven, with plenty of body, and in the reds, structure to last for decades.

It was an uneasy partnership after a few years, because Jim insisted on making wine out of just about anything organic, while Murray wanted to see bottom-line results. At one time, Jim was making more than fifty different kinds of wine at Stoney Ridge.

The Warren-Puddicombe partnership ended in the early 1990s, but Jim found his new partners even less understanding and more difficult. At one stage Jim's financial partner put lock and key on Stoney Ridge's cellars, insisting that he be the only one allowed to bring bottles out for tastings. Those old bottles were Jim's babies, so you can imagine how he felt when prohibited from showing them off!

Jim left Stoney Ridge to become a roving Niagara wine consultant, spreading his expertise to a dozen new wineries. Now Stoney Ridge is under new management yet again—with Vineland businessman Barry Katzman as president—and Jim is back as the consultant who is restoring Stoney Ridge's old style. He has been a great contributor to Ontario's wine revolution.

# Lakeview Cellars

Eddy Gurinskas, a retired CNR supervisor of signals, is another prizewinning amateur winemaker who turned professional. He and his wife Lorraine bought a Beamsville Bench vineyard in 1986, then obtained a farm gate winery licence in 1991 as Lakeview Cellars. Eddy was then right in step with two good friends, John Marynissen and Jim Warren, fellow amateurs turned professional. They shared knowledge and sometimes vine cuttings, much to their mutual benefit. In 1995 and in 2000, the three friends co-operated to create special wines. Each man made a large barrel of Pinot Noir wine in his own style; another large barrel was made by blending one third of each man's Pinot Noir wine together in a fourth barrel. They called the wines "The Three Guys," and collectors snapped up the wine in lots of four bottles, one blended, and one from each winemaker.

Eddy's production at Lakeview was low quantity and high quality. He made powerful wines and aged the reds primarily in American oak, which gave them all a twist of something different. I still have some of his early red wines in the cellar, and they are just reaching their peak.

In 2000, Eddy decided it was time to retire, and sold Lakeview to Diamond Estates Wines and Spirits. He's there as a consultant at least until the end of the 2003 vintage, and then he and Lorraine will do some travelling.

## Henry of Pelham

The brothers Paul, Matthew, and Daniel Speck have created a premium, prizewinning winery from a grape farm that can trace its roots back to 1776 and bugle boy Nicholas Smith, who received his soldier's grant along with others who came north as Loyalists during the Revolutionary War. Nicholas also purchased prime land at a crossroads, where his son Henry opened an inn near the town of Pelham, signing his application for a liquor licence as Henry of Pelham, thus giving today's winery its name.

Henry's original inn has been modernized and expanded to become the winery's headquarters. When the Speck brothers opened for business in 1987, they suffered some early teething problems with the 2,200 cases of wine they produced.

Paul Speck of Henry of Pelham with the winery sign and a sample bottle

By the mid-1990s, Henry of Pelham was rivalling the best in Ontario. Winemaker Ron Geisbrecht left his job in charge of experimental winemaking with Brights to join Henry of Pelham, and made a perfect fit with the Specks. Their secret is pruning grapes to produce a modest harvest. Paul Speck explains that Henry of Pelham makes different classes of wine, with the most expensive coming from vineyards with a harvest of only one and a half tons per acre, and the lower-priced wines from grapes harvested at three to four tons per acre. Quality shows in the degree of fruit concentration found in all Henry of Pelham wines.

In 2002 they produced 75,000 cases of wine. The Speck brothers intend to concentrate on high-end wines. At this writing, Paul was chairman of the Ontario Wine Council and vice-chair of Vintners Quality Alliance.

## Pillitteri Estates Winery

Gary Pillitteri took part in the early stages of Ontario's wine revolution as a grower. He'd been a successful amateur winemaker in the same crowd as John Marynissen, Karl Kaiser, Jim Warren, and Eddy Gurinskas, growing grapes for some of the major wineries, and enough to make his own wine for family and competitions.

Sue Ann Staff, brilliant young winemaker from Pillitteri Estates Winery, examines one of her babies

"Dad was making thirty to forty demijohns a year for family and friends," recalled his son Charlie, "and winning all sorts of prizes for his ice wine."

In 1978 Gary bought some Chardonnay vines from Paul Bosc, planted them, and signed a twenty-five-year contract as a grape grower for Château-Gai.

Gary ran for the Liberals in 1988, but lost, so with his family he decided to make his own grapes into his own wine in his own winery. Of course, Gary won his seat in the 1993 election, leaving son Charlie, daughters Connie and Lucy, and sons-in-law Jamie Slingerland and Helmut Friesen to handle the first vintage. Charlie remembers that they made 4,000 cases of the 1992 vintage, under winemaker Joe Will, who has since left to form Strewn Winery.

These days it's a rare wine competition that doesn't have a few Pillitteri wines on the gold medal stand, and ice wine has become a specialty. Out of a production of 50,000 cases a year, 15,000 cases are ice wine, much of it sold in Asia where prices often top $100 for a half bottle. From the 2002 vintage, Pillitteri produced seven different kinds of ice wine. Sue Ann Staff, who became Pillitteri winemaker in the mid-1990s, has combined her talents with the growing know-how of the family to produce some superb table wines as well as the company's specialty ice wines. Sue Ann's Family Reserve Cabernet Franc table wine is hard evidence that this is a grape that can do at least as well in Niagara as it does in France. Her Merlot, Sauvignon Blanc, and Rieslings are excellent in balance and fruit concentration.

## Vineland Estates

Close your eyes while you sip a Vineland Estates Riesling wine and you'd swear you were in France's Alsace region. The wine is steely dry, and loaded with apricot, peach, and pear flavours, which are perfectly balanced by the acid—just like a good Alsatian. If dry Rieslings are Vineland's signature wines, then they are followed by a host of other whites and reds, among the best produced in Canada, which is only fitting. Vineland was one of the early estate wineries in Ontario, on the cutting edge of the wine revolution.

German winemaker Herman Weiss started things in 1979 when he bought land at Vineland, on the Niagara Bench, and planted his German clone Rieslings. The first vintage was 1982. In 1987 Weiss took British Columbian winemaker Allan Schmidt as a partner. Allan's father Lloyd had been at Sumac Ridge, where Allan learned his winemaking. Allan recalls that Vineland made 2,000 cases in 1987, compared to more than 60,000 cases a year by 2003. There have been major changes since 1992, when entrepreneur John Howard bought the winery. Today Allan's brother Brian is the winemaker and Allan is general manager. The winery has become a showcase for tourists, with a wonderful restaurant, restored period buildings, classy modern facilities for making, displaying, and selling wine—and the best view in Niagara.

Allan Schmidt, of Vineland estates,
with samples of his ice wine

In Allan's view the LCBO is holding back Ontario's small wineries; many of them can't get shelf space for their limited production.

"In Toronto LCBO stores, you can buy two Vineland Estates wines, the dry Riesling and the semi-dry. Do you know how many you can buy in Calgary, where the stores are free enterprise? There are seventeen types of our wine available there," he said. "That's one of the reasons we plan to first introduce every new wine in Alberta."

Vineland sells 10,000 cases a year in Alberta, compared to less than 7,000 cases a year through LCBO stores. The rest of the 60,000-case annual production is sold to restaurants, by special order, or through the retail stores. Such is Vineland's reputation that American wine collectors sometimes arrive to buy ten-year-old Riesling, which from a good vintage year ages just as well as a fine Alsace Riesling.

# BOSC

Paul Bosc and his wife Andree were forced out of their homes after Charles de Gaulle stopped the generals' coup in Algeria. They'd been grape farmers and they fled to Burgundy, where Paul studied viticulture at University of Dijon. He was an experienced diver—so skilled that Jacques Cousteau had offered him a job as a diver on the ocean research vessel *Calypso*. Bosc said later that he'd turned down the offer because his wife Andree was pregnant with Paul Bosc junior at the time, and he knew that if he went with Cousteau and the *Calypso* sirens, he'd probably lose his wife.

Things didn't go very well for the Bosc family in Burgundy, probably because there were hundreds of dispossessed Algerian *"Pieds Noirs"* in France at the time. In 1963 Bosc decided that for his family's benefit he should emigrate to Canada—Montreal, to be specific. Paul spoke very little English, so location was a no-brainer. It had to be Quebec.

The only way Bosc could find to utilize some of his wine knowledge in Quebec was selling. He applied successfully for a job with the SAQ (Société des Alcools du Québec), the province's alcohol monopoly, and wound up as a clerk in a Montreal SAQ store. Paul Bosc is not the sort of man to settle easily into such a job, but a young family has to be fed. He chafed at the bit part he was playing; he was frustrated by the work ethics of a government organization and the future such a career presented.

One day a shipment of wine arrived at Bosc's store from the Ontario Château-Gai winery. He noticed that there was a brown granular deposit in the bottles, recognizing immediately that a secondary fermentation was taking place. When that happens, carbon dioxide pressure from fermentation builds up inside the bottle, just the way it does in the making of Champagne. Champagne, of course, is made in heavy-duty bottles designed to resist such pressure and to preserve the bubbles of gas in solution. When secondary fermentation occurs in ordinary wine bottles, they become potentially lethal bombs, liable to shatter when pressure pushes the ordinary glass to its breaking point, hurling shards of glass in all directions.

Remember my story from my winemaking days, when I had this happen to a batch of homemade white wine in screw-top bottles? One day I noticed a deposit, touched the bottle, and it began fizzing around the screw top. I realized the dozen or so bottles were potential bombs, and thank heaven it was Friday. I called in the neighbours for a delightful party of fizzy, secondary fermented wine, which went down very well, without a single bottle exploding.

When Bosc discovered the potentially dangerous Château-Gai wine, he got on the telephone to Château-Gai in Niagara, found somebody who could speak

French, and told them about the wine shipment. He explained what was wrong, and then told a surprised Château-Gai executive how to stop this from happening again. At Château-Gai, they'd never had anything like this happen before. Imagine a Quebec SAQ clerk caring about something like this, not to mention knowing the cause and the remedy!

Two days later, a Château-Gai vice-president flew to Montreal and hired Bosc to work for them making wines in Niagara. Bosc had been with the SAQ for eight months.

His first creation of any note for Château-Gai was a white wine called Alpenweiss. In those days most Ontario wine was best suited to consumption from brown paper bags under bridges, but Alpenweiss was a pleasant change. It was the first Ontario wine I remember without that foxy taste so characteristic of wines made with native North American grape varieties like Concord, Delaware and the like. Bosc developed a process of putting wines through a system of pressure filters to remove most of the foxy taste. Of course Ontario wine producers made a specialty of pumping as much grape juice as possible from the ground, too, harvesting ten, twelve, and even more tons per acre of grapevines, when these days we know you can't make decent wine with that kind of production. You can only sell that sort of stuff to people who have no acquaintance with wine.

Bosc's Alpenweiss was a decent white wine at a fair price, but it didn't last. Trouble was, once the market got established, the wine seemed to degrade. I remember saying some very complimentary things in a column about Alpenweiss shortly after it was released; the column was clipped, enlarged, and displayed in many Château-Gai stores. When in a few years the quality went downhill, and I wrote about that too, the second, critical, column sure wasn't displayed in Château-Gai stores!

During the fourteen years Paul Bosc spent with Château-Gai, he laid the groundwork for the commercial growing of vinifera grapes in Ontario. He asked around the wine community about growing vinifera grapes in Niagara. He was told that it had been tried by Brights, but it simply wouldn't work commercially.

"Brights and Parkdale had three acres of Pinot and Chardonnay," said Bosc, "and they made some pretty good Pinot sparkling wine. Their vineyard was being worked by an old Hungarian farmer, but the experiment didn't go very far."

While Bosc was still with Château-Gai he heard about Dr. Konstantine Frank in New York's Finger Lakes district, who was having great success with vinifera vines. He remembers saying to himself that everybody claimed that vinifera vine growing was impossible in Niagara climate, and here was this German Russian doing it.

In 1967, Bosc made a trip to the Finger Lakes to visit Dr. Frank.

"He showed me around and we tasted some of his wine, but he was pretty cagey about how he was doing it. I looked pretty well and could see some of what he was doing, enough to take some ideas back to Niagara. Without question Dr. Frank was sort of an inspiration to me," said Bosc.

Back at Château-Gai, Bosc began trying to talk his superiors into giving vinifera vines a try, and after a year or so he succeeded, and planted a small experimental vineyard of Chardonnay, Pinot Noir, Riesling, and Gamay. The wines were so good that a small tasting tour was organized. Toronto wine writer Michael Vaughan went with Bosc to New York and wowed the critics with these Canadian vinifera wines. Don Triggs, now president of Vincor, was at Château-Gai when this happened, and told Bosc he'd never forget it.

Then in 1973 Labatts bought Château-Gai. I asked Bosc what happened to the vinifera project.

"The new directors drank the wines, and that was the end of the experimenting," he said. "I remember an Ontario winery executive saying to me that growing vinifera vines was like having two mistresses. You enjoy them both, but you wouldn't marry either of them. Everybody said growing vinifera grapes in Niagara was not commercially feasible."

Paul Bosc Jr. and Paul Bosc Sr. hoist a glass of their best

At that stage Bosc began planning his own winery. A potential partner, lawyer Roger Gordon, approached him to offer backing, and together they looked for property. They settled on a tract of land just north of St. David's, with soil and drainage judged to be right for growing vinifera vines. They bought sixty acres, and Bosc began planting Chardonnay, Pinot Noir, Riesling, Gamay, Aligote, Cabernet Frank, and Cabernet Sauvignon. It was the first commercial-scale vineyard in Niagara—probably in Canada. Then in 1978 he founded Chateau des Charmes.

Bosc really became a major item for wine writers in Ontario when he produced a Nouveau Beaujolais that was better than the French stuff, and released it just before the magic October French release date. Not only did Bosc make an excellent Nouveau Beaujolais, using Gamay Beaujolais grapes, but he enraged French producers by flying a couple of cases to Paris to be released just the day before the French Nouveau was to go on sale. The Bosc wine was good; the publicity was gold-plated. He's made a nouveau wine every year since that first one, and as far as I can remember, each year Bosc's nouveau has been better than most of the French nouveau products selected to be sold by the LCBO.

Bosc was also one of the leading figures in the race to make a good commercial Chardonnay, competing with Inniskillin and Cave Spring. Again he proved that he knew as much about publicity as he did about winemaking. On the grounds that he didn't know which French oak barrels would be best suited his Chardonnay wines, Bosc invited a whole tribe of wine writers to come to a tasting that would compare his Chardonnays, some aged in each of Alliers, Nevers, and Tronçais oak. As I recall, it was the Alliers barrels that won the day—and every writer at the tasting wrote about it.

In 1983 Chateau des Charmes moved to St. David's and more than doubled in size. Bosc and his partner bought almost 100 acres just west of the town, and built a huge French-style chateau, with production facilities, offices, tasting rooms for visitors, and a well-designed store for wine and curio sales to tourists. Across the road from the new winery sits the Boscs' dream home, like a Burgundian picture, surrounded by vineyards.

I remember in 1983 sitting in the Bosc kitchen tasting marvellous Cabernet Sauvignon, Cabernet Frank, and Merlot wines. The table was covered with glasses, and we decided to see who could make the best Bordeaux blend by mixing these classical wines in various proportions. Some of the results were quite spectacular, so much so that Bosc decided that year to market cases of red wine that would contain four bottles of each variety, so people could either blend for themselves, or enjoy each variety on its own.

Paul Bosc Jr. with a selection of Chateau des Charmes wines

These days Paul Bosc senior spends lots of time with his other passion: riding horseback all over the Niagara region. His older son, Paul Jr., runs the sales and business end of the winery while younger son Pierre-Jean is the winemaker. Both operate under Dad's watchful eye, because he's still at the winery a couple of days a week.

# GAMAY

This is the grape variety of Beaujolais; the two are almost synonymous. The French used to call it Gamay Beaujolais, but then some winemakers, notably Paul Bosc, began making a wine they called Gamay Beaujolais after the grape type, which the French could not oppose. The French answer was to change the grape's name to simply Gamay, so producers like Bosc would have to remove the word Beaujolais from their labels.

Gamay does best in the soil and climate of France's Beaujolais district, where it is prized for the relatively high volume it can produce from the bush-like gobbet vines. At its highest quality, Gamay produces the *cru* Beaujolais wines, like Moulin-à-Vent, Morgon, St. Amour, and six others, some of which will improve with moderate bottle ageing. Next down the Beaujolais quality scale come the wines designated Beaujolais Villages, and finally, the ones we see most, Beaujolais Superior and Beaujolais Nouveau. Don't try to cellar age any Beaujolais Nouveau for more than a couple of months, and don't expect it to improve. Beaujolais wines are mostly intended to be quaffed while they are young and full of the gorgeous fruit and acid combination that has made them famous. You can find everything from strawberries to raspberries to bananas in a Beaujolais, thanks to that delightful Gamay grape. Fortunately for Canadians, Gamay does very well in Ontario's Niagara region, especially in the hands of Paul Bosc.

# NATO NONSENSE

One of the most interesting trips for journalists in the Canadian political calendar is the twice-yearly meeting of NATO ministers. Previously held in Paris, they are now held in Brussels each December, rotating for location in May/June amongst the capitals of NATO countries. That assignment must be even more interesting now that NATO has expanded. In the days when I was a reporter specializing in military issues, the biannual NATO meetings were cold warrior stuff where you got a peek into allied strategy, got to know the personalities of some of the players, and achieved some ability to understand why decisions were made.

Canada's membership in NATO was particularly important to both Europe and the US, because Canadian presence demonstrated that this was not merely an alliance of the US and Europe, but truly an alliance of North Atlantic nations. I made several trips to NATO meetings when Paul Hellyer was Minister of National Defence, and in the process grew to like him very much. Later, when Mr. Hellyer left the Liberals to form Action Canada, and when, finally, he had no seat in Parliament, he joined the Parliamentary Press Gallery as a columnist for the *Toronto Sun*.

Imagine the stir he created when he went to his first NATO meeting as a reporter, in Bonn, back in the days when that was the West German capital. The other NATO ministers and the senior NATO staff were used to seeing Mr. Hellyer as a participating minister, not as a reporter, and they were unsure as to how to handle him. They need not have worried. Hellyer wanted to be treated as just what he was—a working journalist.

To give you an idea of his attitude, here's a small anecdote from shortly after he joined the Ottawa Press Gallery. The annual Press Gallery Dinner is an event where reporters lampoon politicians, and politicians fight back with speeches, usually making fun of themselves. Robert Stanfield and Joe Clark used to love the Gallery Dinner. So does Jean Chretien. (Pierre Trudeau hated it.)

In Paul Hellyer's first year in the Press Gallery, he had a good part in the stage show the Press Gallery does at the dinner. He was cast as the lifeguard for a swimming pool. We actually had a large inflatable pool installed in the Railway Committee Room, where the show was taking place. Hellyer wore a blue bathing suit, with a whistle hung around his neck. One of his tasks was to blow the whistle as the acts changed. Written into the script were several references at different times to leadership. Hellyer, who had by then tried for the leadership of the Liberals, the Tories, and finally led his own Action Canada, would perk up in the show every time the word "lead" was used, and say loudly: "Lead? Did somebody say lead?" Every time he did it, there were gales of laughter. So Paul Hellyer didn't take himself too seriously as a member of the Press Gallery. He could laugh at himself.

On this NATO trip we were staying at the Bristol Hotel, an excellent facility just on the edge of the centre of Bonn, where no vehicle traffic is allowed. The first full day was very demanding, so when we arrived back at the hotel we were tired with a combination of work and jet lag. Paul suggested a swim in the Bristol's pool, and it sure sounded like a good idea. We dumped our notebooks, bypassing the more popular bar, and headed for the pool. The pool was deserted. The attendant told us swim suits were not necessary. The swim was delightfully relaxing. A session in the hotel sauna seemed like a natural finishing touch.

I was leading as we went through the door into the steaming outer room of the sauna, with its showers and hot pool. I stopped motionless with shock in the doorway because right ahead were three or four lovely girls, absolutely stark naked.

"My God, we're crashing ladies' day at the sauna," was my first thought.

Paul couldn't see past me, so he shoved a bit to get me moving. He froze just the way I had when he saw the girls milling about just as nature made them. They didn't seem concerned in the least, so we reluctantly came to the conclusion that this was one of those mixed nude saunas we had heard about. We showered, dipped in the hot tub, then went into the sauna. Lying on the top bench was a gorgeous twenty-something girl, who smiled at us and said hello as we tried to find a spot. There were two other girls there, in various sauna poses, both of them very well endowed.

The problem you face as an unsophisticated middle-aged male with a weight problem, is that you don't know what part of your anatomy to casually cover with your towel or your free hand. You're not sure how long you can keep your tummy sucked in, and neither do you know where to look when a charming, nude young girl is speaking to you. It's essential that you meet her eyes, even if you are unreasonably thankful for peripheral vision.

We stayed in that sauna until our fingers were thoroughly wrinkled with moisture and our chins were dripping with perspiration. That evening at dinner we regaled our colleagues with stories of the sauna, and next day after work, the sauna was particularly busy with journalists, suddenly convinced that steaming the body was much more important than a drink at the bar. A different crop of girls was there, still nude and still lovely.

By the end of that series of NATO meetings in Bonn, most of the press corps had permanently wrinkled fingers from too much time in the sauna. Collectively we must have lost several hundred pounds from skipping cocktail hour in the bar in favour of a healthy session in the sauna with some lovely company.

We discovered later that those girls who liked the Bristol Hotel's sauna so much were government secretaries who lived in an apartment building behind the hotel. The crafty managers of the Bristol Hotel had given all the girls complimentary memberships in the hotel health spa and sauna. I certainly knew where I wanted to stay each time we revisited Bonn. So did the rest of the press corps.

# SHERRY

Vines have grown in the region of Jerez since the time when Phoenician galleys used to make regular stops in the harbour of Cadiz, 1,000 years before Christ. The Phoenicians, who were rather fond of a spot of wine, founded the city of Jerez, perhaps as sort of a last filling station before their galleys headed out into the thirsty Atlantic for the Cornwall tin mines, or down the coast of Africa.

The Greeks replaced the Phoenicians as masters of that fabulous harbour and fertile growing plain, and the Romans took it over from the Greeks. A chap named Hannibal supped from the fruit of the vines of Xeres as he readied his elephants for war with Rome; the Vandals and Goths had a turn at ownership; so did the Moors, from 711 until 1264. When the Spanish hero King Alfonso X kicked out the Moors, wine once again became big business in Cadiz and Andalusia.

Cadiz sits in the south of Spain, on a promontory that looks rather like the head and neck of a goose. The goose's beak points due west, jutting out into the Atlantic, and Cadiz is located on the back of the bird's head. The River Guadalete runs into Cadiz Bay, and the city of Jerez, the home of Sherry, lies some fifteen kilometres upriver. The triangle of land surrounding Cadiz, Jerez, and the port of Sanlucar de Barrameda is one of the most famous and valuable pieces of grape-producing real estate in the world.

Jerez, of course, gave Sherry its name, because the English don't understand what Spanish tongues do with the letter "J." The British experienced less trouble appreciating the wines of the region. There are records of shipments from Jerez to the English as far back as 1485, seven years before Columbus set off for the New World.

In 1587, when Sir Francis Drake attacked Cadiz, there were 2,900 pipes of Sherry included in the booty, something that is said to have helped develop the British taste for Sherry.

Andalusia, the home of Sherry, is almost Spain's most southerly point. It gets hot there in the long summer and mighty wet during the winter rainy season. You might say there are two seasons—sloppy muddy, and sun-baked dusty—both necessary for the production of Sherry.

The soil is of two main types. The most highly prized for vineyards is a fine, calcium-rich chalky stuff, which looks almost white. There are pockets of that white chalky stuff all over the Sherry district, with the main deposits lying immediately north and west of Jerez. The other soil of the district is sandier, and although it is of the same even consistency as the soil of the prime districts, it has slightly fewer complex mineral flavours to impart to the grapes.

It's important that the soil be of even consistency in the Sherry district, because when the rains come, the earth must be able to sop up water like a sponge and hold it against the coming summer. Beginning in May, the sun bakes that soil and forms something of a crust, trapping the moisture. The vines pull moisture from that reservoir, sending their roots down nine metres and more into the mineral-rich chalk. The best grapes come from mature vines, because the roots are deeper, reaching down for more elements to impart the maximum possible taste complexities to the grapes. Sherry's flavour begins in the mud, in those chalk-lime soils of Andalusia, and the sun-baked days of the southern Spanish summer. The wine's unique nature is built on soil, climate, grape variety, and technique.

Virtually all Sherry is made from the Palomino grape, and there are two types. Palomino Jerez, or Basta, is the older variety and is now going out of usage. Palomino Fino, the better of the two in both quality of juice and quantity produced per hectare, is the favourite. Pedro Ximenez grapes used to be fairly widely grown for making for sweet wines, but virtually none of that variety is being planted today. As Pedro Ximenez vines die off, Palomino Fino vines are planted to replace them. Palomino is one of the few great wine grapes that is also superb for eating straight off the vines. That's why as the vines ripen in Jerez, you'll see guards in small wooden huts on stilts in many of the fields. Locally the huts on stilts are called "*bien-te-veo*," or "I can see you," and they are designed simply to curb grape-nappers who are eager for an illicit taste of the sweet, juicy berries.

The Sherry harvest takes place in September, and often the grapes are left to dry in the sun for up to a week to concentrate the sugar and make the eventual wine as strong as possible. As recently as the sixties, the grapes were still tramped out by peasants wearing boots with special nails in the soles, designed to trap the stems and grape pits as the fruit got crushed. The tramping of the grapes used to be done at night so there wouldn't be so many wasps around to threaten those who were cavorting about on the grapes.

The personal touch, peasants tramping the grapes by foot, went out of fashion for two reasons: the price of labour reached reasonable levels in Spain so it became uneconomical to use manpower; and science developed machines that could crush and press the fruit without breaking the pits. Broken grape pits in the Sherry must would impart a bitter taste to the wine, spoiling its traditional flavour.

Until a few years ago, Sherry was fermented in new oak barrels, and because the must worked with extreme violence, the barrels were only partly filled. There's still a delightful smell in the Sherry towns around harvest time, but not nearly as much as there used to be in the days when barrels were everywhere, overflowing with the foaming new wine.

Producers found that during that first violent fermentation, the must sometimes became too hot, imparting a sharp, burned taste to the wine. Sherry makers have moved progressively to a cold fermenting system, using huge fibreglass or stainless steel tanks for the first ferment, with water trickled down the sides of the tanks to keep temperatures low.

The art of cold fermentation makes for better wines, but it has played havoc with another tradition of Sherry: the supplying of barrels to the whisky trade. The first phase of Sherry fermentation used to take place in new casks. Those casks were used again to ship mature wines for bottling. When the casks were empty, they were sold to whisky distilleries, because the Sherry flavour in the barrels was exactly right for ageing whisky.

Imagine the whisky crisis when Sherry makers began switching to the cold fermentation process: Suddenly there was a shortage of old Sherry barrels for ageing whisky. Several years ago it reached the stage where distilleries were supplying new casks to Sherry producers for free, just so they could have the barrels after the wood had been exposed to fermentation for a sufficient length of time to collect the right flavour.

Sherry is unique in the way it goes through its secondary fermentation. It's put in barrels that are deliberately left only seventy-five or eighty percent full, exposing the wine to air. The barrels are arranged so that air can blow through their ranks in the Bodegas. Ventilating the barrels gives the wine yet another aspect of its special flavour, and it begins the process of separating the various types of Sherries one from the other.

What separates a Fino and a Manzanilla Sherry from an Oloroso is the *flor*—that's Spanish for flower—that develops on the surface of the wine after fermentation (see the chapter "Cava, Fino and Spiders"). We've all seen a white layer of scum form on the top of a jar of vinegar left too long in the kitchen. It's much the same with Sherries, only the white coating develops more quickly, and is considered a good thing. The *flor* is a layer of yeast cells, which will grow so thickly it sometimes looks like a wrinkled layer of farmer's cheese. Flor protects the Sherry from air, and also imparts to it that typical Fino taste. Even the Sherry cellar masters cannot tell which cask will grow *flor* and which will not. Those that develop the thick white layer of yeast cells are destined to become either Fino or Manzanilla Sherries; those that do not develop *flor* become Oloroso Sherries.

Manzanilla Sherry is really a Fino that has lain in barrels on the seacoast, exposed to sea air, to acquire a slight salty tang. Manzanilla Sherries are also made from grapes picked just before they are fully ripe, so Manzanilla can be expected to have a special tartness, melded with the typical Fino tang. Wine master Alexis Lachine says that a newly fermented Fino can be moved nineteen kilometres to the Manzanilla district for maturing, and it will become a Manzanilla, while a Manzanilla can be moved to Jerez for maturing and become a Fino.

Sherries begin to show their individual style about six months after fermentation ends. Then the cellar master goes about the task of giving each barrel its first classification test. To sample the wines, he uses a special tasting wand, with a cup on the end of it, called a *venencia*. Use of the slender, springy wand is in itself an art that takes considerable practice to master. The idea is to plunge the *venencia* through the layer of *flor*, knocking aside the scum, and then quickly bring the small cup out again, filled with new Sherry. The wine is then poured from the cup in a single sweeping motion, to fill the tasting glass. Simple? Try doing it without dribbling down your pant leg, or dousing your neighbour with a shot of Sherry. That's what happened to me when I tried it.

Depending chiefly on his sense of smell, the cellar master classifies the new wines into four categories, and marks each barrel accordingly. One downward stroke—"*una raya*"—means light and good wine; one downward stroke followed by a period is "*raya y punto*"—a wine of slightly less promise; two downward strokes is "*dos rayas*"—a must with less style; and three downward strokes—"*tres rayas*"—means "this one isn't worth the trouble it takes to make Sherry; off to the distillery with it."

After receiving its first report card, the wine is racked off the lees and separated from sediments. Wines that have shown good *flor* development are usually less alcoholic than their sisters. They are fortified with brandy to bring their alcohol content up to the required 15 or 15.5 percent. Wines that have been relegated to the lower classes in the first report card, and show fewer signs of breeding *flor*, are dosed more heavily with brandy in a process rather like the wine version of castration.

Extra alcoholic strength kills off the *flor*, and inhibits their potential to develop any more. Classy Sherries are destined to pass along their best qualities to coming generations. The lower-class wines simply get consumed by the thirsty locals.

Sherries need to rest for a few weeks after this shock treatment, before the masters of Sherry take the wines through the rigours of another classification. Wines that still breed *flor* have their casks marked with a sort of flying "V" and become known as "*palmas*"—potential aristocrats. The casks of fuller wines with no sign of *flor* are marked with one downward stroke to designate them as *raya* Sherries. Barrels marked with two downward strokes are judged to be *dos rayas,* and are thus fingered as being inclined to roughness, perhaps destined for castration with brandy. Those that are judged no good for anything but distillation are marked with two downward strokes, crossed by two horizontal strokes in a sign like the symbol for "number," and off they go to the brandy factories.

For somewhere between nine months and three years, the new Sherries are allowed to sleep and develop their individual characteristics, being reclassified at regular intervals. The top marking remains the "V" sign of *palma*. A heavier-bodied *palma* will be marked with a horizontal line through the V and designated a "Palma Cortado."

A plain cross indicates "Palo Cortado," a real rarity, a full-bodied wine that is also delicate, and yet has shown no sign of *flor* development. It's a wine that doesn't occur very often, and is highly prized, because it combines the qualities of a Fino with the characteristics of an Oloroso. Palo Cortado occurs naturally in the vineyard, through a circumstance that is apparently disappearing— there's less each year. A real Palo Cortado is said to need twenty years to mature, so it's not a wine that is made commercially very often. It does marvellous things to your palate, making taste buds behave like a flock of Spanish riding school horses. It also can play weird tricks on your wallet.

At their best, Sherries that fail to develop *flor*, and become Oloroso wines, can be heaven for the nostrils and a symphony of flavour in your mouth. They are heavier, browner, and less ethereal in their bouquet than Fino Sherries. Oloroso means "fragrant," and that's exactly what the wine is. There are good Olorosos and lesser breeds. Usually the lesser breeds—the plain *raya* Sherries—don't get exported. They are consumed by Spaniards at home, or by tourists who often find the mystique of being in Sherry country flavour enough.

At the Fino end of the scale you find the top-quality Sherries. There, too, a wine's development is largely in nature's hands. Some will naturally develop into Fino Amontillados, and others into straight Amontillado Sherries, to become a darker version of a Fino, with an alcoholic content of about eighteen percent. Such beauties can reach as much as twenty-four percent after ageing. Understandably, Amontillado Sherries are subtle, distinguished, and highly prized. The real thing is very expensive. Don't be taken in by some wines sold as Amontillado, which are merely sweetened Finos and bastardized wines. An Amontillado is not sweet. It gets its name because superficially it resembles the wines of Montilla, near Cordoba.

A *solera* is the place where barrels of the best Sherries are stored for blending—the finishing school for fine Sherries. Barrels are stacked in tiers, with the barrels containing the oldest Sherries on the bottom. The *solera* system is the key to the production of fine Sherries, because it takes advantage of a unique property of Sherry: In a very short period of time, a younger Sherry blended with an older Sherry will take on the characteristics of the older wine.

The best Fino and Oloroso Sherries are stored in barrels in the *solera*, according to their ages, with the oldest wines on the bottom of the tiers of barrels. When a company wants to bottle its finest Sherry, it draws wine from casks in the bottom tier—from the oldest barrels—and draws no more than twenty percent at a time from any one barrel. Sherry from the next oldest barrel—from the tier second to the bottom—is then used to refill the cask of oldest wine. Wine from a barrel in the third tier from the bottom fills the barrel immediately below, and the process continues, with each barrel being filled with wine that is a younger sister. Eventually the wine most recently introduced to the *solera* is used to fill the barrels of its immediate senior, and thus the new vintage enters the system.

A decent period of rest must be allowed in the *solera* before the whole process is repeated for another batch of Sherry, so that the old and the new can become united in their casks. When you buy a Sherry made with this blending system, there are actual traces in the bottle of wines fifty, sixty, perhaps even 100 years old, ready to pass on their character to your nose and palate. A good bottle of Sherry will tell you on the label that it graduated from a *solera*.

For visitors to a *solera*, Sherry masters will demonstrate the effect that blending can have by taking a small amount of old Sherry in a glass, swirling it about, and then emptying it. Mere traces of the old wine left in the glass are sufficient to react with a new Sherry poured into the same glass. It will get deeper in colour and richer in nose and flavour while you watch, simply by being mixed with the traces of its elder.

The great Sherry houses blend the products of a number of *soleras* to create the wine that fills the bottles we buy. The proportion of the various wines used in blending is vitally important. Too much old Sherry and the wine might be overpowering; too little and there wouldn't be the necessary character. That blending is the end art in a chain of highly developed skills that go into creating this magic in a glass.

Don't be disappointed if your glass of Sherry in Cadiz falls short of the power the same brand offered in London. Fino Sherries for export are stronger than you'll find them in a Spanish wine bar. Before being shipped out of the country, Fino Sherries are dosed with a half-and-half mixture of wine and brandy, so that their alcoholic content is raised a degree or so. It helps keep the wine stable during shipping, and ensures that there won't be any *flor* developing in your decanter at home. Sherry is also ultra-cooled and filtered before being bottled for export, so that there won't be any tartaric acid crystals present when the bottle is sold. Mind you, a real Sherry lover wouldn't mind the crystals, or even a touch of *flor* in his Fino decanter. Neophytes might complain.

It was in a Jerez restaurant where I first encountered that marvellous Spanish custom that has your waiter will bring a small bottle of Fino Sherry to the table in an ice bucket, so you can sip while you decide on your food. You don't mind lingering over choices when there's Fino to drink. The restaurant wins because your appetite increases.

Sweet Sherry? Yes, it's very popular in North America, and in the United Kingdom, too. It's certainly not the Spanish way to drink the fruit of the vines of Jerez. Sherry was first sweetened for the English trade. Even today, you won't find much of the sweet variety sold in Spain.

There are several ways of producing sweet Sherries. If there's a small amount of brandy in the cask before fermentation begins, then the alcoholic content will be high enough to kill off the yeast while there is still sugar left in the new wine. Some Sherries are sweetened after they've been through the ageing process by the addition of some brandy and concentrated, sweet juice. Some are sweetened by being blended with wine made from Pedro Ximenez grapes.

Drink sweet Sherry if you like. It's a good tipple. Drink it either before dinner as an aperitif, or afterwards like Port. Drink it at room temperature, or on the rocks, as does my wife Jane. Let your own taste decide. There are also some basics that are useful guidelines.

The key to handling and serving Sherry properly, particularly dry Sherry, is recognition of the fact that it is a white wine—a special white wine, of course, but still a white wine. It should not be served in those little glasses marked "Sherry" in your crystal set, because tiny glasses don't give the bouquet a chance to develop. Serve Sherry in generous-sized glasses, and fill the glass no more than one-third full, so the bouquet has room to expand. Serve Finos, Manzanillas, Olorosos, and Palo Cortados slightly chilled. Drink them as aperitifs, or with anything else that you would match with a white wine. Sherries are excellent with Spanish Tapas, and any other spicy appetizer. Fino is perfect with consommés. Suit the type of Sherry to the dish you are serving, according to your own taste. We keep a bottle of Fino in the door of the refrigerator. I love a cold glass before dinner.

Because Sherry is a white wine, you should also remember that it won't last forever once it's been opened. Neither will a Fino or a Manzanilla keep for long periods in your cellar. Once bottled, the experts claim that those Sherries will not improve with age, so drink them up. Unless you have a real taste for it, and your household consumes it quickly, don't buy large quantities of Sherry at the same time.

In their sealed bottles, Finos will maintain their peak for a year or so. An Oloroso or a dry Amontillado will undergo few changes in the bottle when properly cellared, and can be kept for a many years. Sweet Sherries keep even longer in the bottle and will improve somewhat by losing some of their sweetness and enhancing their flavour.

A week or so in the decanter is enough to affect the flavour of a Sherry through oxidization. It's not a bad idea to keep an empty half bottle around, and use it to reclaim any half-bottle leftovers from a Sunday afternoon. Another solution might be to suit the number of your guests and their drinking capacity to the number of bottles you plan to serve, or vice versa.

If some of the Sherry names twist your tongue, particularly Manzanilla and Amontillado, remember that a double "l" in Spanish is pronounced like "e," so Manzanilla becomes "Manzaneea."

The next time you have a dinner party, instead of cocktails before dinner and leading the guests to the table with paralyzed palates, think Sherry. It's a terribly pleasant and highly civilized way to begin a meal.

# PALOMINO

If it weren't for Palomino grapes we wouldn't have any Sherry, or even many imitators of Sherry. This buxom white grape does wonderfully well in the hot, dry climate and crusty soils around the southern Spanish town of Jerez. It even does well producing 4.5 tons of fruit per acre, which certainly suits the growers. The vine is somewhat subject to mildew, so the dry climate of southern Spain works in its favour. It matters not that Palomino juices have a tendency to oxidize, because that's required when you're making Sherry. Remember we discussed that floating white flaky scum, needed to produce Fino Sherry and known as *flor*? That's what gives Fino Sherry its delightful bite on your tongue when you sip it before dinner.

Make an ordinary wine out of Palomino grapes and you wind up with something quite insipid—low in acid, not much on the taste scale, and not even very heavy in alcohol. Put the same grape in the hands of Spanish Sherry makers, to be vinified, fortified, allowed to collect *flor* in barrels not quite full, then put through a complex ageing system in *solera* barrels, and you can get something unique. Serve it very cold. As I've said before, at home we keep a bottle of Fino in the refrigerator door.

Palomino has been so successful making Sherry that you'll find plantings of it in Australia, New Zealand, South Africa, California, and even Argentina, all places where it is used to make Sherry-like wines. Most of them are even called Sherry on the label, although only wines made in the Jerez area are entitled to that name.

# PROPERLY CORKED

Cork oak trees on Portugal's Alentejo plain look for all the world like giant umbrellas. Portugal is the heart of the world's modern cork industry, producing almost half the world's supply of wine corks from cultivated forests, and from roadside trees each carefully marked with the owner's name. I remember driving through Portugal past hundreds of cork oak trees at the sides of the roads.

Cork oak trees in Portugal's central plain area

Cork's commercial value has escalated in step with the world's increasing thirst for wines, despite the fact that screw-top bottles and plastic stoppers are growing in popularity with wineries.

It was the invention of the cork bottle stopper that made possible the ageing of fine wine. Until the cork stopper came along, wine bottles were squat, onion-shaped affairs used for bringing wine to the table from cellar casks, sometimes plugged with a piece of whittled wood or twisted rag. The use of corks made it possible for the bottle to evolve into something more cylindrical, so bottled wine could be stored lying down in stacks. It didn't take winemakers long to discover that those harsh tannin flavours in some wines—like those made with Cabernet or Nebbiolo—would mellow into something very special when the bottles were cork stoppered and allowed to mature for a few years. Before corks were used as bottle stoppers, the mere idea of making and maturing a vintage Port would have been impossible. What delights corks have made possible!

Wine corks are made from the bark of the cork oak tree, an evergreen that thrives in Portugal, Spain, along the Mediterranean coast of North Africa, some places in southern France, lower Italy, and Sicily. Portugal and Spain are the two most important commercial producers, with most of the processing being done in Portugal.

A cork tree must be twenty-five years old before the bark is stripped for the first time. Stripping the outer bark doesn't bother the tree; it simply seems to produce a finer layer of new bark over the area that's been stripped. That first stripping does not produce anything of commercial value. Nine years later the second stripping produces cork of a limited value, for use as powder to make materials like linoleum. It is not until the third stripping, another nine years later, that quality begins to appear.

Every nine years a cork oak tree is stripped of its bark, and the cork is stripped off in large planks and taken to a boiling station to cook off tannin and sap, and then stacked to dry in flattened heaps. Cork oaks live and produce for about 150 years, although some have been known to last more than 200 years. The older the tree the more cork it produces and the better the quality. Cork for making wine bottle stoppers should be as free from pockets of graininess as possible, and without holes created by knots in the tree.

Washed and dried cork is hand sorted by experts into grades, the best going for wine corks, the lesser qualities used for making insulation, cork board, conglomerates, gaskets for car engines, and the like. Planks of cork to be used for wine corks are then cut into various widths, depending on the length of the cork stopper to be made. The longer the cork, the more expensive it will be. These slabs of cork are then put through a punch machine that cuts out the individual cork stoppers, at right angles to the line of growth. These days a computer scans each slab and adjusts the punch machine so that the maximum number of corks can be punched from each piece. Punching must be precise, because if the outer edge of any slab is pierced, chances are the cork will be tainted and will contaminate the wine.

We've all heard of "corked" wine and many of us have smelled that mouldy, slightly skunky odour. Over the years I've sent back quite a few bottles that were corked in restaurants, and even once in a private home. Anyone can be stuck with a corked bottle. You won't get an argument when you refuse a corked bottle of wine in any decent restaurant, and if you get such a bottle at home, your wine merchant will give you a refund on its return, unless you've consumed half the bottle.

The most common cause of a contaminated cork is imperfect washing after the use of chlorine bleach in the cleaning process, which can cause the formation of trichloranisole, that smelly chemical that does the contamination. With increased demand for corks in the 1980s and probably sped-up production, the incidence of corked wines rose to almost five percent—more than a bottle for every two cases—souring the attitudes of many wine producers and leading them to explore other ways of stoppering their wines. The cork industry answered those complaints by switching from chlorine bleaching to hydrogen peroxide, or an even safer process of high humidity heating, for sterilization.

That didn't stop many wineries from switching away from natural cork stoppers, and in truth, most of the world's wines have no need of expensive cork stoppers, because they are made to be drunk while they are young. There's no earthly reason why a delightful, fresh white wine from the Loire needs a cork stopper when a metal twist top will do, except for the fact that consumers equate a cork stopper with quality. That attitude may be changing. You'll run into plenty of decent screw-top stuff these days, and lots of wines with a plastic cork, or a stopper made with compressed particles of cork, with a thin layer or two of real cork next to the wine.

I'm a traditionalist who pays attention to corks. They are, after all, a natural miracle. There are millions of fourteen-sided microscopic cells in every cork, each one filled with air, so the cork is flexible, light, compressible, and easily removed from a wine bottle. I still have trouble removing those plastic jobs and the conglomerate corks are the very devil for a thirsty chap to pull.

Check the cork when buying wine. Sometimes you can see the cork below the foil around the neck of the bottle. If you can, that's an expensive cork and an indication that the wine producer thought enough of his product to spend a few pennies per bottle extra on a long, quality cork. Squeeze the cork when you remove it from the bottle to make sure it's moist and flexible, a sign that the wine has been stored lying down. If there are diamond-like crystals on the cork, clear for white wine, reddish for red wine, don't let that worry you. It's tartaric acid precipitated from the wine—odourless and tasteless. And there's nothing like a peek at the cork if somebody asks you to identify a masked bottle of wine. Usually the name of the winery and the vintage date are printed on the cork.

# FIRESIDE DRINKS

When the weather outside is frightful, that's the time to exercise your artistry by concocting something steamy, spicy, and slightly alcoholic. There's nothing like a noggin of hot toddy, mulled wine, or your own invention to thaw the chills picked up from an afternoon of skiing, skating, or frolicking on a sleigh hill.

Not many years ago, warm winter drinks were most commonly made by plunging a red-hot poker into a tankard of red wine that had perhaps been doctored with spices. The fizzing sound and delightful smell of hot metal being quenched in spicy wine filled many a tavern common room on a winter evening. The very thought makes you feel warm and mellow.

You can still heat your après-ski refreshment that way, provided you are careful to use a clean poker and heat-proof containers for the drinks, but today there are more effective hot drink aids, like, for example, microwave ovens, kitchen stoves, and thermos flasks.

There are a few basic guidelines for successfully constructing fireside winter drinks. Most importantly, you should never *boil* the wine or liquor destined to become the essential part of a hot drink, because alcohol comes off as vapour at seventy-two degrees Celsius (160–165 degrees Fahrenheit). You don't want to diminish the zip of your hot drink.

When wine is to be the backbone of your concoction, heat it carefully in either a glass or stainless steel pot, ensuring that it doesn't become heated higher than the boiling point of alcohol. When you're making a hot toddy with liquor, use boiling water for the heat; add the liquor at room temperature just before serving.

The second secret for successful construction of fireside sipping drinks is to use liquid honey as a sweetener, not plain sugar. It makes hot drinks taste smoother, avoiding the slightly burned taste that refined sugar can sometimes impart. The third successful sipper secret is using lemon in virtually all drinks. Use lemon juice to set up an attractive balance with spicy sweetness; use grated or sliced lemon peel for the zest of the citrus oils in the peel. Lemon and honey by themselves are super. Add wine, spices, or rum/whisky, and wow!

Properly spicing mulled wine is a challenge, because you must avoid those lumpy spice bits that can be so unattractive in the last swallow. With some spices, it takes actual boiling to infuse a liquid with their flavour, but if you can't boil the wine, how do you get spicy flavours into the brew? The answer is to boil the spices in a small amount of water for about five minutes, then strain out the bits so you can add the clean, spice-infused water to the mulled wine. Use about four ounces of water and watch carefully that it doesn't boil dry.

Hot drinks are best enjoyed when they are in proper drinking vessels. Avoid using wineglasses, unless they are the sturdy type. Pottery goblets are excellent; so are pottery mugs. You should avoid using metal tankards for mulled wine because they can sometimes impart a nasty metallic flavour to a warm drink.

Once you become an expert mulled winemaker, guests can have you running back and forth to the kitchen constantly, so make double batches of mulled wine and keep seconds available in a thermos jug. You can even make mulled wine in advance, keep it in a glass container, and microwave it to the proper temperature before serving. You will need experience when using the microwave, so that the mulled wine doesn't get hot enough to boil off the alcohol.

Hot toddy is best served in pottery mugs for the taste and because the mugs make wonderful hand warmers. It's an ideal drink to warm away the chills, and if you've got the sniffles, a mug of this before bedtime is a sure-fire cure. Toddy should be made in individual mugs, adding liquor to spiced boiling water and butter. You can use your favourite spices, particularly ginger, nutmeg, and cinnamon. Heat the water, add spices and honey to the mug, pour in the boiling water, and just before serving, stir in the rum or whisky. If you don't stir, the good stuff stays on top. Avoid microwaving hot toddy after the liquor has been added.

Here are two basic recipes, one for mulled wine and one for hot toddy. Feel free to adjust quantities to your own taste.

## Mulled Wine

Makes 4 to 6 servings.

1/2 cup (125 ml) water

1 tsp (5 ml) powdered ginger

1 tsp (5 ml) powdered cinnamon

1 tsp (5 ml) ground nutmeg

6 cloves

4–6 cinnamon sticks

1/2 Tbsp (7 ml) liquid honey to taste

1/2 lemon

1/2 cup (125 ml) Port wine

1 bottle (750 ml) red wine

Mix the wine, Port, and honey in a large glass or stainless steel container. Put it on low heat. In a separate small pan boil the water. Carve a few strips off the lemon and add half to the boiling water. Add the cinnamon, nutmeg, ginger, and cloves to the boiling water and boil them together gently for five minutes.

Add the juice of the half lemon to the warming wine, removing any seeds. Strain any solids from the spice-infused water and add to the wine, Port, and honey mixture. Stir gently.

Serve in thick glasses or mugs with a sliver of lemon peel floating in each mug, and place a cinnamon stick in each mug.

Get ready to serve seconds!

## Hot Toddy

Makes one serving.

1/2 cup (125 ml) boiling water

1 tsp (5 ml) butter

Pinch cinnamon

Pinch ginger

Pinch nutmeg

Juice of 1/2 lemon

1/4 cup (60 ml) Rum or Scotch Whiskey

1 cinnamon stick (optional)

Boil water in a kettle and while it's heating, put a teaspoon of butter into a mug; add honey, lemon juice, and spices. Pour boiling water into the mug, making sure you've left enough room for the Rum or Scotch. Stir to dissolve the honey and butter, then add the Rum or Scotch, stirring again immediately. Serve it right away, with a cinnamon stick if desired.

# SOUTH AFRICAN SIPPING

Drive the expressway from Cape Town airport to the city and you'll see a horrible South African shantytown of dwellings made with sheet metal and scrap cardboard, hugging both sides of the road for three kilometres, cut off from traffic by concrete barriers. Kids play in the space between highway and shacks. From the car, you get glimpses of the packed humanity and their poverty. With the HIV/AIDS situation in South Africa, just imagine what the disease rates are in these ghettos.

Officials claim the ragged inhabitants are refugees from Zimbabwe, Zambia, and Mozambique, drawn by the hope of a better life. I was told that the turnover of inhabitants is ninety percent annually, as people find a place in the local economy and are replaced as new refugees move in seeking a better break in life. But hey, this is a wine trip, my last as a wine writer for the *Ottawa Citizen*, and we're not supposed to be fixated on social conditions, even when they bite us on the nose.

When I left for this trip to Cape Town in late 2001, my attitude towards South Africa was moderate enthusiasm. After a week in the western Cape vineyards, tasting more than 250 wines in six days, I came home a raving cheerleader for Cape Town, which has to be the most beautiful city in the world, and with boundless enthusiasm for the Cape wines. The wines weren't bad when Canada proscribed South African products years ago because of apartheid. They're much improved and getting even better, thanks to the great South African success story of peaceful transformation from a brutally segregated society to the new Rainbow Coalition democracy.

We saw honest efforts and the beginnings of successful training of black winemakers and managers, coupled with real internationalization of the industry. Rapid expansion is happening in South Africa's wine industry. At winery after winery we saw new equipment that represented tens of millions of dollars in new investment. Huge stainless steel fermenting and storage tanks, along with the best possible presses and storage facilities, have appeared everywhere.

Almost all the investment has come from Europe, primarily Switzerland, Germany and France. You have to conclude that canny investors sat back to watch how stable South Africa would be under a one-person, one-vote democracy. Apparently the investors decided South Africa would make it, and with its great climate and fertile valleys lacing through the mountains like green fingers, the country would be ideal for making a new style of wine for the world.

It's certainly an innovative business. I'll bet we met more than three dozen winemakers, and not more than two or three of them were over forty years old. More of them were under thirty than over forty, and everybody had new ideas.

At the huge Nederburg Wines complex, sixty kilometres outside Cape Town, we were astounded to meet a twenty-eight-year-old Romanian winemaker, Razvan Macici, who was making great wine out of Nebbiolo grapes, an Italian variety. He bounced with enthusiasm as he showed us through the winery, pulling samples from tanks or barrels for us to taste. He didn't want us to write about some of his experiments, in case some other winemaker copied him. His equipment was gleaming new stainless steel, the kind of hardware young winemakers dream of using in pursuit of creating the ideal wine.

We met several black assistant winemakers, and some cellar masters, usually on an industry fast track as the wine business strives for equal opportunity and a stronger black presence. The cellar master at the huge KWV winery, for example, is black. The first black winemaker, a twenty-two-year-old Zulu named Mzukhoma Mvemve, graduated from a program sponsored by the Cape Classics group on Jan. 7, 2002. Money for his tuition, and the tuition fees of a number of others further back in the program, came from collective contributions from the wineries, and from the sale of Indaba wines, some of which are for sale in Canada and the U.S. I liked the Indaba Pinotage best. *Indaba* means "meeting place," and that's what the South African wine industry is striving to be—a meeting place for wine enthusiasts.

One evening we met ten senior people from the Cape Classics group, a consortium of wineries involved in the black wine scholarship program. Dinner thankfully was scheduled for seven p.m.; after a hard day of tasting at half a dozen wineries, we were ready for food. Not so fast . . . Every one of the winemakers present had brought some bottles of his best for us to try, so we went through sniff, swirl, and sip with at least twenty wines before we saw the first course of dinner. That happened to us almost every evening, hence it was no surprise when the most statistically inclined of our group announced as we were leaving that we'd tasted 252 wines in six days. Frankly, I think he missed counting a few.

Everywhere we went we asked to see the housing for winery workers. There was quite a contrast between that shantytown we saw on the airport road to Cape Town and the clean houses we saw for workers at the wineries we visited: homes with electricity and running water. The law says that the homes of workers who have been with a company for five years belong to them and they can't be evicted, not even if they quit or get fired. Wineries are careful whom they hire, and they can pick and choose the best because jobs at the wineries are in demand, thanks largely to legislation protecting workers.

There was a time when rural folk envied the city dwellers, said Johann Kridge, of Kanonkop winery, north of Stellenboch. Not any more. The envy path has been reversed, particularly when it comes to places like Kanonkop. There's a big old cannon mounted at the gates of Kanonkop, which in the old days was used as a signal gun. When a fleet of sailing ships approached Cape Town, guns fired all over the fertile valleys north of the city told farmers to bring their produce to the port to supply the ships.

Tradition may be old at Kanonkop, but their arrangement with the workers is certainly enlightened. For the fifty-person workforce there's modern housing, a daycare centre, and sports facilities. Profit sharing is a major incentive. Policy there is to never employ children until they have matriculated, and then they are guaranteed a job, or help with higher education. The super quality of Kanonkop wines reflects the happy employees. Theirs was one of the best Pinotage wines we tasted during this weeklong trip.

"Pinotage has the heart of a lion and the tongue of a woman," said Mr. Kridge. "After drinking a certain quantity you can talk forever and fight like the devil."

We asked about the HIV/AIDS plague wherever we went. Each winery claimed their workforce was AIDS-free, and all expressed concern about what will happen to South Africa's workforce over the next ten years.

The HIV infection rate is one person in nine. Take into account the much lower infection rate for whites, and apparently for rural workers, and you could estimate rates of infection pushing fifty percent in the shantytowns of refugees. There's a belief among some of the uneducated blacks that sex with a virgin will cure AIDS. The result has been many assaults on girls as young as eighteen months old.

One of our best discoveries was the farm and winery at Thandi, east of Cape Town, where black Africans run a successful cooperative farm operation, coupled with a winery where Andreas Berger, thirty-two, is one of the country's leading black winemakers. His wife Susan expertly conducted a swirl, sniff and spit tasting for us, and explained that Thandi, also the name of their wines, means "love."

The Thandi operation is being fostered by Dr. Paul Cluver, a well-known neurosurgeon and wine farmer, and also by South African government agencies in cooperation with the British supermarket chain Tesco. Thandi wines fly off Tesco shelves in the U.K.

The co-op is expected to be profitable by the end of 2003, we were told.

The black South Africans are earning ownership out of the profits they make. They were producing wine, vegetables, fruit, and even crafts, sold primarily in Cape Town. I spoke with the wiry, energy-rich farm foreman and asked him the name of his tribe. He first explained that he was Cape Malay—a "coloured," under the old apartheid system. Then he quickly corrected himself.

"No, no!" he said. "I'm South African. We all are South African now."

We see some good South African wines in North America today, but baby, you ain't seen nothin' yet. My notebook from this trip is full of triple stars for quality and value. In fact those happy wine experiences began on the plane when the flight attendant served us a wonderfully smooth, complex, and rich Shiraz from a place called Bon Courage, a winery northeast of Cape Town in the Robertson area.

Shiraz, in fact, seems to be the coming king of red grape varieties in South Africa. We tasted some that were good, and more than a few that were terrific. Australia is best known for Shiraz wines, although the grape has its origins in ancient Persia. The Shiraz wines we liked best at the Cape were just a bit higher in acid than most Australian Shiraz wines, with every bit as much fruit and complexity, making them better balanced to my taste.

One of the last wineries we visited was Bouchard Finlayson, quite close to Walker Bay. The setting is magnificent; the modern thatch-roofed winery sits on a hill facing south, with lesser rolling hills cut by deep valleys leading to the southern ocean, right where the Atlantic meets the Indian Ocean. Peter Finlayson led us through a tasting of some great Pinot Noir wines—wines that could well have been mistaken for top-line Burgundies, with a little extra body. As the name implies, Finlayson has a business alliance with Burgundy, as well as quality in common. Bouchard Finlayson wines are available in the U.S., but at prices ranging up to $50 a bottle—out of my reach for all but very special occasions.

Our last stop was Walker Bay itself, a delightful seaside tourist town with whitewashed houses and small hotels, where you can watch right whales playing just a few hundred yards off the seashore walk, waving flukes at the locals and tourists alike. This was our last chance to pick up tourist-type gifts for friends and family, so we scurried from shop to shop eagerly, until thirst took precedence.

Then we stopped for a beer.

# ABOUT THE AUTHOR

Peter Ward has been happily learning about wine through a long career as a journalist covering everything from police stories to local, provincial, and federal politics, to events at international trouble spots. For twenty-nine years he wrote a weekly wine column for the *Ottawa Citizen*. He has written magazine articles on wine, and often leads wine tastings.

Peter lives in Ottawa with his wife, Jane, visiting as often as possible with his daughter Wendy and her family in Welland, and with sons Tim and Mark, who live, respectively, in Washington, D.C., and Orlando, Florida. Tim is the author of four books, so Dad simply had to do something.